Women Who Woke up the Law

Karin Wells

Second Story Press

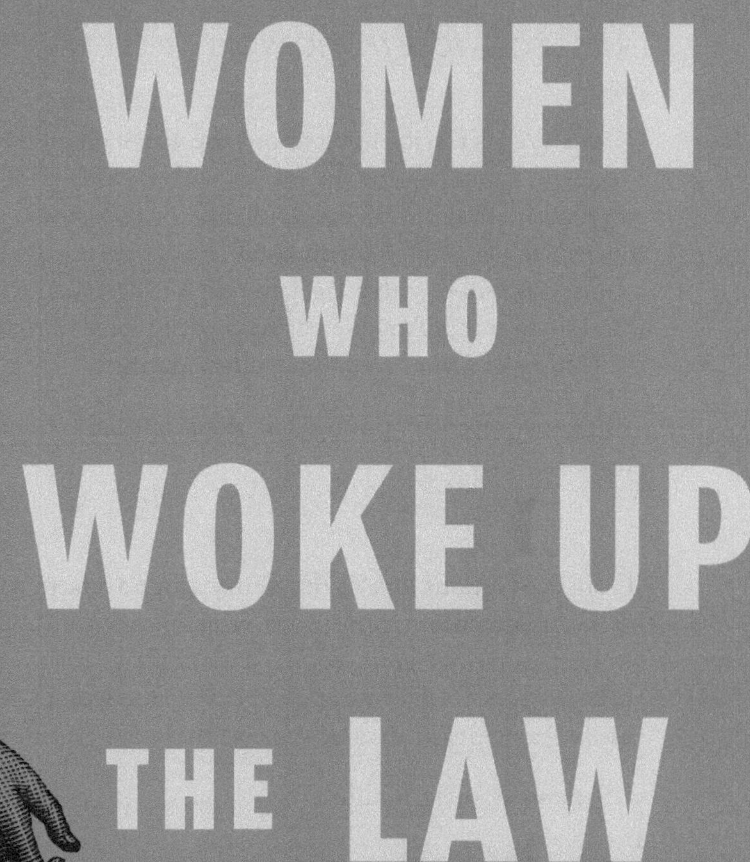

WOMEN WHO WOKE UP THE LAW

INSIDE THE CASES THAT CHANGED WOMEN'S RIGHTS IN CANADA

KARIN WELLS

PRAISE FOR *WOMEN WHO WOKE UP THE LAW*

"Karin Wells's terrific book about the way women have changed the law in Canada grips the reader with the power of a novel. Each story, whether about divorce, violence, or Indigenous rights, is told through the lens of one woman as she comes in contact—usually against her will—with a legal system not designed with her best interests in mind. Anyone engaged with women's rights, the law, or the history of Canada will find it fascinating."

—Elizabeth Renzetti, author of *What She Said: Conversations About Equality*

"From the Famous Five to the frenzy around a farm wife who wanted her fair share, these women were reluctant recruits to the courtroom battles that changed our world. Their chilling stories of adultery, abuse, and abortion came at great cost to the women whose personal cases became public causes. We owe them our gratitude."

—Senator Pamela Wallin

"These are stories of courage and perseverance. Each gem is about an ordinary woman who achieved something extraordinary. We owe a debt of gratitude to these women, but also to Karin Wells for—once again—pulling back the curtain of Canadian history to celebrate the women who sought and achieved justice. These remarkable stories are about unsung Canadian heroes—women who pried justice and fairness from the unwilling grasp of the patriarchy. Brava to Karin Wells and to these women for their courage and perseverance. A beautifully written and compelling book about extraordinary Canadian women, the unsung heroes of history whose personal quests for justice changed the laws for all of us."

—Carol Off, author of *At a Loss for Words: Conversation in an Age of Rage*

"As Wells deftly demonstrates, Canadian history is full of 'defiant and ornery' women who stood up for themselves—often without ever realizing they were standing up for others. Whether it's reproductive rights or women's safety, hope is often hard to come by these days. But *Women Who Woke up the Law* shows us that we have faced these moments before and have come out victorious. Let this book inspire you."

—Julie S. Lalonde, *Resilience Is Futile: The Life and Death and Life of Julie S. Lalonde*

"*Women Who Woke up the Law* is itself a wake-up call; mesmerizing, compelling, and heartbreaking. The battles that these women fought against systemic injustice assert the importance of breaking silence, speaking out, and yes, washing our linen in public. If 'fear makes you feeble,' this fearless tracing of fearless women challenging inequality and injustice roars with strength and resilience. Every thinking woman and man in Canada needs to read this book. An unflinching reminder of women's long and fierce fight for justice under the law."

—Aritha van Herk, writer

"A compelling and illuminating work, readers will be inspired by the fierce, embattled protagonists of *Women Who Woke up the Law* and equally enraged by their circumstances. In our present political climate, I didn't read this book as a work of history but as a call to arms."

—Emily Urquhart, author of *Ordinary Wonder Tales*

Library and Archives Canada Cataloguing in Publication

Title: Women who woke up the law / Karin Wells.
Names: Wells, Karin, 1949- author
Identifiers: Canadiana (print) 20240472179 | Canadiana (ebook) 20240473884 | ISBN 9781772604191 (softcover) | ISBN 9781772604207 (EPUB)
Subjects: LCSH: Women's rights—Canada—Cases. | LCSH: Women—Legal status, laws, etc.—Canada—Cases. | LCSH: Sex discrimination against women—Law and legislation—Canada—Cases. | LCGFT: Case studies.
Classification: LCC KE509 .W45 2025 | DDC 342.7108/78—dc23

Cover design by Natalie Olsen
Edited by Gillian Rodgerson

Printed and bound in Canada

Second Story Press gratefully acknowledges the support of the Ontario Arts Council and the Canada Council for the Arts for our publishing program. We acknowledge the financial support of the Government of Canada through the Canada Book Fund.

Canada Council for the Arts

Funded by the Government of Canada
Financé par le gouvernement du Canada
Canada

Published by
Second Story Press
20 Maud Street, Suite 401
Toronto, ON M5V 2M5
www.secondstorypress.ca

To Janice, Bunnie, Sharon A., and Sharon M.,
Margie, Christine, Brenda, and Milda

CONTENTS

If women lawyers and women judges through their differing perspectives on life can bring a new humanity to bear on the decision-making process, perhaps they will make a difference. Perhaps they will succeed in infusing the law with an understanding of what it means to be fully human.

—Madame Justice Bertha Wilson,
Supreme Court of Canada

INTRODUCTION

I will be master of what is mine own: She is my goods, my chattels; she is my house, my household stuff, my field, my barn, my horse, my ox, my ass, my any thing.

—Petruchio, *The Taming of the Shrew*,
William Shakespeare, 1590

Things didn't start well for women—"She is my goods…my horse…my any thing." That is how it was. She had no property rights: she was the property. When she married, her identity merged with his; merged and disappeared. In ancient Greece and Rome, it was known as the "perpetual tutelage of women"—women were forever under the thumb of their father or husband. It was inconceivable that women could have an identity of their own. Women were less than slaves. Legally, slaves could be emancipated. It was biologically predetermined that women could not. "Rights" of any sort are a very modern concept.

As Bertha Wilson, the first woman appointed to Canada's Supreme Court, said: "Change in the law comes slowly and incrementally; that is its nature. It responds to changes in society; it seldom initiates them." For decades, glaciers moved more quickly than the lot of women under Canadian law. Then, seemingly out of nowhere, comes the "landmark" case that turns the world on its head. Sometimes it's a clear, triumphant victory, and sometimes the big cases capture attention and outrage because the court *does not* respond to changes in society.

Somewhere, lost in the legal verbiage behind those landmark cases, is a woman who decided, late one night, after her partner had knocked her about one time too many, or after she got nowhere with her fifth polite letter to someone in an office in Ottawa, or after she was arrested, or after she simply had had enough of whatever, decided to push back, put herself on the line, and fight for a change in the law. That's what and who this book is about, those stubborn, bold women who plunged in. Few, if any, of the women behind the cases in this book—neither the lawmakers nor the lawbreakers—would have had any idea of what they were letting themselves in for, what getting on the witness stand would mean, how the years of appeals and delay would wear on them. They were certainly not expecting the public attention and, often, criticism, that followed them. Nor could they have anticipated that the process would take on a life of its own, often leaving them alone and on the sidelines. Going to court or being taken to court, if she was a witness or charged with an offence, was sometimes fatally difficult.

+++

It was one of the most unnerving days of my youth. I was a young law student doing my articles—the year of practical training that came after law school. The firm I articled with acted for the local Children's Aid Society, and workers were coming to town to find out more about how courts and trials worked and what would be expected of them if and when they had to testify when Children's Aid made an application to take a child into care.

There was a mock trial. I was on the witness stand cast as the inept young mother trying to hold on to her child. The very senior lawyer, my principal, took me through my evidence while a couple of hundred Children's Aid workers watched. I am a good talker. Not this time. Propped up there at the front of the room, I couldn't say what I wanted to say, couldn't sound convincing, couldn't remember anything at all. Another well-seasoned trial lawyer zeroed in for the kill: the cross-examination. I knew this man; he was perfectly pleasant in real life. Now, he grew fangs, going after me and tearing me limb from limb. And that was "just pretend."

What would it have been like for that woman who was trying to convince a jury in a tiny courthouse in Nova Scotia that it was self-defence when she killed her partner? Or for the young woman walking into the palais de justice in small-town Quebec to argue that it was her choice, not his, to have an abortion? What would the woman who sat watching from the gallery of the Supreme Court of Canada have been thinking as nine white, black-robed men determined whether she could be a Status Indian after she married a white man? What was it that pushed these women, even when their lawyers said their fight was hopeless? Law in Canada is made by both the courts and the legislatures. There is constant tension between the two and frequent condemnation of "activist" courts. "Appointed" judges, it is reasoned, should not overturn decisions of elected parliamentarians. But then there are issues that are too politically hot for elected members of Parliament: Are women persons? Could anyone other than the pregnant woman veto an abortion? It was the courts, spurred on by pushy women, not parliament, that settled those questions. We owe them.

Not surprisingly, all but one of the cases discussed in this book spring from marriages and sex. If a marriage ended—and for decades, not many did—for one thing, women were dependent on their husbands for support. The other reality was that divorce, for a woman, was hard to come by. *Her* grounds for divorce were limited. A woman who managed to circumvent, if not definitively change, the law—like Eleanora Tudor-Hart—must have been exceptional. How did she manage to hold on to her children (divorced women usually lost custody) and divorce her philandering husband at a time when no other women could?

Who was Irene Florence Murdoch, the Alberta woman who fought for half the ranch where she had laboured? And why was she so damn tenacious? Then there's Stella Bliss, the Vancouver hippie in a flowered dress who needed her hundred-and-something dollars a week in government maternity benefits to stay afloat. Little did she know it, her fight for maternity benefits would redefine women's equality under the Charter of Rights. How did that happen? These women are the accused, complainants—what some would call victims, and plaintiffs. All of them, because they went to court, changed some aspect of the lives of women in this country.

There's an assumption that to get anywhere in court you have to have money and alabaster skin; certainly money helps—lawyers' fees are high. But this book is not about access. Suffice it to say that access to the justice system remains imperfect. Lack of money or understanding of how it all works, fear, and sometimes just plain fatigue, all play a role in deterring men and women from pursuing legal remedies. And it is hardly revelatory to point out that racialized men and women do not fare as well when they are charged with a criminal offence and are charged more often. In 2018, Indigenous women made up 40% of women inmates in federal prisons, but only 4% of the population of women in Canada.

And yet, the women in this book, who in various ways changed the law, were not the privileged and the well-heeled. It's unusual for a socially well-positioned woman to draw attention to herself by washing her dirty linen in public. There is one bona fide heiress in these stories and one stoutly upper-middle-class woman with very good political connections, although those connections did not get her what she wanted. The rest of these women did not have either money or privilege. They were more often simply defiant and ornery. Their lawyers took their cases either on a contingency basis—a percentage of the winnings—or acted pro bono, for nothing. One woman even argued the early stages of her case herself. These are stories about the fight that a waitress, a nurse's aide, a ranch wife, a young receptionist, a flight attendant, a teacher—working class women—put up to change the law.

The stories of these landmark cases do not happen neatly, decade by decade. Changes to the law do not happen in an inevitable forward flow. Sometimes it's one step forward, two steps back. When it came to women's rights, there was a pipeline of frustration running from the days of the early suffragettes until it eventually burst fifty years later with the second wave of feminism, showering cases on the Supreme Court of Canada in the 70s and 80s.

For decades, too, there was a dearth of women judges hearing cases. In 1970, there were 889 judges and magistrates in Canada; 14 were women. Only one—a Quebec judge—was a member of a Superior Court. Bertha Wilson was appointed to the Supreme Court of Canada in 1982, an appointment that coincided with the repatriation of Canada's Constitution and the passage of the Charter of Rights and Freedoms. Wilson's appointment to the Supreme Court in retrospect seemed politically inevitable. Nonetheless, it was widely opposed, even by one of the most liberal judges the court had known, Bora Laskin. "Was she ready?" he asked. "Weren't there more qualified candidates?"

Wilson—never a flamboyant figure—gave a talk in 1990 asking what difference, if any, women judges would make to the law. Her answer, in part, was contained in her judgement in *R v Morgentaler*, which found the criminalization of abortion violated a woman's Charter right to security of the person. Wilson said that,

> It is probably impossible for a man to respond, even imaginatively, to such a dilemma, not just because it is outside the realm of his personal experience...but because he can relate to it only by objectifying it, thereby eliminating the subjective elements of the female psyche [that] are at the heart of the dilemma.

Beverley McLachlin became the third woman appointed to the Supreme Court of Canada in 1989. She wrote in her memoir that when she was sworn in, Bertha Wilson pulled her aside and whispered, "Three down, six more to go." In the fall of 2023, when Mary Moreau was appointed to the highest court, Wilson, had she been alive, would have whispered, "Five down, four more to go." For the first time, the majority of judges on the Supreme Court of Canada are women.

It's not possible to predict which cases will become "landmarks." David Mossop, a forty-year veteran of the Community Legal Assistance Society in Vancouver, said, "Most of these cases, the big ones, happen by accident." And when it comes to women's rights, the big ones aren't always the winners. There's a difference between a legal loss and its political fallout. Irene Florence Murdoch and Stella Bliss both lost in court, but the political fallout pushed change faster and further than anyone expected.

One last thing: This book was not intended to be a tirade against abusive men. They just kept showing up. Regrettably, there are more manipulative threats, loaded guns, broken jaws, and unconscious women in these pages than I ever intended.

The law can be a blunt instrument. The consensus is that these days, society expects more of a solution-oriented form of justice, a justice system that is less adversarial, where winners and losers give way to common lessons learned. Nonetheless, judges and juries can, should, and do change the law, and women and their lawyers must and will continue to advocate.

—Karin Wells, Collingwood, Ontario, 2023

1. The Utmost Prudence

Where will this country come to in twenty-five years if we are going to grant divorces simply because some woman has been disappointed in regard to her husband, and comes here and asks for a dissolution of her marriage?

—E.A. Lancaster, Member of Parliament, 1905

Come spring, with leaves on the bushes, Eliza Campbell's grave is hard to find. The obliging man in the Mount Pleasant Cemetery office stretches an arm up over the counter with a map in his hand.

"Here." The cemetery man has clearly done this before. He has penned an *X* on one of the medium-sized squares not far from the Mount Pleasant Road entrance. "This is the Scott memorial. Then cross the road and walk straight back to the fence."

He pulls the map back and marks another *X* on a much smaller square.

"That's her." Casting a disapproving glance down at the shoes the visitor is wearing, he adds, "Watch your step."

Don't fall over, is what he's saying.

There are 168,000 graves in Toronto's Mount Pleasant Cemetery, some dating back to 1876. Massive granite monuments and mini-Greek temples for the rich and powerful; that's what gets noticed. Eliza Campbell is tucked away among the insignificant. The ground in the section where she is buried is pitted with tiny, sunken grave markers, some less than a foot square. Breaking up the grass are a few upright, government-issued stones memorializing soldiers killed in the world wars and clusters of stones inscribed with Chinese characters, graves of members of the China Inland Mission. Then there are little, flat stones marked "Mother" or "My beloved wife" disappearing into overgrown lawn. No, that wouldn't be Eliza. She was no one's "beloved." Anyone searching for the last resting place of Eliza Campbell could not be blamed for thinking that she, like so many others, has sunk into obscurity, her grave maker merely a pothole after more than a hundred years in the ground.

Eyes to the earth, walking back to the brown wooden fence, there's still no sign of Eliza Campbell. All that's left to search is the ground under the bushes by the fence. Push the branches aside, brush off the dirt, and there she is, the inscription clear and clean: "Eliza Maria Campbell, 1844–1910," and across the bottom of the stone, writ deep and loud enough to be heard a century later, are the words "I did <u>not</u> commit adultery."

Eliza Campbell's grave marker, Mount Pleasant Cemetery, Toronto.

No, Eliza—the Parliament of Canada voted and passed judgement in 1877 and agreed that you did *not* commit adultery. Trouble was, your husband said you did. And that's how it all started. As her home town newspaper, the *Whitby Chronicle* reported,

> The resistance of an intelligent, brave and virtuous woman...against the persecution and ill treatment of a coarse, ill-natured, penurious and unprincipled husband, has made the Campbell Divorce Case, not only a cause celebre, but has conclusively established...that in Ontario...a married woman has few rights which a husband is bound to respect.

+++

[T]he family of J.T. Byrne were held in very high estimation in the community and there was never a whisper of scandal against the lady until the time when the defendant chose to make the accusation.

April 6, 1863, was a Monday. Eliza was nineteen, tall for the times, with dark hair and eyes that glowed with joy on her wedding day. Her father, the Reverend John Thomas Byrne, beamed as he stood waiting to officiate for his favourite daughter. Byrne, Whitby's Congregationalist minister, was well-liked, well-respected. His son, James, was on his way to becoming Whitby's druggist; his elder daughter, Bithiah, was already well-married; and now here was Eliza taking her first step toward becoming a respectable Whitby matron. The Reverend Byrne had raised his children to think for themselves, both the boys and the girls. Years later, when things went sour, Eliza said she was liberal in her views, at least when it came to church matters. "Spirited," her friends said of her—a word that came back to haunt her.

There she stood on that spring day in her best dress. There was neither the budget nor the inclination to buy a wedding dress, a dress that would only be worn once. No frills, no fancy. The Congregationalists were first cousins to the Puritans, after all, and austerity was next to Godliness.

The Reverend Byrne cleared his throat and looked at the pair of them, his Eliza and her groom, Robert Campbell. His daughter had made a good match—or so he thought. Campbell, ten years older than his fiancée, had a baby face and a deceptively innocent look about him. He was an enterprising, conservative Presbyterian who, with his younger brother, James, and his sister, had arrived in Whitby from Scotland in the 1850s.

Robert Campbell established a dry goods store—hats, clothes, dishes—and then the year he married Eliza, he made his younger brother James a partner, giving the enterprise "increased energy and means." The Campbell brothers had a nose for business and were doing well. Very well. (When James Campbell left Whitby more than thirty years later, the *Whitby Chronicle* reported that he departed "so well supplied with this world's goods that he can live in comfortable leisure and luxury anywhere he chooses to go.") With their new store in the middle of town, the Campbell brothers epitomized professional success. What Robert needed next was a wife.

Marriage and a family were essential steps for a rising young businessman. The Campbell brothers had views of women rooted in

Robert Campbell

the teachings of John Knox, founder of Scottish Presbyterianism; to wit, God created women as servants and subjects to men.

When Robert looked at his bride, he saw a modest, pious—he wanted pious—young woman who he never doubted would be a good and obedient wife. When Eliza looked at him, she saw "her guardian and her guide," as she referred to him when she testified in court years later. And she accepted his guidance; Eliza was no radical. She also saw a man with good prospects. Marriage, she knew, meant work and risk; it would be her job to give him children—her mother had had nine but only four lived past infancy. What she did not realize as she stood in front of her father, on the verge of becoming a wife, was that the moment the Reverend Byrne pronounced them man and wife, she would lose her legal identity. Her name would be gone. She could no longer manage or dispose of any property, sign legal documents, keep any salary she might earn, or obtain an education without her husband's permission. It would also be almost impossible for her to leave her marriage and stand on her own. But like most brides, Eliza did not think for a moment that she would ever want to leave her Robert, nor he her.

The ceremony was brief—the celebration briefer.

+++

Thank God the people of Canada know how to estimate...value and cherish the sacred character of the matrimonial tie, the purity and sacredness of the family—they know these sentiments—attributes of the higher law—are the source and life of Christian civilization and without them no nation can permanently prosper.

—Senator Robert Gowan, 1888

When Eliza married Robert in 1863, only four couples in what would eventually become the province of Ontario in the country of Canada had ever been divorced—all at the instigation of the husband. Four couples—eight people. Marriage was sacrosanct. It was the foundation of this new country. As feminist legal scholar

Constance Backhouse wrote, "Canadians became obsessed with the notion of the institution of marriage as the structural underpinning of a stable and healthy society." And if there was a little weakness in your personal structural underpinnings, your family, you must never let it show. Appearances were everything. Families, strong united families, were the building blocks for the future prosperity of the nation. In 1868, a year after Confederation, divorce was denounced as an unchristian practice.

The dissolution of marriage was also a serious political issue. Divorce, everyone came to believe, could stain the social fabric and potentially tear the country apart. Under the British North America Act, which defined Canada as a country, marriage and divorce were federal matters. However, divorce was a political hot potato. Catholic-dominated Quebec had its Civil Code, and the Code was clear: "Marriage can only be dissolved by the natural death of one of the parties; while both live it is indissoluble." Therefore, there was no divorce in Quebec, and when Upper and Lower Canada were united in 1841, Quebec Catholic legislators could and would block any attempt to introduce a Divorce Act in this new federation. It was more politically expedient for the federal government to ignore the issue and, despite the British North America Act, let the provinces get on with it. Divorce in Canada, as it expanded and added provinces, was a patchwork mess. Prior to World War I, Nova Scotia, New Brunswick, and British Columbia had divorce courts (they had been established before Confederation). It was impossible to get a divorce in Quebec, given the strength of the Catholic Church, and next to impossible in Ontario, where there were no divorce courts.

In the beginning, British and French settlers brought the laws of their respective countries with them. With the exception of Quebec and its French-based Civil Code, Canadian law followed English law. For centuries, with some exceptions, divorce in Britain could only and rarely be obtained through an Act of Parliament (the old ecclesiastical courts forbade divorce completely). And that's the way it was in what became Ontario. A husband or, theoretically, a wife who wanted and could afford to divorce had to go to Ottawa, present their evidence—their witnesses—to a committee of the Senate, and then listen as their marital future was debated and voted on, first in the Senate and then in the House of Commons. Finally, their Act of Parliament, their divorce, was shipped off to England and signed by Queen Victoria.

The British handed divorce over to the courts in 1857 and set out grounds for divorce in legislation. That was in Britain. Nothing changed in Canada. Not surprisingly, and much to the distress of many Canadian legislators, the number of divorces in Great Britain rose very quickly. Member of Parliament and future chief justice of Ontario, William Mullock, said of the British situation, "The divorce court in England is one of the greatest scandals of British life today."

In the United States, divorce was a state matter, and in some northern states, the grounds for divorce were expanded from the standard adultery, desertion, and cruelty to include bigamy, impotence, felony conviction, and even drunkenness. Between 1870 and 1880, the American rate of divorce increased by 79%. The Canadian prime minister, Sir John A. Macdonald, was aghast:

> The number of divorces, the corruption of society, and the number of collusive trials increase to the annually increasing degradation of the public mind.... I prefer our system here, which offers very considerable impediments to the granting of divorces, to the systems which prevail elsewhere.

Political leaders across the board maintained that they did not object to divorce per se but did not want "additional facilities," i.e., courts, granting divorce. Parliament managed to make it as difficult as possible for couples to divorce.

Sanctimonious, hypocritical Canada. It wasn't about the happiness of the people. Rather, it was about preserving the image of a morally upright nation. Not surprisingly, Canada had one of the lowest divorce rates in the western world. In the thirty-three years from 1867 to 1900, Parliament granted sixty-nine divorces: a little more than two per year.

Download that attitude to the drawing rooms of the middle class, and there was a sharp intake of breath if the "D word" was uttered in polite society. A well-brought-up woman like Eliza Campbell was expected not to know, let alone talk, of such things. Newspapers went out of their way not to write about marital matters. Words like "indignities" and "brutality" were code for wife-battering and sexually abusive husbands, and if a newspaper had to call a spade a spade, it would apologize to its readers.

There was also a grotesque imbalance when it came to who could divorce whom and why. In those four pre-Confederation divorces, the husbands had cast off their wives on the grounds of adultery. Wives, on the other hand, were encouraged to ignore a husband's marital indiscretions. The other reality was that if she divorced her husband, a woman risked losing not only her means of support but also her children. Husbands were almost always granted custody. Children were property. A philandering husband was something to be endured.

John Alexander Gemmill, who wrote the first Canadian textbook on divorce in 1889, was not unsympathetic to the plight of women:

> Divorce at present is a perquisite of the man. The law empowers the man, however monstrous his marital conduct may have been, to turn his wife into the street and separate her from every intercourse with her children, or leave her to starve in the workhouse, if in a moment of weakness she forgets her marriage vows. But a woman who has been subject to open and continual adultery, even under the conjugal roof, is unable to obtain a divorce, only unless he has been guilty of cruelty or two years desertion as well as adultery.

If a wife had the bravado and audacity, not to mention the means, to try to rid herself of an adulterous husband, she found that the playing field was not even. Adultery alone was not enough. She had to prove, as Gemmill said, adultery *plus* cruelty or desertion. (It was ruled in 1826 that a husband had "a right to chastise his wife moderately" and that, for her to be justified in leaving her husband, "the chastisement must be such as to put her life in jeopardy.")

To the English Law Lords, this kind of inequality hardly needed justifying. At the beginning of the nineteenth century, the most influential and learned lawyer in the land, Lord Chancellor John Scott, spelled it out: "It is to be considered that the adultery committed by the wife and the adultery committed by the husband are entirely different in their consequences." The adultery of the wife, he went on, might "impose a spurious issue on the husband." ("Issue" being the polite word for bastard child.) And the great Lord Eldon adjusted his wig, fixed the room with a penetrating gaze, and dared anyone to disagree. In Canada in 1893, Ontario's Chief Justice of Queen's Bench, John Douglas Armour, summed it up neatly: "the adulterer retains his place in society, while the adulteress loses hers."

It would be tall, sharp-eyed Eleanora Tudor-Hart of Montreal who would go on the attack and become the first woman in Canada to be granted a divorce by Parliament on the grounds of adultery alone.

Eleanora, privileged, impatient, and insistent, was an American aristocrat, the daughter of one of the sixty listed Boston Brahmin families. Her father, Frederic Tudor, known as the "Ice King" of Boston, made his fortune shipping ice all over the world. Thanks to Frederic Tudor, there was ice cream in India. At forty-nine, realizing that he needed a family—and therefore a wife—to complete the picture, he found nineteen-year-old Euphemia Fenno. But Effy Fenno didn't want babies. Ultimately, she was locked in her room and confined to bed, where she produced six children. Eleanora was the last born.

Young Eleanora lived life on her own terms: she came from a family of independent women, and wealth helped. While modest little Eliza Campbell was quite content to be married in her best dress in small-town Whitby, that would not have been good enough for Eleanora Tudor. Her social position demanded she be corseted, bustled, and wrapped in creamy white satin, a bride in full battle dress when she married Canadian Frederick Levey Hart in 1871. Seventeen years later in 1888, having proved her husband "a constant and habitual frequenter of houses of ill-fame," she washed her hands of him, successfully divorcing him on the grounds of adultery alone. It was a radical step forward in Canadian law and an early flirtation with gender equality.

The Hart divorce marked the first debate in Parliament on the rights of women. But a decade earlier, Eliza Campbell had laid the groundwork. Not that she intended to.

Eleanora Tudor-Hart and baby William Owen, 1876.

♦♦♦

Just received, Port Wine, Whiskey—4000 gallons, 140 gallons Jamaica rum, fresh oysters, English black and Japan teas, English tweed.

—*Whitby Chronicle*, 1862

Whitby, principal town in the then-county of Ontario, was buzzing when the Campbells set up house. They were an abstemious couple, but with four thousand gallons of whiskey swilling about in a town of three thousand, there was a lot of life going on around them.

The front page of the *Chronicle* featured ads for twenty different hotels. A piano maker and a manufacturer of sewing machines catered to growing domestic needs. The Royal Adelphi dramatic company spent a week performing in Whitby. At the invitation of the *Chronicle*'s founder and publisher, William Higgins, Thomas D'Arcy McGee, the Irish Catholic journalist, politician, and poet, lectured on the novels of Sir Walter Scott. McGee would be assassinated by the Fenian Brotherhood six years later.

The newspaper ran articles on the American Civil War raging a thousand kilometres to the south, and on page three, Robert and James Campbell announced a sale of their winter stock to make room for spring dress goods and "large amounts of readymade clothing."

Whitby was a burgeoning town of dirt streets—well-watered in the summer to keep the dust down—surrounded by farms. William Gordon, another Scottish immigrant, owned a hundred acres on the shore of Lake Ontario south of the town. The Gordons and the Byrnes had been friends since Eliza's childhood—she played the piano and sang at Gordon get-togethers. The Reverend Byrne officiated the wedding of the eldest Gordon son, and another son, James Keith Gordon, was one of the fourteen lawyers advertising in the *Whitby Chronicle*. When he opened his practice—the year that Eliza Byrne married Robert Campbell—the *Chronicle* said that he, "like his father, will, we feel assured, deserve public favor by strict rectitude of principle." The best-known Gordon, Adam, was a member of Parliament who made his reputation with a proposed Bill on the

"Better Celebration of the Sabbath." The Gordons were every bit as morally upright as Eliza's family. Yet it was the youngest son, George Brand Gordon, whom Robert Campbell ultimately accused of seducing his wife.

+++

In 1873, one of the wettest years on record, Robert Campbell arrived back in Canada after a buying trip to England for the business. He disembarked from his ship just before the deadliest hurricane in Canadian history made landfall in the Maritimes. A thousand people died, twelve hundred ships sank, and countless bridges and roads were destroyed. It was a cataclysm worthy of the Old Testament. Perhaps the ever-pious Robert Campbell saw it as God's punishment for the evil wreaking havoc on his domestic life.

In the early years of the marriage, all had seemed well. Eliza had three children, two boys and a girl, and furthered the Campbell line. The R. and J. Campbell Dry Goods business thrived. The brothers bought more property and James, the younger Campbell, got into local politics. (He was elected first a Whitby councillor, then deputy reeve, and ultimately mayor of Whitby.)

Eliza had gone with her husband on an earlier buying trip to England and had the effrontery to make what was described as a "walking, nodding, bowing acquaintance" with a man on the ship. Robert thought the worst. It was a harbinger of what was to come.

This time he had set off for England in June of 1873 by himself, leaving Eliza, now twenty-nine, and the children on their own for the summer. She was three months pregnant with their fourth child. They were by now ten years married, and it had become increasingly apparent that they were not well-matched. That summer of 1873 provided her with a break from her increasingly dour husband. As William MacDougall, later her lawyer, said,

> Mrs. Campbell is a person of great social aptitudes, always disposed to entertain her friends...she was fond of music and the society of young persons...these

> were more congenial than the cold, morose, negligent, absorbed husband who seems to have thought that all his wife should think of was how to manage his house, look after his children, and wear a pleasant face when he came home late at night.

That summer, she spent time with her Byrne family and the Gordons. There were no friendly invitations from her brother-in-law James and his wife while her husband was away. This isn't to say that James wasn't keeping an eye on his brother's household. For two months, he, along with John Anderson, who was married to the Campbell sister, kept watch on Eliza, spying on her from the local alleyways. They watched her and she watched them watching her. "They prowled about the house like thieves in the night until after midnight," she said. It was unnerving and did not bode well.

Robert returned to Whitby on August 25, 1873, greeted his wife, and told her he wanted to take the three children, then nine, eight, and six, to Saugeen on the shore of Lake Huron for a "change of air." He wanted to go immediately, not even pausing to spend the night at home. Eliza went with them partway, then he kissed her goodbye. The children turned and waved to their mother as they rode away. It was the last she ever saw of her two eldest boys and her daughter.

Unbeknownst to Eliza, her husband had gone to see his brother before he arrived at their house. James had reported on his summer surveillance, telling Robert that he had seen a man enter the Campbell house late at night when Eliza was alone and that he had the evidence to prove that he was up to no good.

Robert Campbell, by all accounts, was a demon when his temper was roused. All of his suspicions were reinforced and his anger fuelled by his brother James, a notoriously suspicious, unforgiving, graceless man. It was said of James in the *Whitby Chronicle*, "if Mr. Campbell lacked some of the popularity which is the aim of most men, it was because he never sought after it, having an independent and rather curt style of dealing."

Was it that hair-shirt brand of Protestant piety that the Campbells brought with them from Scotland that made Robert Campbell believe the worst of his wife? There is no credible explanation, but he jumped on his younger brother's accusations and immediately filed an action for "criminal conversation," the legal euphemism for sleeping with another man's wife, against twenty-five-year-old George Gordon, the man James said he had seen "at home" with Eliza. ("Criminal Conversation" was on the books in Ontario until the mid-1970s.) Eliza was blindsided. She did not deny that young George had come by for a visit. He was a family friend—they had known each other for years. Her husband was not interested in explanations, and neither was the law. "Under the law of Ontario," as her lawyer described it, "the petitioner [Robert Campbell] in this action has the case all to himself. He produced his own witnesses and they cannot be contradicted." There was no "two sides to the story."

James Campbell testified in support of his brother saying that not only had he seen George Gordon entering the house, but that young George had also confessed and he, James, had heard "suggestive" goings-on while he was lurking outside the house. (The maid, Jane Newsome, testified that she heard no such thing; but, the lawyers argued, given that she admitted she had "lost her virtue," her "veracity" could not be trusted.) The wife, in this case Eliza Campbell, had no right of rebuttal, no right to call witnesses.

Not surprisingly, Robert Campbell won his case. George Gordon had to pay him, the wronged husband, damages for infringing on his property—his wife. She was now labelled an adulteress. It had been little more than a month since her husband returned home. Eliza Campbell was reeling.

Alone and by now nearly seven months pregnant, she holed up in the house—her husband's house. She had no claim to the property and he wanted her gone. At first, he tried to starve her out, telling Whitby merchants not to extend any credit. The Byrnes closed ranks. Her mother, her sister, and her brother the druggist looked after her. They were all present at the house when Robert Campbell returned, accompanied by a local constable, to remove his wife. He even had a doctor's note saying that he could forcibly remove her without jeopardizing her health. Eliza's mother testified in the court action that followed: "Mr. Campbell told me he came to put Mrs. Campbell out of the house and likewise put me out. I told him it would be very difficult to do so." Mrs. Byrne went on,

> Mr. Campbell ordered her to get out of bed and leave the house. He then took hold of her and tugged at her in the bed. He succeeded in raising her up. She resisted and struck at him and said, "Go away from me; don't hurt me." She called him a villain...I then saw him take her by the lower limbs and take her out of bed which I thought a very painful experience for a woman in her situation. She asked if he was not ashamed of himself. He said "No: It was she who ought to be ashamed...." He came at her with violence.... She was scarcely able to stand. They then got her to the stairs and...took her down the stairs. I saw her thrust out by Robert Campbell.... She was put out at quarter to ten at night.

Eliza collapsed into the arms of her brother outside the front door. The *Whitby Chronicle*, doing its best to sound even-handed, summed things up:

> Mrs. Campbell is a refined well-educated woman very much admired for her beauty and her accomplishments. She has resided since her earliest childhood in the town and never before has the breath of scandal whispered against her good name. Mr. Campbell is a highly respected businessman and in bringing such a charge against his wife and breaking up his household must believe himself to be grievously wronged.

Years later, when the *Campbell* case was over and done with, Eliza Campbell's lawyer William MacDougall's address to the Senate was published in the *Whitby Chronicle*. It went on for pages but there was one key question: "What protection," he asked, "does the law extend to this discarded wife?"

On December 13, 1873, two and a half months after her husband had physically removed her from what she had thought was her home, Eliza Maria Campbell gave birth to her fourth child, Francis William Campbell.

+++

Two weeks after baby Francis made his appearance in Whitby, Ernest Percyval Hart was born in Montreal. Percyval, as he was always known, was the second baby for twenty-three-year-old Eleanora (Tudor) Hart, the Boston heiress. Effie (Mary Alice) had been born the year before, and Edith would come along three years later. Francis William in Whitby, Percyval in Montreal—two squalling boy babies who grew up without much sympathy or affection for their mothers, women who each had a part in changing divorce law in Canada.

It was Percyval who, years later, would tell Eleanora's story. It was a jaundiced view. When she was eighty-six, he wrote his mother a letter taking her to task for inflicting the social stigma of divorce on him and his sisters. What business did she have, he implied, leaving her husband and casting shame upon her children? Not only did the law offer next to no help to a woman who wanted to leave a bad marriage, "society" and her own children condemned her as well.

When Eleanora had married Frederick Hart in Massachusetts in 1871, she was a fine catch, reportedly worth $200,000 (the equivalent of $5.3 million in 2024) in her own right. The couple moved to Montreal where the children were born and then to Tallapoosa, Georgia—"Possum Snout," as it was also known. Frederick called himself a mining engineer and set about making his mark on the world, or trying to. He and his brother-in-law, William Tudor, set up an ill-conceived copper mine in the middle of nowhere. If there was copper, there was no way to get it to market. The family lived a very rustic homesteading life in the shadow of the Civil War. Eleanora had been born into luxury, yet she managed well in Possum Snout. Years later, Percyval would say that his Georgia childhood days were his only happy memories of family life.

The happiness didn't last long. First, William Tudor bailed on Possum Snout and the mine and moved back to Boston. Eleanora and Frederick and the three children were not far behind. They returned to Montreal and moved in with Frederick's father; the children were shuffled between boarding schools and their Boston grandparents'. Eleanora and Frederick tolerated each other. It was a marriage "without affection," one of the senators hearing the divorce application said later. Old Frederic Tudor, Eleanora's father, had died in 1864, leaving a substantial legacy to his children. Now there were money arguments. When the Hart divorce came before Parliament in 1888, no one disagreed that Frederick Hart had married Eleanora for her money. But that was just a sidebar. There was something else in the air, some other problem in the marriage. Percyval, looking back as an adult, could not say, or chose not to say, what it was. By the mid-1870s, Eleanora's marriage was rotting away. Eliza's had exploded.

+++

The lawyers, as they usually do will reap a plentiful harvest from the misfortune of their neighbors.

—*Whitby Chronicle*

In all likelihood, it was James Keith Gordon, the older lawyer brother, who pushed Eliza to fight back and counter her husband's charge of "criminal conversation" by bringing an action for defamation—slander. She was desperate to clear her name. The Campbell brothers had besmirched both the Byrnes and the Gordons. Still nursing her baby, Eliza was back in court in the spring of 1874. James Campbell's testimony, she charged, was a pack of lies.

The *Whitby Chronicle* devoted an entire edition to the trial. The Toronto courtroom was "deeply crowded," it reported. There is nothing like a scandal to cultivate a crowd. Witnesses lined up on each side. One testifying for Eliza Campbell said that her husband had known the young George Gordon for years and welcomed him into his house. A Whitby woman testified against her, saying that "a woman in that condition was likely to forget herself." The newspaper reported that James Campbell and his brother-in-law John Anderson "asserted that they heard language of such a disgusting nature"—as they listened at Eliza Campbell's downstairs windows—"that one would have supposed that it could only have proceeded from a common prostitute. And yet," the *Chronicle* went on, "it came from the daughter of a clergyman who could scarcely have been acquainted with such language." Whitby hung on every word.

Eliza sued for $10,000 in damages (more than a quarter of a million dollars in 2024). On April 2, 1874, the all-male jury—women would not be allowed to serve on juries in Ontario until 1952—found that James Campbell had indeed perjured himself and defamed Eliza's good name. They awarded her $1,000. One juror told a reporter that ten of the twelve jurors were inclined to give her the full amount. Whitby was jubilant. The *Chronicle* had a field day:

> [Q]uite a demonstration took place. A torchlight procession headed by the Whitby band paraded the principal streets and halting in front of the residence of James Byrne [the druggist]...gave hearty cheers for Mrs. Campbell, Mr. Byrne, and Mr. M/G. Cameron [the lawyers]. There was also a display of fireworks in honor of the occasion after which the large crowd thronged the streets.

No sooner was the defamation case won than Eliza Campbell was back in court, asking for alimony. An adulterous woman in nineteenth-century Canada was not entitled to alimony, but she argued that the charges against her were based on perjured testimony, and therefore, she was not an adulterous woman. It's difficult to understand today, more than a hundred years later, but what Eliza Campbell really wanted, for the sake of her good name and her children, was the restoration of her marriage and her respectability.

The judge, Vice-Chancellor Blake, described by Constance Backhouse as one of the most vigorous supporters of patriarchal marriage, pondered the case for seventeen months. For nearly a year and a half, he hummed and hawed. "I am unable to force my mind to the conclusion," he finally wrote, "that I can stamp Mrs. Campbell with the indelible stigma" of adultery. Instead, he called her behaviour—entertaining a man while her husband was absent—"frivolous and indiscreet." "Frivolous and indiscreet" did her in. Eliza Campbell was chastised for a breech not of law but of decorum. Once again, it was the "well-being" of society that came first. Rather than use his judicial authority to make a potentially precedent-setting decision in favour of the wife and grant her alimony, Blake wriggled out of it. He passed the ball back to Robert Campbell and put the onus on her.

> I appeal to Mr. Campbell's feelings as a husband to allow his wife that opportunity of explanation which she so beseechingly asked for in her appealing letter of August 28 read by her counsel...I appeal to Mr. Campbell to spare himself and his wife this ordeal.... May he now not rest assured that his wife warned by the fearful ordeal she has undergone, will in the future seek more diligently to cultivate that spirit of obedience to his wishes which is her duty to exhibit; will learn more carefully to look after her children and her household duties and perform her part of a good wife and mother.

Robert Campbell could not, would not, "spare himself and his wife this ordeal." He did not believe that Eliza had learned her lesson, that she would "diligently cultivate that spirit of obedience." Even though evidence of adultery had been proved false, Vice-Chancellor Blake found that her "frivolity and indiscretion" was enough to deny her alimony.

Robert Campbell was not finished with his wife. He was bound and determined to grind her into the dirt. With his jaw firmly set, he served notice that he was applying to Parliament to divorce his wife on the grounds of adultery. Eliza said it again and again, "I did <u>not</u> commit adultery."

+++

The action of Mrs. Campbell has certainly not done her case any harm. When she was telegraphed for, an elderly gentleman and a friend, one Mr. Gross of Whitby, who believed in her innocence, accompanied her immediately.

—*Whitby Chronicle*, April 6, 1876

In the spring of 1876, a telegram summoned Eliza Campbell to Ottawa to appear before a committee of the Senate to defend herself.

A little more than a year earlier, her father, the Reverend Byrne, overwhelmed by all that had been said and written about his daughter, fell against a fence in Albany, New York, staggered a few steps, and dropped dead. The *Chronicle* reported that the "notorious case of *Campbell v Gordon* aggravated as it has been by the unwarranted language employed in a notice for divorce, had their share in bringing the venerable grey hairs of the Reverend Mr. Byrne to a premature grave." Whitby's sympathy for Eliza grew.

Mr. Gross, a seventy-nine-year-old Whitby hardware merchant, stepped into the breach and became her protector. *Campbell v Campbell* was attracting attention far beyond Whitby. Eliza Campbell and Mr. Gross took the train to Ottawa and checked into the Russell House, Ottawa's most high-profile hotel where he shielded her as best he could from public attention. The *Whitby Chronicle* had sent a reporter to Ottawa.

> [In] five minutes, everyone else in the room was staring at her as she sat modestly beside the old gentleman. She was arrayed in the deepest mourning and seemed to keenly feel her unenviable position. Mrs. Campbell is tall and very slight in figure and a pronounced brunette with large black eyes. Her face though pale and evidently worn by nearly three years of all she experienced is interesting and expressive...she always brings a book and when not engaged in conversation seeks diversion in its pages.

The Russell House was across the street from the not-yet-complete Parliament buildings. (Canada had been a country for less than ten years.) Eliza Campbell, subdued and mourning both her marriage and the death of her father, testified before the Senate Committee. The case, her lawyer argued, was about more than the Campbells. Its significance should not be underestimated. "The decision in this case will have an important bearing not only on the rights of these individuals and their future happiness and position in society," MacDougall said, "but a powerful moral influence upon other families and individuals, far and wide." Moral influence eclipsed any question of rights. Ten years later, Senator Richard Gowan echoed MacDougall when he said that "the function of the legislators are in reality, not legal but moral." Divorce law was muddy, to say the least.

William MacDougall, who took Eliza Campbell's case to Ottawa, was a former member of Parliament and cabinet minister in Sir John A. Macdonald's government. He was considered a progressive, but "progressive" in the early years of confederation did not mean championing a wife's rights. Rather, it meant giving her an opportunity to explain herself and to promise, as Vice-Chancellor Blake suggested, to "mend her ways." She will, MacDougall assured Parliament, "cultivate that spirit of obedience to [her husband's] wishes which it is her duty to exhibit...[she] will learn more carefully to look after her children and her household duties and to perform her part of a good wife and mother." There was never for a moment any suggestion of equality between husband and wife.

MacDougall had two legal objectives: first, to defeat Robert's allegations of adultery and second, to get what Eliza wanted, a judicial separation, never a divorce, on the grounds of cruelty and desertion, as well as financial support. She was asking for a third of her husband's salary and "an amount for the support of any children allotted to her." (MacDougall had asked the Committee to "Let her keep the child [Francis William, who was now three] and the little girl. Let the husband keep the boys.")

William MacDougall argued well. Parliament dismissed Robert Campbell's application for divorce, gave Eliza a judicial separation, ordered Robert to pay her $500 a year, and gave her custody of little Francis William but not her daughter. They threw in $50 a day to pay their old colleague, MacDougall.

As she and Mr. Gross left Ottawa and trundled through the countryside, Eliza Campbell contemplated her situation. There she was, barely into her thirties, and what was she left with? Three of her children were gone. Her husband, in name only, despised her. Her father was dead, her brother James, the druggist, would die less than a year later. The only consolation—she had restored her good name, and her friends were still behind her. They made sure that MacDougall's submissions to the Senate on her behalf were published in the *Whitby Chronicle*, but she knew a cloud of suspicion would always hang over her. It was a bumpy ride back to Whitby. The law had not changed. Small consolation, but Eliza Campbell had given the country something to think about.

+++

...an unpardonable social offence.

When Percyval Tudor-Hart wrote to his elderly mother in 1936, condemning her for the social stigma she had inflicted on her children, he pointed out her every fault: her irascibility, her incorrigible nature, her neglect. His biographer, Alasdair Alpin MacGregor, writing decades later, referred to Eleanora as "the evil genius of the family." All four of the children, MacGregor maintained, were brought up to despise their father rather than to "love and revere him."

Toward the end of that memorable letter to his mother, Percyval wrote,

> you married our father no doubt because you thought it advisable as well as your pleasure and there can be no blame attached to your doing so. Five years later you were in misintelligence with him, each of you living in different parts of the world.... During one of your absences from us, you divorced our father in Montreal, at a time when divorce, certainly in the province of Quebec, was considered an unpardonable social offence. We had to share with you and our father the stigma.

Eleanora Tudor-Hart was the first woman in Canada to successfully sue her husband for divorce on the grounds of adultery alone. She made legal history. To her son, however, she had committed "an unpardonable social offence."

William Owen, the youngest of the Hart children, was born in 1884. (The children added the more prestigious "Tudor" to their name as young adults.) Shortly after his birth, Eleanora Tudor-Hart decided that she had had enough of her marriage. The lives of Eleanora and Frederick had degenerated to a point well beyond repair. The family was living in Montreal and the older children were in boarding schools. Frederick Hart would disappear at night and return looking increasingly the worse for wear. It was "because of wine and women," he would admit and go on to describe himself as "a blackguard," living the life he wanted, unashamedly visiting his favourite Montreal brothels. Eleanora Tudor-Hart moved out, something that nearly proved fatal to her case. Frederick Hart disappeared. Quietly, she hired a private detective and then a lawyer, filed her petition for divorce with Parliament, and slipped away to Ottawa to appear before the Senate Committee. Not until all was said and done did Eleanora Tudor-Hart go to Boston to talk to the children.

The older three, by then teenagers, presumed their mother had found their father, and when they met her at the railway station, Percyval recalled, they excitedly asked after him. "You no longer have a father!" she replied. "Is he dead?" asked the eldest, Effie, in great distress. "No, he's not dead," her mother replied, "but he has gone out of our lives forever. We are having nothing further to do with him." All three declared that they weren't going to allow their father to be taken out of their lives "in this pitiless way," as Percyval described it.

Eleanora Tudor-Hart had arrived at the door of the Senate seeking her divorce in 1888, nine years after Eliza Campbell had returned to Whitby. She knew nothing of the Campbell divorce, but her husband's lawyer certainly did. He was John Alexander Gemmill, the man who would publish the divorce textbook the following year. A book in which both the Campbell and Hart cases featured prominently.

Eleanora was "a woman of an exceedingly nervous temperament," remarked the senators after she testified. And they added that she was "a lady of a somewhat difficult temper." She hesitated and haltingly struggled through her story in front of the senators. Her lawyer then called a startling parade of witnesses: a man who was leaving the brothel as Frederick was arriving, as well as "an inmate of the house" who corroborated the testimony of the earlier witness and added that Frederick Hart seemed to know the girls of the house "the same as any person else that came in."

The facts of the case were one thing. Adultery had been proved. Frederick Hart frequented brothels, that was clear. The law was another. Eleanora was breaking new ground in asking for a divorce, alleging only adultery, never cruelty. "I cannot say that I have received any actual violence," she answered when asked, "and although he at times had very violent fits of temper and would sometimes threaten people's lives and cursed his father terribly to me in private, he only once threatened me with violence and then I ran and he could not do it." Adultery was sufficient for a man to divorce his wife but not enough for a woman to divorce her husband. Eleanora Tudor-Hart was asking for a little bit of equality.

+++

With respect to divorce in England one is struck with the marked, and I must think unjust, discriminations made between the sexes in respect to matrimonial offences, and the prejudices which existed, and still exist, against equal right of relief to the woman as well as the man.

—Senator J.R. Gowan

James Robert Gowan has been credited with organizing the Canadian court system and coordinating the new country's laws. He drafted statutes, underwrote the first law journal in the country, and funded John Gemmill's book on divorce. He chaired half the divorce committees while he was a senator. He was appointed to the Senate in 1885, and at age sixty-nine, was just hitting his stride when the Hart Bill of Divorce case came before the Divorce Committee.

"What should we be doing then if we refused to pass this bill?" wrote Gowan when Eleanora Tudor-Hart made her bid to change the law and divorce her adulterous husband.

> What but saying to a virtuous woman: "You are to remain to your life's end under the dominion of a

Sir James Robert Gowan, lawyer, judge, senator, and chair of the Senate Divorce Committee.

> profigate [sic] man who could only desire to retain his hold for unworthy purposes...." Under the dominion of a shamless [sic] man, who uncovered his evil doings to his wife and flaunted his impurities in her face! Is the maintenance of a decent society, the preservation of purity in family relations a matter of slight concern.... Will the Senate of Canada affirm by its decision that adultery may be practiced with impunity by husband and father in our Christian community, in the midst of our Christian homes?

It was a high-flown speech with its protestations of "the preservation of purity in family relations," but it had a hypocritical ring. It was widely known that Gowan had had an affair with his cousin Ogle Gowan's wife, and even more widely known that the newly elected, married leader of the Opposition, and future Prime Minister Wilfrid Laurier, was involved in what became a twenty-year love affair that has been described as the "most celebrated liaison" in Canadian political history.

When the Hart divorce was reported in Hansard, the official record of parliamentary debate, it occupied more than fifty pages. This at a time when the country was in the last throes of the Pacific bribery and corruption scandal, British Columbia and Manitoba were still new to Confederation, and the economy was in recession. Yet Parliament remained preoccupied with the moral upkeep of the nation.

+++

The Honourable Gentlemen have read the evidence, they can come to no other conclusion than that there was no justification for this woman deserting her husband.

Because she had money of her own, Eleanora Tudor-Hart was able to leave her husband, or "desert him" as at least one senator insisted, and that was a problem. When was a woman justified in leaving the marriage?

> Hon. Mr. Abbott—He told her on that occasion also that she was quite right in leaving him.... She is evidently unwilling to come out and state in the broad language of the streets what she found her husband did.... A gently nurtured woman, being asked in a room full of men what she had discovered, will not answer with the same candour that a woman of a different character will. He made many remarks to her which a virtuous man would not make to a virtuous wife.... On one occasion he told her that he was thoroughly bad and that he respected her for leaving him.

Other senators, however, argued that rather than leave her husband, she had a legal duty to correct his behaviour:

> She had proved no acts of cruelty; she had simply shown that the man had been out late at night card playing, and had doubtless been squandering her money.... The proper course for her was to have endeavored by her own conduct to reclaim him from those haunts...she never reasoned with him, never took the means that a woman should take to re-claim an erring husband.... If we admit that diversity of temperament, and other causes which prevent people from living happily together, furnish sufficient grounds for divorce, the applications for relief will increase enormously.

Was it proved that he committed adultery before she "deserted him"? And if she had left him, was he, therefore, justified in frequenting his favourite brothels? Back and forth the argument went, lobbing Eleanora Tudor-Hart's life over the net.

Whatever finally swayed the vote—it might have been the fate of the children—Eleanora Tudor-Hart got her divorce. In 1888, divorce bills were not "judged," they were voted on. The vote in the Senate was 32–9 in her favour. Theoretically, Eleanora Tudor-Hart changed the law, but the Hart divorce did not establish a strong precedent. A woman's right to sue for divorce on the grounds of adultery alone was not legislated until 1925—thirty-seven years later.

+++

William Owen Tudor-Hart, Eleanora's youngest child, never married. Her eldest son, Percyval, married three times (his first two wives died). Wife number one, Nellie, was his cousin, the daughter of his mother's sister and a Polish aristocrat. Effie, his elder sister, also married, but in 1896, Eleanora wrote to her second daughter, Edith, and swore her to a vow of spinsterhood. Why? The goal of every Victorian mother was to see their daughters well-married. What was going on in the Tudor-Hart family? Sixty-five years later, Percyval Tudor-Hart's biographer could still not bring himself to say why Eleanora had told her daughter that she must never marry.

Percyval grew up and became a respected artist, much to the displeasure of his father. When he was in his early twenties, Percyval returned to Canada briefly from Italy, where he had been living, and went to see his father. It was 1896, mere months before his mother told Edith she must never marry. Percyval found Frederick Hart in the Verdun Protestant Hospital for the Insane, set up just five years earlier. Psychiatric treatment in that era amounted to not much more than restraint, violence, and isolation. More than one retired doctor has called "the Verdun" a snake pit. Percyval wrote to his biographer that his father was "a hopeless case, with delusions of grandeur" and unable to recognize his son. Frederick Hart was forty-four and had been committed the year before. Was it very early onset dementia? Some congenital condition? Or was it "the loathsome disease," a consequence of those habitual brothel visits? Tertiary syphilis was rampant. Up to 45% of Canada's North-West Mounted Police force was reported as infected in the mid-1880s.

Victorian women who didn't know where babies came from, who weren't allowed to talk about adultery, had no idea what syphilis was. And if they did, they could never admit it. (There was no reliable test for syphilis until 1906, ten years after Percyval visited his father, and no cure until the 1940s with the advent of antibiotics.) Had Eleanora figured it out? Was that why she told her daughter never to marry? And when she appeared before Parliament petitioning for divorce, did some Honourable Gentlemen have their suspicions? Frederick Hart never left the Verdun Hospital for the Insane. He died in 1916.

+++

The Campbell divorce proved too much for Whitby, or Whitby proved too much for the divorced Campbells. Robert upped stakes in May of 1885 and bought a dry goods store in Marshall, Missouri, a town rebuilding after the Civil War. He took his three eldest children and his sister with him. The youngest, Francis William, the child "given" by Parliament to his mother, wound up in Missouri as well. In 1950, at the age of sixty-seven, "Frank" Campbell applied for American Social Security benefits.

As for James Campbell, the younger brother who had been convicted of perjury, pragmatic Whitby elected him reeve in 1881 and mayor ten years later. Then he too left for the US, landing in Chicago where he made a second fortune. Young George Gordon, the alleged seducer who, it was said, looked "handsome in military uniform," left Whitby shortly after the trial that implicated him. He enlisted in the Red River expeditionary force and went to Manitoba to put down the North-West Rebellion.

Eliza Campbell was left on her own with no children, no family. She moved to Toronto and lived in a neat little house at 256 Major Street, died in 1910, and was interred in Mount Pleasant Cemetery. She had left instructions for that grave marker that forever shouts, "I did <u>not</u> commit adultery." Three years later, Robert Campbell came back to Canada from Missouri and, now a widower, married another Whitby girl, Clara Emma Shier. She was seventy, he was nearly seventy-nine. He had known Clara Shier as long as he'd known Eliza. Exactly how well had they known each other? That was the question.

+++

Eleanora lived on and became a white-haired woman given to cameo brooches and lace. Living in London in 1935, she wrote to her son wishing him well in his third marriage. "I hope my dear son that you may eventually find peace and comfort in this life though they may come from a quarter least expected." In that letter, she also announced that she was going to give herself an eighty-fifth birthday party on July 1: "Ice cream will be served at 4:00 p.m. There must be a splendid Tudor-Hart reunion." She commanded the attendance of Percyval, his children, and importantly, the grandchildren.

One of those grandchildren, Alexander, Percyval's only son, was cut of very different cloth from his father and his grandmother. He was a doctor and an active member of the British Communist Party. Alex Tudor-Hart had studied medicine in Vienna, where, in 1933, two years before his grandmother's birthday invitation, he married a young Viennese photographer and fellow Party member, Edith Suschitzky. She was a Jew who had trained as a Montessori kindergarten teacher in London and returned to Vienna. With Hitler poised to annex Austria, she and her new husband fled for England within months of their marriage.

It wasn't until the 1990s that the full story of Edith Suschitzky came out. Not only was she a Party member, but she had also been working for the NKVD (Narodny Komissariat Vnutrennikh Del), the Soviet secret police, since she was twenty-one. MI5, the British domestic counter-intelligence agency, had her under surveillance for years and dismissed her as "a rather typical, emotional, introspective and somewhat intellectual Viennese Jewess." They underestimated Edith Suschitzky Tudor-Hart. Her job for the NKVD was to recruit spies. A year before Eleanora's ice cream birthday party in 1935, she led Kim Philby into Regent's Park for his first meeting with his Soviet handler. A year later, she delivered up Anthony Blunt. Philby and Blunt were two of the "Cambridge Five," the most famous spy ring in UK history. In 1964 when he confessed, Blunt said of Edith, "She was the grandmother of us all." She was never caught.

Did Edith and Eleanora eat ice cream together in the garden on Dominion Day (what would become Canada Day) in 1935? Quite possibly. It was, after all, a command performance, a "splendid Tudor-Hart reunion." Perhaps Edith brought her newborn son, Eleanora's great-grandson. What would they have talked about? Edith would have had no time for Eleanora's American pedigree and her wealth, but she would have approved of her chutzpah in divorcing her husband.

A year after the birthday party, Dr. Alexander Tudor-Hart went off to the Spanish Civil War as part of the Spanish Medical Aid Committee where he worked with Canadian surgeon Dr. Norman Bethune, and they each made major advances in battlefront medicine. When Alexander Tudor-Hart came back, Edith Suschitzky divorced him. In England it wasn't difficult; the double standard had disappeared. As of 1923, a woman could go to court and sue for divorce, citing the same grounds as men.

Edith Suschitzky Tudor-Hart

Canada did not pass a federal Divorce Act until 1968, standardizing divorce across the country. Only then could women in Quebec go to court and get a divorce. Eleanora Tudor-Hart had both the money and the courage to stand up for herself, beat the law as it stood, and get her divorce eighty years earlier. She was ninety-one when she died a self-contained, single woman.

2. A Contented Woman

Whenever I don't know whether to fight or not—I always fight!
The world loves a peaceful man, but gives way to a strenuous kicker.

—Emily Murphy

It was a fall evening in 1878, and the Ferguson children were wriggling with anticipation, barely under control. Emily was ten, then there was her little sister, Annie, and that herd of brothers. They were outdoor kids full of frolic; Cookstown called them the little Ferguson "divils." But this night was special. The boys were in their velveteen suits, and Emily wore her silk dress. The green dining room curtains covering the deep windows were drawn, and the tasselled curtain cords hung down.

The children didn't know quite who, but important visitors were due. The oldest brother, Thomas, saw their shadows through the little panes of glass surrounding the front door. Then came a knock, and their father strode down the hall, flung open the door, and boomed out a greeting. The young Fergusons watched as Sir John A. Macdonald, once again prime minister, and two of his friends made their way in. There was backslapping all around. Macdonald and his Conservatives had just been reelected after five years in Opposition. His protégé, D'Alton McCarthy, the newly elected member of Parliament for the district, was close behind along with Charles Tupper, who was about to be named Minister of Public Works. Isaac Ferguson, the children's father, knew powerful people.

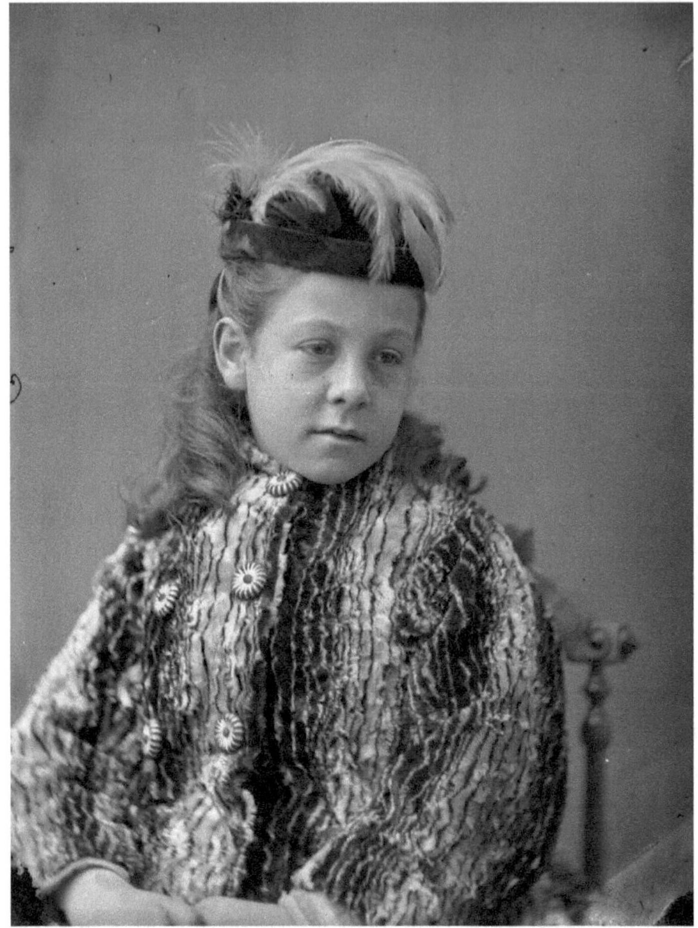

Emily Ferguson, the little girl who grew up to become Emily Murphy, first woman magistrate in the British Empire.

The dining room table was well-set—china from England, crystal, and silver. The maid cleared the final course and then, when the adults moved back from the table, the children were summoned. "Well," said Sir John, "who can recite something for me?" He pointed his beaky nose in their general direction. The boys melted away but not sturdy little Emily. She smoothed her dress and climbed up on the table (the story is part of Gowan–Ferguson family lore, and in some versions, Sir John lifts her up on a chair). Her dark ringlets bounced—ringlets, not pigtails, that night—and she recited an epic poem. Emily was never one to miss an opportunity. Sir John had another brandy, and the evening went on.

Reflecting on her childhood decades later, she wrote, "Those were wonderful times"—you can hear her smile—"when I wore copper toed shoeboots and had only the rudiments of a soul—those carefree days when my hair was done in fierce little pigtails, and I was not so much as halfway wise. For that matter who was wholly wise? Even my father wasn't wise, Mother was sure of this."

"Mother" was Emily Gowan, who brought her own strong political connections to the marriage. She was a cousin, through illegitimate family connections back in Ireland, to Robert Gowan, the same lawyer and senator who, ten years later, became the reigning expert on divorce and Eleanora Tudor-Hart's champion. Robert Gowan was a great friend of Sir John's, staying with him every time he went to Ottawa. Gowan was not only a friend but an influential force in Macdonald's government, doing more than anyone in laying the groundwork for the country's legal system. He lived in Barrie, thirty kilometres down the road from the Fergusons. When Emily was born, Gowan was a judge. He had already restructured the Ontario court system and was celebrating his twenty-fifth anniversary on the bench. When he was appointed at twenty-seven, he became the youngest judge in the British Empire.

Three of the Ferguson boys became lawyers (one rebelled and was a doctor). An uncle and a brother-in-law were judges and would regularly hold forth at the family dinner table. The Ferguson children were weaned on a steady diet of law and politics. As a child, Emily was intelligent and, given her upbringing, opinionated. It's not altogether surprising that even if she was a woman, Emily Ferguson—Emily Murphy, as she became—made a place for herself in that very male world.

Those Gowans: Robert Gowan was the youngest judge in his day, and his little cousin Emily would become the first female magistrate in the Empire. As one of "the Famous Five," she redefined the legal status of women under Canadian law and advanced women's property rights in Alberta. Emily Murphy changed the law for Canadian women—at least, for women who came from her world.

+++

Edmonton will have its first woman police magistrate and Alberta will have taken another step in the path of social reform, leading every other province in the Dominion, when on July 1st Mrs. Arthur Murphy takes her seat on the bench as the specially selected official to adjudicate upon the cases of women and girls arising in the community.

—*Edmonton Bulletin*, June 14, 1916

Becoming the "first female magistrate in the British Empire" in 1916 was remarkably easy. Emily Ferguson grew out of her pigtails, graduated from Bishop Strachan School—the elite school for young (Anglican) ladies in Ontario—and at nineteen, married theology student Arthur Murphy. She wore white silk and was surrounded by five bridesmaids in "rainbow tints." A hundred guests raised their glasses in the giant marquee on the lawn of the family home in Cookstown. It was a safe bet that there wasn't a Catholic, let alone a Jew or a Muslim, among them.

Emily's mother, Emily Gowan, was the youngest daughter of Irish-born Ogle Gowan, who sat in one Canadian legislative assembly or another for much of his adult life. Her grandfather, Hunter Gowan, was the man who led "The Black Mob," a band of Protestant marauders that chased down and killed Catholic rebels in Ireland. Ogle Gowan established the Protestant Orange Order in Canada, the largest public association in Canadian history. He turned the Orange Order, with its anti-Catholic sentiment, into his political base in Upper Canada.

Every July 12, the anniversary of Ireland's Battle of the Boyne, the day in 1690 when Protestant King William of Orange defeated Catholic King James II, the bugles and drums of the Cookstown Orange Band arrived at little Emily's childhood home, and the local chapter of the Orange Order paid homage to the Gowans and all that they stood for. The town turned out, waved their banners, and cried "No Surrender," while the Ferguson family rode in a "chariot" in the Cookstown Orange Day Parade. Young Emily was in the thick of things, enjoying herself. Her youngest brother was

Emily Murphy's mother, Emily Gowan, 1866.

baptized with streamers of the Orange Order pinned to his christening gown.

Anti-Catholicism was virulent and violent. Toronto's *Globe* newspaper claimed the city's Irish Catholic immigrants "fill our poorhouses and our prisons and are as brutish in their superstitions as Hindoos." In 1875, when little Emily Ferguson was seven, two thousand Catholics were stoned and shot at by Orangemen as they walked through the streets of Toronto. Protestant raiders burned out Catholic settlers east of Cookstown.

Cousin Robert Gowan had been grand secretary of the Orange Order as a young man, and he capitalized on the political power that came with it. When he grew older, Senator Robert Gowan acknowledged the not-so-savoury aspect of the Gowan legacy: "the Irish Protestant gentry were guilty of a great wrong," he wrote, "in not recognizing...that Roman Catholic and Protestant were entitled to equal rights before the law.... [O]n the contrary some of them would even have desired to perpetrate, if not enlarge the unjust penal laws under which Roman Catholics suffered, and I must say, were degraded." That atmosphere of Catholic degradation surrounded Emily

Ferguson at she grew up. In her world, Anglo-Irish Protestants were "guardians of the race." It was bred in the bone.

Newly married, Arthur and Emily Murphy spent ten years ministering in small-town Ontario. Emily learned how to organize and navigate feuding factions—there would have been plenty in any small-town church. After the Reverend Murphy climbed out of the pulpit every Sunday, Mrs. Murphy was with him at the church door shaking hands with the congregation and inquiring, "How is old Mrs. Fowler?" and asking an exhausted young mother, "Is your little boy getting better?"

Then came the night when Arthur Murphy was the Anglican Church's featured speaker at the still-new Massey Hall in Toronto. It had been a difficult few months. They had both had typhoid, and their six-year-old daughter Doris had died of diphtheria. He was exhausted. She watched him from the audience as he readied himself to speak. Then she saw him fumble, hesitate, and fall apart in front of the assembled audience. Overwhelmed, Arthur Murphy decided he needed to reinvent himself. He gave up saving souls, and the Murphys went west, first to Manitoba, and then in 1907, the Padre, as Emily called Arthur (the family called her "Tubby"), decided to move further west to Edmonton, population eighteen thousand. Alberta had been a province for two years. Men outnumbered women, horses outnumbered everyone. Arthur Murphy became an entrepreneur, went into life insurance, and began speculating in land, mines, and timber. Emily Murphy, back in the bosom of a (small) urban elite, traded church committees for women's groups and set about running whatever she joined.

In 1916, she and a small group from the Edmonton Local Council of Women went downtown to the courthouse to watch the trials of prostitutes. They were thrown out of the courtroom in short order. The language of these "slatterns," they were told, was too coarse for a gentlewoman's ear. Mrs. Murphy went home and wrote to the attorney general: "If the evidence is not fit to be heard in mixed company, then the government must set up a special court presided over by women to try other women."

Because it was a new province, Alberta was not hidebound by tradition. Remarkably, in a matter of months, Emily Murphy had her women's court and without much ado, she was appointed a police magistrate. Her appointment was in direct violation of the Police Magistrates and Justices of the Peace Act, not because she was a woman—that came later—but rather because she was not a lawyer. She didn't see that as a problem: "Legal knowledge one needs and must acquire, but many women who have adjudicated for a family or club have as good a training for the bench in some particulars as lawyers."

The only law Emily Murphy knew had been picked up from her brothers at the family dinner table. If Alberta was prepared to ignore its own legislation, so was she.

+++

Emily Murphy practised her own brand of "maternal justice," handing down decisions based not on the law but her personal values. Her aim was to "civilize" those who came before her. There were complaints. On one occasion, she referred to an accused as "a gypsy." Rather than an ethnic description, it was an insult widely flung about a century ago. The woman's lawyer wrote to the deputy attorney general saying, understandably, that he felt "quite certain that [Murphy was] prejudiced against the accused and all her class and [was] predisposed to find against her." Her friend and colleague in women's causes, Nellie McClung, said that Emily had a "burning love of justice, a maternal desire to protect the weak. Mrs. Murphy loved a fight and as far as I know never turned her back on one." But it was a "burning love" of her own brand of justice.

Looking down from the bench (or across her desk when there was no courtroom), she divided the women who appeared before her into two camps: those who were "criminal by choice" and could be reformed, and the irredeemable, the genetically "feeble-minded," who were, in her estimation, born criminal and could never be cured. Murphy wasn't alone in her born-criminal views. It was a respected academic theory that had been around since the 1870s. But what to do with these born-criminals and other "degenerates" and "mental defectives" who were housed in mental institutions?

Emily Murphy

Release them, Murphy would say, and they would "father" and "mother" more "degenerate" children.

Like many of her fellow Alberta suffragists, Emily Murphy was a strong advocate of the province's Sexual Sterilization Act of 1928. The argument was that everything from mental illness, alcoholism, and epilepsy to prostitution, sexual "perversion," and even what was called "pauperism"—poverty—was genetically determined and could be eliminated from society by sterilizing the afflicted. Under the Act, the medical superintendent of any mental hospital could refer a patient to the Eugenics Board, which had the power to "prescribe" sterilization as a condition of release. Ninety-nine percent of all referrals were approved. The Board ordered the sterilization of a disproportionate number of women, domestic servants, Catholics, and Indigenous people.

All of the Famous Five were in favour of sterilization, but Murphy was adamant. "Insane people are not entitled to progeny," she would say at women's meetings. "We protect the public against diseased and distempered cattle. We should similarly protect them against the offal of humanity." She was equally as convinced that the public needed protecting against non-white immigrants. In her 1922 book *The Black Candle*, Murphy went on a racist rampage: "white women in close proximity to racialized men would lead to their inevitable downfall and would threaten the white Christian nation." She said that these immigrants, particularly Asians, would "bring about the degeneration of the white race" through drug trafficking. It's thought by many that her rantings against marijuana—"the victims...are dispossessed of their natural and normal willpower, and their mentality is that of idiots"—led to its criminalization in 1924, fifteen years before it was banned in the United States.

All of which makes Emily Murphy a complicated and dubious feminist icon. For the most part, her racist, discriminatory bent has been overlooked and outweighed by her fight for the rights of women—at least, the rights of Anglo-Protestant women.

\+ + +

The government of Alberta might not have had a problem ignoring their own legislation and putting Emily Murphy on the bench, but others did. On her first day as a magistrate, an Edmonton lawyer named Eardley Jackson objected that Murphy was not competent because the law said only "persons" could be magistrates, and, as a woman, she wasn't a "person."

The next year, the same objection was thrown at Alice Jamieson, the first woman appointed a judge in juvenile court and the first woman magistrate in Calgary. Defence lawyer John McKinley Cameron said that Jamieson was "legally incompetent and incapable," given that she was a woman and, therefore, not a "person," and he took the argument to the Alberta Court of Appeal. That court ruled that in Alberta, women were persons. Still earlier, in 1891, the Law Society of Upper Canada had rejected a request from Clara Brett Martin to be admitted as a law student on the same grounds. She was not a "person." The Ontario legislature passed a bill that said the word

John McKinley Cameron, lawyer, 1918.

Clara Brett Martin, Canada's first women lawyer.

"person" in the Law Society statute should be interpreted to include women, and Clara Brett Martin became the first woman lawyer in the country. When Montreal's Annie MacDonald Langstaff applied to take the Quebec bar exams in 1915, she was turned down because she was a woman. She took her case to the Quebec Superior Court where Mr. Justice Saint-Pierre explained, in all sincerity, why a woman could never be a lawyer: "in a case of [rape] and putting to complainant the questions which must of all necessity be asked.... No woman possessing the least sense of decency could possibly do so without throwing a blur upon her own dignity and without bringing into utter contempt the honor and respect due to her sex." Quebec did not admit women to the bar until 1941.

Although Alberta and Ontario had held that women were indeed "persons," a piecemeal approach to the "persons" question was not enough. There needed to be a constitutional ruling that covered the whole country.

+++

The three women [Nellie McClung, Emily Murphy, and Alice Jamieson,] emerged triumphant into the chilly spring air, and linked arms as they strolled down Jasper Avenue.

Alberta women were on a roll. They had been given the same voting rights as men in 1916, two years before Ottawa enfranchised women (who were not Indigenous or Asian) federally.

Historian Charlotte Gray in her biography of Nellie McClung describes the celebration following the reading of the bill in the Alberta legislature:

> The three women [Nellie McClung, Emily Murphy, and Alice Jamieson,] emerged triumphant into the chilly spring air and linked arms as they strolled down Jasper Avenue. Emily, a stout woman with what a contemporary described as "the lusty sea-going roll of a sailor" caught sight of a hat shop and let out a whoop of glee. She shepherded her two friends through the door. Nellie chose a broad-brimmed hat decorated with a white ribbon and an enormous artificial flower, Alice selected a dignified bonnet with a velvet furbelow, and Emily plonked a feathered straw cloche on her head. Then the three women continued down the street to a photographer's studio. There they posed, resplendent in their thick wool coats and victory bonnets.

Now that they had secured the vote, they reasoned, "personhood" was the next logical step. Murphy aspired to be a senator, an impossibility if she was not federally recognized as a "person." Other women's activists put her name forward, thousands across the country backed her, and newspapers endorsed her. She had written to and petitioned the Conservative Prime Minister Robert Borden for the better part of a decade. The prime minister replied, somewhat disingenuously, that, much as he would like to, he could not declare women "persons." He was hog-tied, legally speaking, by a nineteenth-century British common law ruling that "women were eligible for pains and penalties, but not rights and privileges." What could he do? Murphy didn't get any further with Borden's successor, Arthur Meighen, or the next prime minister, Liberal William Lyon Mackenzie King.

They needed another way forward. Emily Murphy's brother, William Nassau Ferguson, was by then a judge on the Ontario Court of Appeal. He wrote to his sister, pointing to Section 60 of the Supreme Court Act. It said that any five living people could petition the court for a ruling on a constitutional matter. (William Ferguson died less than a year later and never saw the result of his legal advice.) By this time, 1927, Emily Murphy was well-known in Alberta. She was a popular author, having written the best-selling "Janey Canuck" books, as well as a speaker and women's activist involved in everything from the Women's Institute to the Women's Press Club. She had also become a friend and ally of Nellie McClung, originally from Manitoba, by then living in Edmonton. The pair talked tactics and chose and approached three other women to sign the petition to the Supreme Court—Henrietta Muir Edwards, child of evangelical parents and an advocate of women's education; Louise McKinney, the first woman elected to a legislature in the British Empire and now a former MLA, a lay preacher, and devout prohibitionist; and the tall, elegant child of the British Raj, Irene Parlby, Alberta's first woman cabinet minister and in 1927, still a sitting MLA. Now they were "the Famous Five."

On August 27, 1927, a warm summer day, they sat on Emily Murphy's verandah in their hats and their gloves, drank tea, ate nut bread, and traded war stories of the fight for women's suffrage. Then they went inside, signed the petition, and sat back and waited.

Arguments were presented to the Supreme Court of Canada in Ottawa on March 14, 1928. The five women never left Alberta. There are no witnesses, no emotional tirades at the Supreme Court. This is the place for legal argument. The court came down with its decision six weeks later. The Canadian Supreme Court judges who heard the persons case were an "originalist" court of the view that legal texts, including the British North America Act that defined

Nellie McClung, Alice Jamieson, and Emily Murphy on the day Alberta gave women the vote in 1916.

Canada, should be given the meaning that the original legislators had in mind. In their opinion, when the BNA Act came into being in 1867, no one could have intended "persons" to include women. Women were not, could never be "persons." British Columbia's Ellen Smith, the first woman cabinet minister in the Empire, said it well: "The iron dropped into the souls of women in Canada when we heard that it took a man to decree that his mother was not a person." (When Smith was elected, the newspapers discussed at great length whether a woman should be allowed to wear a hat in the legislature.)

It wasn't over.

In 1927, the Supreme Court of Canada was not the ultimate arbiter. Until as late as 1949, some cases could be appealed to the Privy Council in Great Britain. The five Alberta women did just that.

Viscount Sankey, Lord High Chancellor of Great Britain, delivered the judgement in *Edwards v Canada* ("Edwards" because

Henrietta Muir Edwards's name came first in the alphabet). The son of a grocer and a Labour politician who, as a lawyer, specialized in workmen's compensation cases, Sankey applied a different theory to the interpretation of the British North America Act. Canada's constitution, he said, was "a living tree capable of growth and expansion within its natural limits." The "living tree" doctrine, as it became known, meant, and still means, that Canada's constitution must be looked at within the context of a changing society. It must be adaptable.

The light reflected off the silver buckles on the Lord High Chancellor's shoes as he led the parade into the court. John Sankey, his judicial wig grazing his shoulders and long red brocade robes trailing behind him, pronounced that women were persons, that "the exclusion of women from all public offices is a relic of days more barbarous than ours...and to those who ask why should the word ["persons"] include females the obvious answer is why should it not."

Would that all judgements were as succinct.

Today, the Famous Five cast in bronze, stand on Parliament Hill in Ottawa (and in Calgary). Emily Murphy rests her hand on the back of a chair, inviting any passing stranger to sit and join the discussion.

+++

I wanted the law to grant women our share as well as the man. I felt humbled to take anything off my husband in a way although I knew it was rightly mine.... I always felt I wanted the law to make it straight for me.

—Elizabeth Clark, ranch wife

The "Persons" Case was a massive victory, a triumph. It was a clean, intellectual fight as much political as legal, if not more. For Murphy and the others, it was easy sailing compared to an earlier battle they had waged over women's property rights.

Ever since they arrived in Alberta, the Murphys had travelled outside Edmonton, chasing down Arthur's mining and lumber claims. Those expeditions brought Emily face to face with abject rural poverty. She met ranch women who were barely holding their heads above water, and as she became well-known, many more of these ranch wives wrote to her. Mrs. John Sturling, in her letter, said she was "hovering between life and death." Her husband, she said, had forced her to "do a man's work in the fields…[and had] driven her about with a horsewhip and drawn a gun," and now he was planning to "sell out" and return to England. Mrs. Fred Clarke wrote that she had loaned her husband $1,000 to purchase the ranch. He had then sold the farm and pocketed the money, leaving her and the children "with the wind blowing through the cracks in the house and $3.90." The letters kept coming.

To Emily Murphy, with all those lawyers in her family, it seemed there should be a legal remedy. These ranch wives should have a legal interest in the property. This was early days—Murphy had only been in Edmonton for two years, however, she was already "Convenor" of the committee on law for the Better Protection of Women and Children with the Edmonton Local Council of Women. Women's property rights were all about protecting women and children, keeping a roof over their heads. This was her territory.

In another place and another time, there was something called "dower." It was a traditional legal right that dated back to before the Norman conquests in England in 1066. Dower gave a woman a life interest in her husband's property, meaning that, after he died, she would have a place to live for the rest of her life. Dower still existed in Eastern Canada but had been abolished in the development of the West. That meant prairie women were starting from scratch. Henrietta Edwards, who had been working on women's property rights since before Alberta was a province, recruited Murphy and Irene Parlby to campaign for dower for Alberta women. It was Murphy's first attempt to change the law. "Dower" was all about the *husband's* property and his bounty in giving his wife a slim slice. It was 1909. The idea of "matrimonial property" wasn't even a gleam in Murphy's eye.

Initially, Edwards, Murphy, and Parlby pushed for a law that would give wives and widows a one-third share of the property owned by their husbands. The idea was not well received. "Why should women worry about possessing some of their husband's property during his lifetime?" said the province's first attorney general, Charles W. Cross. "Time enough after he's dead." The bill didn't pass.

They pushed harder. In 1915, the Alberta legislature passed the Married Women's Home Protection Act. It gave a wife the right to register a document on title preventing the "homestead" (the ranch house, *not* the ranch) from being sold, mortgaged, or leased. It wasn't an automatic right. The wife had to know the law and get herself to a lawyer to make a claim. How often would that happen?

They pushed harder still. What they got was the Dower Act of 1917. The Act gave wives a life interest in their husband's estate and the right to prevent a husband from selling, leasing, or mortgaging the home—*the* home or *his* home, not *their* home. The *Edmonton Bulletin* opined that "this act coupled with all the beneficent legislation that the...government had already passed in the interest of women, place[d] the fair sex of Alberta on a very high plane indeed." Alberta women were better off than any in the world, the newspaper said. Henrietta Edwards thanked the government and said that if there were laws that "disqualified women because of sex," they were the fault of Ottawa, not Edmonton. 'Twas ever thus.

As Alberta historian Catherine Cavanaugh wrote, "If the Alberta Dower Act can be said to have in any way recognized the pioneering partnership of women and men in the West, it was partnership by concession and that was no partnership at all."

◆◆◆

It was one thing to pass legislation, quite another to make it stick. Finding that point where change in the law lines up with the change in the culture of the community can lead to many a misstep. The West was a male frontier—it was there in the rhetoric: "three years in the Northwest would raise a farmer higher on the scale of manhood." In the West, men were "hardened into sterner stuff." And on it went. Women were not given land grants by the federal government, not allowed to "homestead." To "admit women into the opportunities of the land grant would be to make them more independent of marriage than ever," said the Federal Minister of the Interior, Frank Oliver. Men owned property, and property in Alberta (and the rest of the prairies) equalled livelihood. A ranch was how and where family income was generated. Despite the work a woman put into the ranch, if a couple split, a woman not only lost her small property claim under the Dower Act, but she also lost any income from the ranch. That meant she also lost her children. A judge was likely to say to her, "You have no means to support your children. The kids go with the father."

Courts were not enthusiastic when it came to enforcing the Dower Act. Husbands regarded dower as an obstacle to circumvent, a provocation. Murphy, Parlby, and Edwards were disillusioned, concluding that dower was worse than the illness it was intended to cure. Now there was a new opportunity for domestic tyranny. Or, in the more down-to-earth words of the provincial land registrar, "when a farmer's wife puts on her bonnet and spends a day in Town at some lawyer's office on some mysterious mission, there is bound to be trouble at home."

Emily Murphy died in 1933, and fights over dower rights continued to rage.

+++

In 1968, more than half a century after the act was passed, dower was the final straw in a marriage that had been going bad for a decade or more. The ranch was the Brockway property, three quarters of a section, 480 acres near Turner Valley, southwest of Calgary. Looking out the kitchen window every morning, the ranch wife could see wide vistas, big skies, cattle on the land. Turning her head, her eyes rested on the outbuildings and horses waiting to be saddled up. She loved this place. But her husband wanted to sell and move farther away. They had been together for twenty-five years, and she had worked this ranch, put sweat and money into it. No, she wasn't moving or giving up her stake.

Four years earlier, she had put her foot down and told her husband that she would not sign away her dower rights. Without her signature, he couldn't sell the ranch. That night in 1968, he was going at her again. "Sign the goddamn papers," he shouted, spit flying across the room. Sign the papers and relinquish her claim? No. Her mother, a little bird of a woman, sixty-nine years old, was visiting. She sat in the kitchen, backing her daughter. He later said the fight was the mother's fault. "He pulled my hair out," she testified in court. He had already pushed her over and given her a black eye. Then he went for his wife. He wrapped his strong cattleman's arms around her face and squeezed. Squeezed so hard that he broke her jaw in three places.

The admitting nurse who checked her into the hospital that night took one look at her swollen, bloody face and knew she couldn't talk. Was she even conscious? The nurse turned and asked her mother, "What's her name?"

"Florrie—Irene Florence Murdoch."

The case of Irene Murdoch changed women's property rights forever.

3. "Not even a spoon."

...a revolution was born. It was called Murdoch v Murdoch.

—Beverley McLachlin,
Chief Justice of the Supreme Court of Canada

The Holy Cross Hospital in Calgary kept Florrie Murdoch for a few days—wired her jaw shut, stitched up her face, and gave her something for the pain. Her lip was paralyzed, and she would have a speech impediment for the rest of her life; nothing could be done about that. They might have kept her longer, but she wanted to get back to her twelve-year-old son, so she put the cervical collar the hospital had given her around her neck and went back to the ranch. She pushed the key into the lock and twisted—nothing. Jiggling the lock, pushing the key, still nothing. Alex Murdoch had changed the locks. Locked out, Florence Murdoch stood outside the ranch house still wearing the torn and bloodstained clothes from the night before.

It had been this way for years. Her mother, Florence Nash, told the court that she had seen Alex Murdoch pick his wife up by the back of her neck more than once. He had thrown hot cocoa in her face. The fights and the beatings were part of the scenery. But the *Murdoch* case wasn't about domestic abuse; it was about a wife's property rights. That's what Florence Murdoch was intent on from the beginning: her share of the ranch.

Her paralyzed lip and speech impediment could not be hidden or ignored. The injuries were debilitating—"life-altering" in modern parlance—but they barely seemed to count. Alex Murdoch was convicted of assault in relatively short order. That was a straightforward criminal case. The legal debate over a married woman's property rights was something else again. The *Murdoch* case went on for five years and went all the way up to the Supreme Court of Canada. There was only one name on the deed to the ranch, James Alexander Murdoch, but they were husband and wife. Irene Florence Murdoch had put money into purchasing the property and she had worked the ranch; she had worked hard. Did any of that give her a share in the property? In 1973, the highest court in the land was asked to decide what claim she had.

None, said the Supreme Court.

The Supreme Court of Canada decided it was bound by the law as it stood, much as it had forty-five years earlier, in the "persons" case. This would turn out to be an instance where the court lagged behind the country. Public opinion was changing. By the 1970s, women's voices were much louder. But almost because *Murdoch v Murdoch* went the wrong way in the minds of many, it became the catalyst for change. Five years after the *Murdoch* case was decided, legislation had been introduced in every province giving husbands and wives equal rights to property acquired during a marriage. It was a revolution a long time in the making.

***

Florence Murdoch (she was "Florence" or "Florrie" to those who knew her, "Irene" in court documents) was an unlikely and a reluctant champion. It took a long time for the media to discover her, and when they did, they saw her as a traditional, conservative woman with a bee in her bonnet about the ranch. Florence Murdoch didn't fit the feminist mould, and she did not enjoy being the poster girl for women's property rights. She gave her last interview to the press in 1976, and then turned her back on the world.

Fred Nash, back from WWI, Calgary, 1918.

+++

In the spring of 1925 when Florence Nash went into labour, she and her husband were living in a log cabin in Bighorn, Alberta. The cabin was fifty miles from anywhere and had no electricity and no running water. They were well up in the foothills of the Rockies, with tracks rather than roads to connect them to the outside world. Fred Nash was one of Alberta's first forest rangers, men who, in the words of the *High River Times*, "labor for the love of trees, shrubs and wild flowers." His job was to watch for fires, build and maintain a network of lookouts, and rescue anyone lost in the bush. The family's only company was an assistant ranger, an American named Lloyd Waikle, who lived an even more lonely life out in the bunkhouse.

Fred Nash was a British immigrant who arrived in Canada before the First World War. He was a teenager with dreams of becoming a cowboy and he realized those dreams by becoming a star cowpuncher at the legendary Bar U Ranch. When the war broke out, he signed up, shipped out, and, against the odds, came back to the Bar U unscathed. (In 1919, the Prince of Wales, the future King Edward VIII, made a grand tour of Canada. While hungover from a raucous night at the Ranchmen's Club in Calgary, he spent twenty-four hours at the Bar U—long enough for Fred Nash to get his photograph taken with the future king.)

A year later, as summer began, twenty-year-old Florence Butterfield disembarked from the *Empress of France* in Montreal. Miss Butterfield was on the ship's passenger list as a "fiancée" and the purpose of her trip was "marriage." She and Fred had met in London when he was back from the trenches on war leave. On the strength of a promise, she made the transatlantic voyage, got on the train in Montreal, and travelled to Calgary to marry a man she couldn't have known for more than a few weeks. Irene Florence Murdoch had parents who were prepared to head down new paths. The apple didn't fall far from the tree.

Irene Florence was born in that log cabin on May 18, 1925. She had a sister, Evelyn, two years older, for company. When she was four, the family moved to a slightly less remote station. Nearly a hundred years later—she was ninety-five when she died—Irene Florence Nash Jesperson's (as she became) obituary described her childhood: "They [she and Evelyn] lived a life of riding, roping, shooting, fighting fires and supplying lookout stations and more."

Out there in the foothills, Fred Nash taught his daughters everything he would have taught a son. She grew up infused with the mythical image of Alberta women—the myth that Irene Florence Murdoch and so many other women who could ride, rope, shoot, and do anything a man could do, were equal partners with men.

\+ + +

We don't have what we thought we had.

—Henrietta Edwards

In 1925, a few months after baby Florrie was born, Irene Parlby introduced a revolutionary bill into the Alberta legislature in Edmonton. It was "An Act Establishing Community of Property as Between Husband and Wife." Parlby, another English immigrant and a woman with a lady-of-the-manor pedigree, grew roses in her garden out in front of the ranch in Alix, Alberta. She had come to Canada on a whim in 1896, fallen in love, married, and stayed. Initially, she subscribed to the wonder of, as she wrote, "the clear-eyed man, the real pioneer type...content to travel with a good stout axe and make his road as he went along." That idea faded with the

Irene Parlby, Alberta's first woman cabinet minister.

roses, and she became a crusader for women's rights and an organizer. Parlby became president of the United Farm Women of Alberta in 1916 and came to know Henrietta Edwards and Emily Murphy. She had helped push the Dower Act through in 1917. But Dower gave Alberta women only a life-interest in what was referred to as their husband's home. They were growing tired of crumbs from the table and wanted their own piece of the cake: shared ownership of marital property. Even doughty Henrietta Muir Edwards, who had politely thanked the premier for the Dower Act, changed her tune. "We don't have what we thought we had," she said rather poignantly. They didn't have matrimonial property *rights*. They had no claim to the furniture, the cattle, the seed, the farm equipment, or most importantly, the ranch. Rural women were pressing for a half interest in all matrimonial property half a century before Irene Florence Murdoch filed her suit.

It was the story of Lela O'Leary in the early 1920s that got Alberta women going, just as it would be *Murdoch v Murdoch* that got women across the country going in the 1970s. As Catherine Cavanaugh of Athabasca University tells it, Lela O'Leary left her husband, alleging "various acts of cruelty." As in *Murdoch*, Lela's husband had been found guilty of assaulting his wife—she was then a few months pregnant with her fourth child. However, the judge would not grant her alimony, saying that she was complaining "a little too much…about her husband's behaviour" and that she "nagged him a little bit" and that in a quarrel, she "did not lie down to him at all." Lela O'Leary was living in a Calgary rooming house and taking in sewing to earn a living. Days before Christmas of 1921, she went out to the farm to see her children. Synott O'Leary threw her out in minus-fifteen-degree weather, and he had every right to do so. She was trespassing. She had no property rights in the farm.

Many women followed the case in the newspapers, and they were angry. Remarkably, there was a legal flip-flop. Lela O'Leary went back to court, and three years after it all began, she was awarded alimony and custody of her children.

But the anger did not die down. Politicians grew nervous. The lawyer representing Synott O'Leary wrote to the attorney general, alerting him to rumours that Calgary women were about to "ask for legislation further determining the rights of women." He went on to say that their "totally unconsidered and impractical suggestions" could mean that some members of the legislature "might not appreciate the great dangers of such legislation." When they were asked for an opinion, lawyers in the attorney general's department reported that indeed, the laws as they stood were not equal between men and women. But, they added, any move toward "community property" would be "too costly, too radical, inconvenient, unjustifiable as well as generally too disruptive to the economy and therefore bad for business."

For anyone who didn't quite understand where this line of thinking was coming from, Edmonton lawyer S.M. Gwendolyn Duff spelled it out in a talk to the Edmonton branch of the Alberta Women's Institute:

> [The wife's services] belong to the husband and [are] his property the same as those of his horse or other animals...[thus] the wife's work in the home is not recognized legally as having economic value.... Because the husband is the one usually whose labor brings in the money...[the wife] is made to feel that his work is of importance while hers is not.

Thus things were, leading up to 1925, when Irene Parlby introduced her bill advocating equal property rights. Parlby, who had been elected to the Alberta Legislature in 1921, was a cabinet minister, the second woman cabinet minister in the Empire in a majority government. On paper, she had power, nonetheless, the bill was shuffled off to a committee chaired by Parlby for further study. The committee included Henrietta Edwards and Emily Murphy, but strangely and puzzling to many, when the committee reported to the legislature, it backed away from the idea of a fifty-fifty split of matrimonial assets, what was known as "community of property." Had they lost their nerve and decided that Alberta wasn't ready for something so radical? If Parlby, Edwards, and Murphy had stuck to their guns when the baby who became Florrie Murdoch was crying in her cradle up in the foothills, it might have made her adult life a lot easier.

+++

It was 1943, the middle of World War II, when seventeen-year-old Irene Florence Nash married James Alexander Murdock (it's "Murdock" in the census records of 1926, "Murdoch" in the court records). Alex Murdoch was a twenty-three-year-old range rider chasing cows for the forestry service. He owned twenty-five or thirty horses, plus eight cows. Teenage Florrie brought two horses to the marriage. Both had ambition, both were prepared to work hard. Young Florence Murdoch was no prairie princess. She had been bucked off more than one bronco. During the war years, men would have been in short supply, and a hard-working woman with calloused hands, who sat easy in the saddle, was particularly valued.

For the next four years, they hired themselves out and worked on other people's ranches. Alex Murdoch broke horses and looked after the cattle; Florence cooked for the crews and worked with her husband outdoors. "They" were paid $100 a month, the money handed to Alex, plus room and board. In 1947, Fred Nash retired from the forestry service and he and his son-in-law bought a dude ranch for $6,000. It was registered in the names of the two men. Florrie worked the ranch, setting up the guests, guiding them on pack trips, and running fishing and hunting hikes. Four years later, Fred Nash became ill, and they sold the ranch. Alex pocketed a $500 profit, the equivalent of $6,000 in 2024.

When Fred Nash died in 1952, his wife inherited a tidy sum in life insurance. She gave her daughter a portion of that money, and the Murdochs purchased "grazing rights," with some of the money coming from Florence. Around the same time, Alex began working for a stock association at a ranchers' grazing co-op deep in the foothills. He worked and lived on the grazing grounds five months a year for the rest of their marriage. In 1956, their son William "Bill" Murdoch was born, and by the time he was two, the Murdochs had bought the three-quarter section of land, 480 acres near Turner Valley for $25,000. Alex Murdoch continued working up in the foothills, leaving his wife at home to look after the baby and handle everything that needed to be done at the ranch.

That is where they still were, just outside Turner Valley, in 1968, the night that Alex Murdoch broke Florence's jaw.

+++

Les Duncan [the lawyer for Alex Murdoch] often told me, "Look, I knew this was going to be a bombshell of a case." I didn't.

—Ernest Shymka

Florence Murdoch went shopping for a lawyer almost as soon as she got out of the hospital. With her jaw wired shut, wearing a neck brace, and frequently bursting into tears, she was a mess. And she didn't have much money. She was living in a motel, unemployable and relying on her mother for support. Vanessa Gruben, Angela Cameron, and Angela Chaisson wrote about Florence Murdoch in *Property on Trial*. As they said, she needed a lawyer who would either take her case for nothing—pro bono—or who would share the risk, taking the case on a contingency basis.

Mumbling out of the corner of her mouth, Florrie Murdoch nonetheless made it clear to each of the lawyers she visited that she wanted a share of the ranch. She was unwavering. But her name was not on the title deed, and there was no written evidence that the land was ever intended to be registered in her name. It was seen by most lawyers as an impossible case.

Ernest Shymka

Leslie Duncan was just beginning his practice as a commercial lawyer in Calgary when he became Alex Murdoch's lawyer, before Florence Murdoch found someone to represent her. The Legal Archives Society of Alberta interviewed Duncan about the *Murdoch* case more than thirty years after the fact. He said then that he didn't think Florence Murdoch's advisors "always agreed with her because I think in total I heard over the years twelve different counsel represented her.... I could never get anyone to talk about a lump-sum settlement. They wanted an interest in the farm."

There she was: a physically disabled, impoverished woman with an unwinnable case. But she would not be dissuaded. It was a share in the ranch or nothing. Florence Murdoch shopped around for a lawyer until she finally found Ernest Shymka.

In the decades following *Murdoch*, Shymka was often asked about the case. He spoke willingly but with some regret—you can hear it in his voice—that it had become sensationalized. Shymka was a small-town boy from Smoky Lake, Alberta, north of Edmonton, born of Ukrainian and Polish parents. Many of his clients were central-European immigrants who brought unconventional issues through the door. "You weren't dealing with esoteric legal problems," he said. "You were dealing with very human problems." Out of necessity, he became inventive, not afraid to push and stretch the law. It made Ernest Shymka a good fit for Florence Murdoch.

> At every meeting that I ever had with her, she was always in tears...it was very sad...first of all she wanted the marriage to be put together...to be reunited with her husband and her son. Now I guess this became impossible...it was not fair, and it was not right that she was without an interest in the land.

She was advised, repeatedly by friends, family, and lawyers, that the logical, sensible thing to do was to sue for divorce and support payments. Earlier that year, 1968, the federal government had passed Canada's first Divorce Act. Divorce and support would have been quicker and the outcome more certain. But Florence Murdoch held fast. She did not want to divorce her husband. She wanted a share in the ranch.

Northern Alberta, where Shymka was from, had a more liberal approach to women's rights in his estimation. He saw it in his own family. He grew up with a mother who had a big role in the Shymka family's network of small stores throughout the north of the province. Farther south, as he saw it, things were different.

> This was cowboy country, this was ranch country, this was cattle country, and [Florence Murdoch] had her dower rights, she had a right to make a claim for alimony...I think it was maybe a foregone conclusion with some people, some lawyers...that [the case] wasn't going to go anywheres [sic]. Because she adamantly did not want to do anything other than establish that she had an interest in that property.

In his 2015 interview with the Alberta Legal Archives Society, Shymka explained that to Florence Murdoch, the ranch, *their* ranch, was key to her marriage. She still had hope.

> [She] didn't want a divorce, that I think was clear, she was hoping...to keep that ranch...that they would get together. And she had great affection for her son that was just tearing her up. The boy was at the age when he preferred to be with his father because he had the ranch and he liked riding horses and all of those things...as opposed to...living in some basement suite with his mother. So she was trying to just return things to the way they were. It might have seemed far-fetched on her part but that is what she wanted...to restore things to the way they were, if only her husband would acknowledge that she was entitled to something here.

There was another reason why Shymka took Florence Murdoch's case. His wife, Nancy Shymka, wouldn't let him turn her down.

> I had some doubts about it, you know. [Nancy] always said, "You can't drop this case. You have to help this poor soul." I had to do it. I just had to help this poor lady.... It was just so unfair, that she was—how could this be?!... [Put] out in the cold and with nothing.... And, really, [Nancy's] version of it was prophetic because that's how women in Canada reacted to this

> case when it was adjudicated by the Supreme Court of Canada.

He agreed to represent Irene Florence Murdoch on a contingency basis. Then came the hard part. Ernest Shymka wasn't at all sure just how he was going to make the case for his client's claim. This was new territory.

The property was held in her husband's name. Therefore, Shymka had to look for a way for the court to infer that she had a stake in the property. His first argument revolved around money. The law recognized that if she had made a financial contribution to the purchase, then she had a valid claim. Money had come from her account but proving it went directly to the purchase of the ranch would be difficult. If that didn't succeed, then he argued his second point—and this was where Shymka was pushing the boundaries of established law—he would have to convince the court that her physical labour on the ranch amounted to a contribution to the purchase. That her sweat equity meant something.

✦✦✦

No doubt it did cross my mind…you know, does she really have a case? Until you've dug into the law and into the facts and so on, you really didn't know.

—Ernest Shymka

For the next two years, Florence Murdoch regularly made the sixty-kilometre drive from the Turner Valley motel, where she was now living, into Calgary to see Shymka. Then there were the medical appointments. Not only her jaw but also her teeth were wired shut; several were removed. Next came the bone grafts. On it went. By the time they went to trial, she owed $3,000 in medical bills and $800 to her mother for the motel bills.

Shymka, in turn, "dug into the law." He had been reading American cases, which were often well ahead of Canadian law when it came to "community property"—equal division. Canadian courts don't tend to look to American decisions for precedents, but those cases convinced Shymka:

> Well, this is the law in so many of the states...and it was a sort of an appeal to legislators and to judges to say, "Look, this is not satisfactory. This is the way the law should be leaning towards...." How could it be that the husband ended up with everything...? So, just that factual situation led me to think that she would, she'd get something. I never thought that she would get fifty percent.... My thought was, well, maybe she's entitled to twenty-five percent, or a third, based on what she had contributed—and it was worth taking it to trial division.

He started two actions, the first for custody of her son and judicial separation (not divorce). It wasn't only that she did not want to divorce her husband; if they divorced, she lost her right to dower—that life interest in the house which was the only certain property claim she had. The year after they separated, Shymka filed the second suit—and this was the big one—for half of the ranch, the land, the cattle, and even the cattle brand. Irene Florence Murdoch was claiming half the business. Shymka argued that Florence and Alex were partners in business as well as in life and that although the land was in Alex Murdoch's name, the courts should recognize he was holding half of it in trust for his wife.

Florence Murdoch was concerned with the end result and didn't care how they got there. She was also still dealing with her medical issues. When the cases, combined now into one, came to trial in February of 1971, she was still on a liquid diet.

Alex Murdoch was not a city man. He wore his Stetson and his jeans; he was seldom, if ever, seen in a shirt and tie—even a bolo tie; and he didn't think much of bankers and lawyers on principle. But Les Duncan was his friend even if he was a lawyer. He owned land not far from the Murdoch place. Duncan had been born in a fly-in community in northeastern Manitoba where his father looked after the horses at a gold mine. He studied law at the University of Toronto in the early 1960s and then went west, buying what became his ranch in 1967. Within a few years, he was living on the ranch and kept 125 head of cattle. He and Alex (he called him Alec) connected through horses and ranching:

> I met him in that capacity. He was quite a character and he held this ranch out southwest of Turner Valley. And so he first came to see me about that, the breakup of his marriage and some related activities, and initially I referred that to others in the office.

Duncan was not a family law specialist. But,

> Alec just wasn't comfortable with the others.... And so finally when it was going to trial, I decided to do it myself. The case was greatly complicated by the mother. The mother was quite a sophisticated lady from Edmonton, and she was quite strongly opposed to Alec, and whether or not she had separate legal counsel that had helped her to come up with this strategy of claiming an interest in the ranch, I don't know.

Ernest Shymka simply said that his client's mother "encouraged her, stood behind her all the way."

These days, in twenty-first-century Canada, courts urge couples and their lawyers to work out their matrimonial differences, negotiate a settlement, and move on. Very few cases go to trial. Even in 1971, as Shymka said in his interview with Cameron and Gruben, "We had discussed settlement many times."

Duncan did not think there was a chance. "This case was not the kind of thing that was easy to settle. It was headed for trouble."

On the day the trial began, the lawyers shepherded their clients into the courthouse in Calgary. Perhaps there was a hint of conversation, even a conciliatory gesture.

"We have our parties here together—and they're just outside the courtroom door and we were chatting to both of them, I think, separately, and we both felt that if we could have maybe a half an hour or so," said Shymka, they could perhaps settle things on their own. He requested a delay, which "somewhat infuriated the judge. 'What? Are you not ready? Why would you be asking?' But he was upset that I was brazen enough to ask for an adjournment of a half an hour." Judges, Shymka pointed out, "were not always warm and cuddly. They were stern and curious, no-nonsense, and the trial judge was surely that."

Had they settled, reform to married women's property rights might well have been delayed even longer.

The half hour was up. Judge Hugh John MacDonald—described as tough but fair by Shymka—glared down from the bench as Shymka called his first witness.

+++

It was, not surprisingly, a combative trial. Florence Nash, Florrie's mother, testified about the assault and the previous "physical skirmishes." But when Shymka asked Alex Murdoch about the fight, he repeated that it was his mother-in-law who started it. "[Florence Nash] was very prim and proper...so was Florence," Shymka told law professor Angela Cameron. "To say that she started it didn't make sense. Florence Nash was skin and bones."

Shymka moved on to the insurance money, Florence Murdoch's contribution to the purchase of the property. But Alex Murdoch said it was a loan to him from his mother-in-law. The Murdochs were careful bookkeepers, and indeed there was an entry concerning the purchase of the grazing rights—$2,000 from Florence Nash (the mother) "borrowed for land deal." Shymka argued that the idea of a loan did not make sense: Florence Nash intended that money to benefit her daughter, not the man who had given her a black eye and broken her daughter's jaw. The careful bookkeeping would come back to haunt Florence Murdoch.

Then came the legal arguments. The claim for a partnership in the ranch. That would be a tough argument. Shymka put forward that there was an unstated partnership between husband and wife and that even though the property was in Alex Murdoch's name, he held half in trust for his wife. She had, after all, contributed the disputed insurance money and her labour. So much labour. The courts had previously ruled that sweat equity didn't count. But just before the Murdochs went to trial, the case of another farm couple named *Trueman* came before the Alberta Court of Appeal. It was, like *Murdoch*, a divorce case where the wife was asking for a share of the ranch.

The Truemans had been married for a few years when they, like the Murdochs, bought property. Mr. Trueman became ill, and his wife took on the bulk of the farm work, "cutting the crop, stooking, cutting hay, raking hay, discing, harrowing, anything there was to do," as she said at trial.

Mrs. Trueman maintained the loan payments and became the "hired man," keeping the farm going. She also pounded in nails, painted, and papered, and helped build the farmhouse. The Alberta Court of Appeal held that through her labour, she had made a substantial contribution to the property and gave her a half-interest in the homestead—the house and the land immediately surrounding it—not the entire ranch.

No two cases are ever exactly the same. Shymka knew it. Precedent is about the fine distinctions. He also knew that *Trueman* wasn't a popular decision in Alberta. His fingers were crossed.

When Florence Murdoch took the stand, Shymka asked her what she did around the ranch. What exactly was the labour she contributed. Her answer has become legendary:

> *A. Haying, raking, swathing, moving, driving trucks and tractors and teams, quietening horses, taking cattle back and forth to the reserve, dehorning, vaccinating, branding, anything that was to be done. I worked outside with him, just as a man would, anything that was to be done.*
>
> *Q. Was your husband away from these properties?*
>
> *A. Yes, for five months every year.*
>
> *Q. So that you would do the chores and other work around the farm?*

> *A. I did until our son was old enough, then he helped, but until we had him I did it on my own.*

Alex Murdoch, in his testimony, did not disagree. He just saw things differently. When he was asked what his wife did around the ranch, he said, "Oh, just about what the ordinary rancher's wife does. Most of them can do most anything."

Three decades later when Les Duncan was asked about the trial, he dismissed the importance of both Florrie's evidence and what she did around the ranch.

> It's true that she did jobs, like she could drive a tractor and all those things, but it's not as if it was a healthy partnership that she got thrown out in the cold. Because there were lengthy periods where she wasn't available to help with the tractor and...theirs wasn't a working farm or ranch in the sense that there was a lot of work to be done. So the work that was done at the farm, or the ranch as it was, was feeding the cows in the winter and calving them out in the winter, and Alec was always at home for that.

Feelings still ran high more than three decades after the fact.

Florence Murdoch got her judicial separation (Alex Murdoch had not contested the separation), and she was awarded $200 a month in support payments. But Judge Hugh John MacDonald gave custody of their son, Bill, now fifteen, to his father. It was a catch-22: because Alex Murdoch owned and operated the ranch, the very thing Florrie was fighting for, he had the income to pay support to her and look after the boy.

> From the evidence that I have heard, I am satisfied that Mr. Murdoch has been a capable and a successful rancher and has built up a substantial holding from a very small beginning and that, directly or indirectly the success, and that the money to which Mrs. Murdoch is entitled has to come from his ability to farm and ranch this land and run the cattle successfully.

As for her claim to half the ranch, it was dismissed out of hand. Having examined the account books, Judge MacDonald agreed with Alex Murdoch that the money Florrie contributed was a loan from her mother to him that he had paid back.

Nor, ruled Judge MacDonald, did Florence Murdoch's labour count as a contribution to the purchase of the ranch. Mrs. Trueman in the *Trueman* case cut the crop, stooked—bundled—and raked the hay, harrowed the soil, and did "anything there was to do," much as Florence Murdoch did on their ranch, but there was a difference. Mrs. Trueman asked for, and the judges of the Court of Appeal gave her, half of the home*stead*—the house and the land that immediately surrounded it. Florence Murdoch was asking for a share of the ranch, 480 acres. She was asking for half of the business. Shymka wasn't surprised:

> They were okay with giving a wife some interest...in a matrimonial home. And Trueman was 160 acres...a home on a small home quarter. And the scuttlebutt I heard was, there's no way this is going to happen to businesses—and not ranches, for sure. This was a man's domain.

Finally, Judge MacDonald said no as a matter of principle to the argument that it was only fair or equitable, that husband and wife were partners in whatever venture they embarked upon:

> Were I to declare that the plaintiff had an equitable interest in the farm lands and farm assets, it would be tantamount to establishing a precedent that would give any farm or ranch wife a claim in partnership. I have read nothing and nothing has been referred to me that suggests that this is either public policy or the intention of any legislation that exists.

Allow Florence a half interest in the ranch, and the floodgates will open. *All* wives will want half. Indeed.

The decision came and went. There was very little public attention, no sense of outrage over the fate of Florence Murdoch. As

Nancy Shymka said to her husband, "The temperature wasn't high enough."

✦✦✦

I wasn't just a potted plant. I felt it didn't strike me fair that the husband would end up with all the assets.

—Ernest Shymka

Florence Murdoch was deeply discouraged. She barely saw her son, she was working as a cleaning lady, and sinking deeper in debt. When Shymka said she could appeal the decision if she wanted, she said yes.

Shymka was as disappointed as her but determined. Perhaps thinking of the *Trueman* case, which had succeeded on appeal, he filed the appeal with the court in Edmonton.

It was what he saw as the fundamental unfairness that was preoccupying Shymka. How could Florence Murdoch have worked the ranch the way she had and not come away with anything? She had purchased the furniture and the bedding and the kitchen pots and pans out of her own money, and still she had nothing.

Given the usual pace of legal matters, things moved quickly. The trial judge handed down his decision in February of 1971, the case was heard by the Court of Appeal, and their decision was handed down less than a year later. There were no complex "reasons for judgement." Shymka's appearance at the Court of Appeal was over and done within twenty minutes. He was cut off before he even launched into his argument. The Court of Appeal said because Irene Florence Murdoch had accepted the support payments from her husband, she could not now come back and ask for half the farm. Once again, she was out on her ear.

What to do next? Whether to go on and appeal to the Supreme Court of Canada in Ottawa was a big decision. It would be both expensive and intimidating. (In the early 1970s, there was an automatic right to appeal to the highest court. Later, civil cases had to be granted leave to appeal. There are around five hundred requests each year, and forty are granted.) Ernest Shymka had never taken a case to the Supreme Court, but as he saw it, there were three good reasons to go to Ottawa this time; first was his nagging feeling that things, as they stood, just weren't right.

> Just the sheer factual situation.... How could it be that the husband ended up with everything?!...just that alone felt, that can't be right. That can't stand. It just can't stand. She's got to be given something.

Second, the insurance money from her father via her mother, he continued to maintain, was not a loan to her fist-waving husband. And third, instinct. Shymka thought that the timing was good, that the women's movement was strong, and that attitudes toward women were changing: "You didn't have to be a Philadelphia lawyer to figure that out." He filed the notice of appeal to the Supreme Court of Canada on March 24, 1972. "If they hadn't abolished appeals to the Privy Council," he said later, "I would have gone all the way to the Privy Council."

+++

We went to the Supreme Court of Canada and...there wasn't a soul, there wasn't a reporter, there wasn't a single soul in the courthouse when that case was argued.

—Les Duncan

Murdoch v Murdoch attracted very little attention as it continued up the judicial ladder. The temperature, in Nancy Shymka's words, *still* wasn't high enough. No one had ever heard of the Murdochs, no one knew where they came from, and the lawyers were not well-known. It wasn't seen as a test case—although it turned out to be exactly that—and it snuck up on everyone. This was pretty esoteric stuff. Could a spouse, a wife, whose name was not a on a deed, could she convince the court through the law of trusts, that she had a stake in the property? Ernest Shymka never saw *Murdoch* as a headline grabber.

Leslie Duncan did:

> I could see that this was headed for headlines for its own reasons. It was timeliness, it was the fact that [Alex Murdoch] had been convicted of assault, it was the fact that the ranch was in his name alone, even though in total dollars and cents the value of the ranch, by today's standards, wasn't that much.

Florence Murdoch, at home in Turner Valley, didn't hold out much hope. The trial judge's decision was rubbed in her face every month. At the bottom of each support cheque, Alex Murdoch wrote, "alimony—ha ha." She wasn't expecting a legal victory and she certainly did not expect the deluge of publicity that came when the Supreme Court handed down its decision. She just didn't think anyone cared. For that matter, the court itself didn't seem to see this as a major case. For big cases, the Supreme Court usually pulls out all nine judges. There were only five men (the first woman, Bertha Wilson, was not appointed to the Supreme Court of Canada until 1982) sitting on *Murdoch v Murdoch*.

Yet when the court issued its ruling, everything turned upside down. The decision itself changed nothing, and that was the point. The majority of the Supreme Court of Canada justices basically agreed with the trial judge, Hugh McDonald. It is the trial judge who examines the evidence, listens to the witnesses, and makes findings of fact. Supreme Court Justice Ronald Martland, also from Alberta, wrote the decision and quoted McDonald when he said that, Irene Florence Murdoch's twenty-five years of cutting hay, moving, dehorning, vaccinating and driving cattle, and more "was the work done by any ranch wife."

Her work, and for that matter the work of any housewife, the Supreme Court was saying, was what a wife owed her husband by virtue of being married. That work did nothing to earn her a share in "her husband's" property.

It was the dismissive nature of that phrase "the work done by any ranch wife" that outraged women's groups and resonated with the media. This was 1973. Women's groups of all sorts were gaining strength and self-confidence. As Leslie Duncan had said, and Shymka had sensed, it was about timeliness.

The Supreme Court of Canada's judgement did not colour outside the lines. It was what is known as "black letter law"—a strict interpretation of the law as it existed, which is exactly what many, including Duncan, thought the highest court in the land should deliver. Even then, the Supreme Court's decision might not have attracted as much attention were there not a strong dissenting judgement. The Honourable Mr. Justice Bora Laskin, who had only been on the court for three years, had been a human rights activist before he was appointed to the bench and was a judge who thought the court could and should change the law when fairness demanded. Future Chief Justice Brian Dickson said of Laskin that he was "ever sensitive to injustice and ready at all times to reject the notion that whatever is, is right." It was an attitude that dovetailed with Shymka's argument. In his dissenting judgement, Laskin said what women's groups wanted to hear. First, that he did not think the amount of labour contributed by Florence Murdoch to the ranch was ordinary; rather, "the wife's contribution in physical labour...can only be described as extraordinary." Nor did he ignore the consequences of Alex Murdoch's assault on her, and he referred in his judgement to "a physical clash which resulted in the wife's hospitalization." Very importantly, he found that she had made a financial contribution to the purchase and he concluded that,

> In making a substantial contribution of physical labour, as well as a financial contribution, to the acquisition of the successive properties culminating in the acquisition of the Brockway land [the 480 acres near Turner Valley], the wife had established a right to an interest which it would be inequitable to deny and which, if denied, would result in the unjust enrichment of her husband.

Laskin's dissenting judgement had far-reaching ramifications. There was every expectation that Ronald Martland, the respected senior judge on the court, would be the next chief justice. Instead, less than three months after the *Murdoch* decision, Prime Minister Pierre Trudeau named Bora Laskin chief justice. The appointment sent a strong political message and opened the door to a more activist court. Something that was not to everyone's liking—Les Duncan, for one. A few years earlier, when Laskin taught at the University of Toronto Law School, Duncan had been one of his students and he knew when he stood up at the Supreme Court, where Laskin was coming from. "It was obvious," Duncan claimed, "during the course of our argument that I had a four-to-one court, and that Laskin was dead against." When Laskin questioned him from the bench about the "fairness" of the case, Duncan refused to engage and instead answered at length that the courts

Bora Laskin, Chief Justice of the Supreme Court of Canada from 1973–1984.

had no business dealing with this matter. It should be politicians, legislatures, that made policy—not the courts.

Laskin's dissenting opinion attracted public attention. But the reality was the Supreme Court had made a 4–1 decision *against* Irene Florence Murdoch. Sitting at home in Turner Valley, she still had nothing, exactly what Ernest Shymka said in the documents he had submitted to the court. Florence Murdoch got nothing, "not even a spoon."

\+ + +

> *As rural women, we are seriously and justifiably alarmed at the Supreme Court decision in the case of* Murdoch v Murdoch.
>
> —Calgary Local Council of Women

After five years of legal battles, the media finally discovered Florence Murdoch. The CBC's Adrienne Clarkson, later Governor General, interviewed both Ernest Shymka and Leslie Duncan. Shymka, never a rebel, was not angry with the court's decision. He understood how the system worked, and he was careful:

> Justice Martland showed sympathy but he just felt that, within the law, this is just how it'd have to work; so this [is]...the correct decision in the law, you know. And in a sense, that is true...what's the old saying, the law can be an ass? You know, and just that you can have unjust results.

Shymka was so careful and understanding of the Supreme Court's ruling against his client that his interview never made it to air. Leslie Duncan's, however, did. Martland echoed in his decision what Duncan had argued: "It seems to me that the better course would be to attain this object by legislation rather than by the exercise of an immeasurable judicial discretion." The trial judge, John Hugh MacDonald, had pointed in the same direction and so, for that matter, had Laskin:

Ronald Martland, Supreme Court of Canada Judge from 1958–1982.

> No doubt, legislative action may be the better way to lay down policies and prescribe conditions under which, and the extent to which, spouses should share in property acquired by either or both during marriage.

However, Laskin went on:

> The better way is not the only way; and if the exercise of a traditional jurisdiction by the Courts can conduce to equitable sharing, it should not be withheld merely because difficulties in particular cases...may result in a slower and perhaps more painful evolution of principle.

Everyone wanted government to take care of things but it wasn't happening. It's worth remembering that Alberta women's groups had been pushing the legislature for "community property"—equal shares—for the previous fifty years.

+++

Where does court get off saying that the usual duties of a ranch wife are to castrate calves, ride bucking broncos, cook for hired men, and wash their clothes and accept his beatings, summer-fallow, rake hay, pitch bales, keep books and whatever else he asks of her—does it follow that a farmer can divorce his wife on the grounds that she refuses to or is unable to perform this labour?

—Farmer Sarah Rau, in a letter to the Murdoch trust fund

Those words, "the work done by any ranch wife," rang out as chauvinistic and regressive, out of step with the times. The decision angered not only feminists and eastern urbanites but also what were seen as more traditional women's organizations. In Alberta, a partnership had developed between the Calgary Local Council of Women (a women's group formed in 1894) and Irene Parlby's 1916 United Farm Women of Alberta (later renamed the Women of Unifarm). Both were conservative, old-school organizations. In 1977, a substantial number of the Women of Unifarm remained anti-alcohol in the tradition of the Women's Christian Temperance Union, and a significant faction referred to Planned Parenthood as an "abortion referral agency." Whatever they felt about alcohol and abortion, they had always pushed the law to recognize and respect the labour of farm wives like Florence Murdoch. They were furious with the Supreme Court of Canada's decision.

Florence Murdoch was the touch paper for the #MeToo movement of her time and place. Her story was their story. She was respectable, easy to identify with, and going through what so many of them understood firsthand. "The land" was what their lives were all about, but the much-touted saga of the pioneer wife who earned the respect of her husband as she built fences, rode the range, and hauled water beside him, had been proved farcical one too many times.

When the Women of Unifarm came together for their annual convention in 1973, their president, Betty Pedersen, read from the transcript of the Supreme Court decision. She pointed out that the Calgary trial judge had found, in part because Alex and Florence

United Farm Women of Alberta Board of Directors, 1921.

Murdoch did not have a formal agreement, that they were not legally "partners." Pedersen then turned to the group and asked, "How many of you would have drawn up a legal partnership agreement with your husband in the first throes of romance?" The place filled with laughter. The Unifarm women sent the following resolution to the provincial cabinet:

> As rural women we are seriously and justifiably alarmed at the SCC decision (Oct 2, 1973) in the case of *Murdoch v Murdoch*.... As rural women who contribute in many ways to the building of a viable farm or ranch operation, we feel that we have an indubitable right to a legal share in the assets of that operation. Therefore, we demand that upon the dissolution of a marriage, either by divorce or legal separation that assets accumulated during the marriage must be divided on a half and half basis.

It took an article in *Time* magazine to inflame the more urban Calgary Local Council of Women. Upon reading the piece, Patricia de Krasinski, the British-born granddaughter of a militant suffragette and the mother of four daughters, got in her car, drove out to Turner Valley, and knocked on Florence Murdoch's door. De Krasinski (she reclaimed her birth name "Stansfield" in the 1980s) was the Citizenship Convenor of the CLCW. She had come to talk to Florence Murdoch woman to woman, to find out if all that she'd read was true. It was and then some. Because she had lost, Florence Murdoch was saddled with a portion of her husband's legal costs on top of everything else.

De Krasinski went back to the Calgary Council and asked the CLCW president, "What are you going to do to help this woman?" On March 27, 1974, the CLCW set up a trust fund to help Florence Murdoch and thank her. They said "her actions brought the unjustness of our laws on matrimonial property into the open." The money started coming in—some fat cheques, some donations of no more than a dollar. As American writer Anne Enke said, many women, particularly traditional and conservative women, had heard of the women's movement—they just didn't know where to find it.

The Murdoch trust fund was endorsed by the still-new Alberta Human Rights Commission, which sent a letter to Ottawa asking that the court's decision be reviewed. The two-year-old National Action Committee on the Status of Women said that the case of Florence Murdoch had become a national symbol of unjust matrimonial property law. There was a groundswell of public opinion backing Florence Murdoch.

It wasn't merely hit-and-run empathy on de Krasinski's part. She and other CLCW women went with Florence Murdoch to meetings with lawyers for the better part of a decade. In 1979, eleven years after it had all begun and when the options of any further legal action had been exhausted, they drove out to Turner Valley one more time and gave her a cheque for $1805.91, the equivalent of more than $7,300 in 2024.

In the meantime, more farm wives' launched claims for a share in "their" ranches. In 1978, the Saskatchewan Court of Appeal awarded Helen Rathwell half the farm. Her husband appealed to the Supreme Court of Canada. This time the court was ready: all nine judges were sitting. The circumstances were similar to the Murdochs. Helen Rathwell had milked the cows, looked after the garden, canned the produce, driven farm machinery, baled the hay, kept the books, and driven the school bus. Her husband agreed that they had always talked about "our" ranch and worked as a team. His appeal was dismissed. She got half the farm.

The Court also prodded the provincial legislatures across the country one more time. As Justice Brian Dickson wrote in *Rathwell*, "Canadian legislatures generally have given little or no guidance for the resolution of matrimonial property disputes with the result that laws applied are per-force judge made laws."

+++

In 1975, Florence and Alex Murdoch were divorced. Alex Murdoch got in there first and served her with the papers. She counter-petitioned and asked for a lump sum payment. It was seen by the outside world as an adequate substitute for her claim to a share in the ranch. But it wasn't the same. She had argued for a right to half the farm—a lump sum payment as part of a divorce settlement was at the discretion of the judge. This judge awarded her $65,000, about a quarter of the value of the ranch. "The court, I think under a lot of pressure from the headlines and so on, was very generous to her"; Les Duncan never saw the justice in the $65,000 award. "[She] ultimately got more than what I think she should have, but in any event that's the law."

It was a substantial amount and soothed the financial pain, but it did nothing to establish a ranch wife's right to the matrimonial property.

Women across the country continued to speak out and to lobby, and by the end of 1978, nine provinces had passed legislation that guaranteed, with some exceptions, a fifty-fifty split of all assets acquired during a marriage. Too late for Florence Murdoch.

Neither Ernest Shymka nor Leslie Duncan ever appeared before the Supreme Court of Canada again. Shymka did not represent

Florence in the divorce action for "health reasons" and came away with next to nothing by way of payment for his services. Florence Murdoch stayed as far away from the public eye as she could. By 1983, she had remarried and was living in Calgary as Florence Jespersen. That year, *Chatelaine* magazine published "Farm Wives: 10 years after Irene Murdoch," by Suzanne Zwarun. (Doris Anderson, the magazine's former editor and champion of women's rights and also an Alberta woman, was running the National Action Committee on the Status of Women.) Zwarun reported that Florence Murdoch was in "poor health" and "would give anything to get back to the country."

> The embittered Murdoch will likely never recover from the physical and psychological scars inflicted on her by a divorce that became a Canadian cause.... When asked whether she feels a sense of accomplishment at the change that case set in motion, Murdoch says flatly, "I am sorry to have started it. It did more harm than good."

She resented the article and said that she had been quoted out of context. Together with Patricia de Krasinski she wrote a reply that *Chatelaine* published two months later:

> What I said was that I do not want to start it up again after 14 years. This is where it will do more harm than good.... Since my divorce what I have said over and over again is that I want to forget those eight miserable years that led up to it. I have a new life now and I want to forget the old.

She might have wanted to forget but Canadian women did not. The *Murdoch* case became an object lesson. It was commented on by individuals and institutions for years. Ernest Shymka remembered one provincial Law Reform Commission, saying that "the conscience of Canadians was shocked." Law students across the country studied *Murdoch v Murdoch*; women, urban and rural, rich and poor, thanked her for pushing so hard.

Alex Murdoch lived on the ranch for the rest of his life. He died when he was seventy in 1988. Florence Murdoch outlived both her husbands and her son Bill. She died in 2020 at the age of ninety-five in Vulcan, Alberta.

4. No Means No

There is one more, at least one more, Alberta story stemming from Florence Murdoch, Emily Murphy, and the others of Alberta's Famous Five, that begs to be told.

Les Duncan, Alex Murdoch's lawyer in *Murdoch v Murdoch*, had said in his interview with the Legal Archives of the Alberta Law Society that there were many lawyers who represented Florence Murdoch, some of them very briefly, during her five-year journey to the Supreme Court of Canada. They were good lawyers who suggested that the most likely way in which she could succeed and gain some "relief" would be to divorce her husband and claim support under the "new" 1968 Divorce Act. "No, thank you," she might have muttered out of the corner of her mouth and she put her coat on and went from law office to law office until she found Ernest Shymka, the lawyer who would do what she wanted. That is the client's prerogative. At least two of the lawyers she rejected (or who rejected her) went on to become respected advocates and noteworthy judges who made their own mark on the rights of women.

\+ + +

I think in total I heard over the years twelve different counsel represented her. Jack Major was the first. I've never asked Jack why he didn't continue to act.

—Les Duncan

John C. "Jack" Major was a Calgary lawyer ten years into his career and already involved in complex cases. He represented the Province of Alberta before the Supreme Court on constitutional issues, and he was counsel for the Calgary Police Service. No one knows why he did not take on Florence Murdoch's case, although family law wasn't his area of expertise. Almost twenty years after *Murdoch,* in 1991, Major was appointed to the Alberta Court of Appeal, and the next year he was elevated to the Supreme Court of Canada where he presided over, he estimated, more than a thousand cases. Jack Major wrote the Supreme Court's reasons for judgement in this "one more case," *R v Ewanchuk.* A case that settled the law of consent in sexual assault and resulted in the most unseemly judicial fracas Canada has ever seen.

Then there was John Wesley "Buzz" McClung. Florence Murdoch considered him, too, when she was lawyer-shopping but moved on.

"McClung" was a big name in Alberta when it came to the rights of women. John Wesley "Buzz" McClung was the third man in his family to bear the name. The first was the red-haired husband of Nellie McClung—the best known of the early Canadian feminists; the second was their eldest son, born in 1897. That John Wesley McClung fought in WWI and came home deeply affected, shell-shocked. His mother said he had a "hurt look in his clear blue eyes." He regrouped, married, and became a provincial prosecutor. John Wesley "Buzz" McClung, his only child and Nellie's first grandson, was born in 1935. But Nellie McClung's eldest son was an unhappy man. He drank more than anyone should, and in 1944 he died. Six years later, his wife followed him to the grave and at fourteen, "Buzz" McClung became an orphan.

He too shook off the trauma, grew up, and became a criminal lawyer, a very able criminal lawyer. In 1975, he was ranked one of the country's ten best by *Weekend* magazine. This John McClung

John Wesley "Buzz" McClung, Alberta Court of Appeal judge from 1979–2004.

married late (at thirty-eight), and died early (at sixty-nine). Tributes praised his "brilliant legal career" and his prowess as a hunter. In photographs, he has a jaunty air about him. Those who knew him on his days off talked about him as a golfer with an excellent "short game," and described him as outspoken and a man's man.

McClung was also a respected legal historian and like his grandmother Nellie, he had a prodigious memory. For twenty-eight years, he sat on the bench, first in the trial division of Alberta's provincial court and then on the Court of Appeal. But as an Appeal court judge, McClung, despite his strength as a litigator and his much-praised memory, was "the object of criticism." It was the Honourable Mr. Justice John McClung who wrote the Alberta Court of Appeal's reasons for judgement in *R v Ewanchuk*.

+++

To start at the beginning: Steve Ewanchuk was the accused and Jane Doe the complainant, the woman it happened to. This was a sexual assault case, and the identity of complainants is almost always protected. So it was in *Ewanchuk*. She was never known by any other name than "Jane Doe."

In the summer of 1994, this Jane Doe was seventeen with a six-month-old baby at home. (The age of consent to sexual activity in Canada was then fourteen. It was raised to sixteen in 2008.) On this particular day in June, she was wandering through a shopping mall in Edmonton, looking for a job. There was Steven Ewanchuk, sitting in his van in the parking lot. He was forty-four, seemingly friendly, with a head of curly dark hair. They got to talking and he said he might have work for her advertising his woodworking business in a booth in the mall. She was interested. "Come back tomorrow for an interview," he said. She found someone to look after her baby and went to meet him the next day. The interview, she told the court, was conducted in a businesslike manner but she kept the van door open. She was careful.

"Have a look in the trailer. You can see what I make," he must have said, and Jane Doe went into the trailer attached to the van. She left that door open, too. Steve Ewanchuk closed it when he followed her. Then he asked her if she'd like a massage. It was becoming a strange job interview. He massaged her feet and his hands gradually travelled up her legs. She said no and he stopped—and started again. She said no again, he stopped again—then became more insistent. He climbed on top of her. His penis was out of his pants—a flaccid penis, the defence pointed out—and his hand was inside her shorts. She said no one final time, wriggled out from under him, and got the door open. Steve Ewanchuk gave her a $100 bill and told her not to tell anyone.

Jane Doe wasn't bought off. She reported what had happened. That alone made her an exceptional young woman. As late as 2019, only 6% of sexual assaults were reported. A miniscule number were investigated and even fewer came to trial. Jane Doe, whoever she was, was a gutsy seventeen-year-old, prepared to stand up for herself and get on the witness stand when the case went to court.

But Steve Ewanchuk was acquitted. Somehow, the sexual assault charge against him became all about her. His lawyer cross examined

Jane Doe about how she was dressed. It was summer, she was wearing shorts. She was asked and she answered that yes, she had a baby; no, she wasn't married; yes, she and her boyfriend lived with another couple. And when Ewanchuk's fingers were climbing up her leg she said "No" or "Please stop" but did she fight? *We all know what that means* was the subtext implied by the prosecution: *she really meant yes*. The Crown countered that she was inside a small trailer with an insistent man who was bigger than her. Could be she felt foolish for getting herself in this situation in the first place. She decided, as he ground himself into her, that it was wiser to project a relaxed and confident manner. Ewanchuk had asked her if she was scared. Jane Doe had tears in her eyes when she said yes.

All of which added up in the mind of the trial judge to "implied consent," and consent is a valid defence to a sexual assault charge. Even though she said no, Alberta Queen's Bench Judge Moore ruled at trial that Ewanchuk was justified by virtue of the circumstances—what she was wearing, that she had a child—in thinking that "no" meant "yes." Steve Ewanchuk smiled his thanks to his lawyer, zipped up his jacket, and walked out into fresh air.

R v Ewanchuk (R stands for Regina, the Queen, or Rex, the King. In the United States, it would be "The People" or "The State") was appealed. This was the 90s, and public pressure was building. Too many sexual assault cases were failing. Women knew they would be humiliated on the witness stand and either never reported the assault or backed down if and when it went to trial.

Public pressure or not, the judges of the Alberta Court of Appeal upheld the acquittal 2–1 on the grounds of "implied consent." Legal judgements are seldom easy reading. Wading through the analysis, the discussion of precedent, previous cases, cited legislation, and references to academic papers can be a tough slog, a journey through intellectual fog. The Honourable Mr. Justice McClung, however, wrote with as much flair and clarity as his grandmother Nellie. His judgement in *Ewanchuck* was memorable. (Thirty years later, while vacationing in the Arctic, a former Chair of the Alberta chapter of the Canadian Bar Association could still quote its opening lines.) The acquittal alone sparked outrage, but McClung's ability to turn a phrase turned spark into fire.

John "Jack" Major, Supreme Court of Canada judge from 1992–2005.

His judgement opened, "It must be pointed out that the complainant did not present herself to Ewanchuk or enter his trailer in a bonnet and crinoline." He then described Ewanchuk's behaviour—when he had finally desisted, he said to Jane Doe, "See, I'm a nice guy"—as "clumsy passes" that were "far less criminal than hormonal." McClung went on to suggest that "in a less litigious age, going too far in a boyfriend's car was better dealt with on-site—a well-chosen expletive, a slap in the face, or, if necessary, a well-directed knee...before turning to the courts."

There was a dissenting opinion in the appeal. The chief justice, Catherine Fraser, the first woman chief justice of a provincial appeal court in the country, and at forty-four, the youngest chief justice in Alberta history, was having none of this idea of "implied consent"—something between yes and no? The Honourable Chief Justice Fraser saw implied consent as a legal fallacy and wrote that Canadian law does not expect women to be "walking around...in a state of constant consent to sexual activity."

To no one's surprise, *R v Ewanchuk* was appealed to the Supreme Court of Canada.

\+\+\+

A year later, all nine Supreme Court judges, seven men and, by now, two women, filed in and took their places on the bench to hear *R v Ewanchuk*. The "Supremes" are often photographed in their red robes trimmed with white fur, their dress uniform, but on a workday, as this was, it's standard, stern black robes. This was the case that everyone knew would establish the definition of consent in sexual assault cases. If a complainant said no but her shorts, her baby, suggested—in the mind of the accused—that she didn't really mean it, then was it or wasn't it consent? Was there such a thing as "implied consent," as both the trial judge and the Alberta Court of Appeal had found?

No. All nine judges agreed. The principle point of law was straightforward: there is no such things as a defence of implied consent. No means no.

And things might have rested there. At that time, the most senior judge who volunteered to write the judgement was usually given the assignment. Quebec judge Claire L'Heureux-Dubé had the seniority and put her hand up. Instead, the Chief Justice Antonio Lamer asked Justice Jack Major to write the majority judgement. Going back to the days of *Murdoch*, Jack Major and John McClung were colleagues—lawyers together and, briefly, judges together on the Alberta Court of Appeal. Perhaps Lamer thought an Alberta Supreme Court judge overturning the decision of the Alberta Court of Appeal would soften the blow. Supreme Court Justice Ian Binnie was more direct, according to Constance Backhouse in her biography of Claire L'Heureux-Dubé. He said, "If the Court of Appeal of Alberta was going to get straightened out, it was good to have an Alberta judge do it." Backhouse added that Lamer and McClung were hunting buddies. Jack Major wrote a well-reasoned, logical judgement, and the majority of the court signed on.

And things could have rested there.

Claire L'Heureux-Dubé, however, was fuming. She agreed with the outcome but felt strongly that there was more that needed to be on record from Canada's Supreme Court. It was McClung's language that she felt was inappropriate. "It was just as if they were approving what he said," she told Backhouse. "I found it so offensive." L'Heureux-Dubé wrote, as was her right, her own "concurring opinion." She began,

> Violence against women takes many forms: sexual assault is one of them. In Canada, one-half of all women are said to have experienced at least one incident of physical or sexual violence since the age of 16.

And she went on,

> Violence against women is as much a matter of equality as it is an offence against human dignity and a violation of human rights.

She was unequivocal. This case wasn't about consent, she said, it was about myths and stereotypes: myths that women must fight back if they really mean no; that if their clothes reveal a little flesh, they're "asking for it"; that if there's a baby and no wedding ring, then they're of "easy virtue"; and if they are firm but composed while saying no... then no means yes. It all spoke, Madame Justice L'Heureux-Dubé wrote, to what should be expected of the justice system and judges.

> Complainants should be able to rely on a system free from myths and stereotypes and a judiciary whose impartiality is not compromised by these biased assumptions.... It is part of the role of this court to denounce this kind of language unfortunately still used today, which not only perpetuates archaic myths and stereotypes about the nature of sexual assaults but also ignores the law.

It should have rested there.

Claire L'Heureux-Dubé was the second woman appointed to the bench of the Supreme Court of Canada, where she served from 1987–2002.

But John McClung, rather than following the age-old advice—write your angry letter in the evening then sleep on it—must have written his very angry letter moments after he read the report of the Supreme Court's judgement in the *National Post* newspaper and put it in the mailbox before the ink was dry. McClung's letter appeared in the *National Post* the next day. In a profession where civility and etiquette are everything, it was unprecedented. He attacked L'Heureux-Dubé for her "feminist bias" and her "graceless slide into personal invective," then incongruously and inexplicably added that her remarks contributed to the increasing "number of male suicides being reported in the Province of Quebec." The last was a step too far.

His polemic on feminism and the judiciary was echoed by others. The prominent defence counsel Edward Greenspan wrote to the paper in support of McClung:

> By labelling Judge McClung, in effect, the male chauvinist pig of the century, the chief yahoo from

> Alberta, the stupid, ignorant, ultimate, sexist male jerk, Judge L'Heureux-Dubé did an unnecessary and mean-spirited thing...Judge L'Heureux-Dubé drew first blood and whatever he said will not be recorded in Canadian judicial history like her vicious comments about him will.... The feminist perspective has hijacked the Supreme Court of Canada and now feminists want to throw off the bench anyone who disagrees with them.... Madam Justice L'Heureux-Dubé has disgraced the Supreme Court.

Judges are human. In her 1987 article "The Dynamic Nature of Equality," Judge Rosalie Abella who would be appointed to the Supreme Court in 2004, said that "every decision maker walks into a courtroom armed not only with the relevant legal texts, but also with a set of values, experiences, and assumptions that are thoroughly embedded." Abella questioned whether judges could ever be truly impartial. But how far can those thoroughly embedded assumptions be allowed to go? McClung's initial words were controversial and inflammatory, but the suicide remark was unforgivable.

Claire L'Heureux was one of the first women lawyers to practise divorce law in Quebec and became the first woman appointed to the Quebec Superior Court, then the Quebec Court of Appeal. She had married Arthur Dubé, a metallurgist, in 1957. He taught at Laval University. He also suffered from depression. The couple had two children. In 1978, their eighteen-year-old daughter Louise went downstairs and discovered her father's body. He had shot and killed himself. Arthur Dubé's suicide was widely known in the legal community. Judge John McClung wrote and said he did not know and apologized for the suicide remark. What was not widely known was that John Wesley "Buzz" McClung's father had also shot and killed himself. What demons were lurking in McClung's mind?

There were complaints against both judges (twenty-four against McClung, one against L'Heureux-Dubé) to the Canadian Judicial Council, the body that judges the judges. The complaint against Madame Justice L'Heureux-Dubé was dismissed in short order. Mr.

Justice McClung got a slap on the wrist and remained on the bench until his death in 2004.

***

Edmonton's Jane Doe might have read about the Supreme Court decision when it was reported in the newspaper in the winter of 1999. If she did, she must have felt vindicated—after all, the Supreme Court of Canada had backed her up. No does mean no. But she didn't have much time to dwell on the victory. She was busy. Her baby was by then in kindergarten, and with any luck, she was working and perhaps even had another baby. No one knew what happened to Jane Doe—and we still don't. Steve Ewanchuk was a different story.

The police are frequently criticized for not pursuing sexual assault complaints. They had acted on Jane Doe's complaint because Steve Brian Ewanchuk was "known to the police." To protect his right to a fair trial without prejudice, his criminal record could not be entered into evidence. The police, however, knew that Steve Ewanchuk had sexual assault convictions going back to 1969. Then, it had been the rape of two sixteen-year-old girls two months apart, for which he was sentenced to three years in prison. That was followed by a ten-year sentence for the rape of an eighteen-year-old nursing student. (In 1982, the Criminal Code was amended and the charge of "rape" was replaced by the more inclusive "sexual assault." The Crown no longer had

Steve Ewanchuk, 2020.

to prove penetration and the "flaccid penis" defence was no longer of any use.) When Steve Ewanchuk was released in the early 80s, he reportedly sexually assaulted an eleven-year-old girl repeatedly over the next four years. Her parents chose not to pursue charges. In 1989, he got fifteen months for assaulting a fourteen-year-old. Along the way, Ewanchuk violated two court orders ordering him not to employ women under eighteen. Following the Supreme Court of Canada ruling, he was back in prison.

Around the same time that Edmonton Jane Doe was testifying against Steve Ewanchuk, another Jane Doe, a Toronto woman, was battling the Metropolitan Toronto Police Force. In the summer of 1986, a man had sexually assaulted Toronto Jane Doe in her apartment while holding a knife to her throat. He was known as "the balcony rapist" and had, on at least four previous occasions, entered women's apartments via their balconies and assaulted them. This Jane Doe was outraged at the lack of information from the police. Women were not warned. After it happened to her, Toronto Jane Doe began to speak out. She and her friends created their own "warning" and put posters up in the neighbourhood. The police department, in turn, threatened to charge Jane Doe with mischief for interfering with an investigation. The Toronto police maintained that if women were warned and the presence of the balcony rapist was publicized, "women would become hysterical and the rapist would flee the area." The "balcony rapist" Paul Callow was apprehended, charged, and entered a guilty plea to five counts of sexual assault with a weapon in 1987. He served a twenty-year sentence.

With the help of two feminist lawyers and the newly formed Women's Legal Education and Action Fund (LEAF), Toronto Jane Doe took on the police department. After an eleven-year court battle, she won a $220,000 civil lawsuit. The court ruled that investigators were negligent in their failure to protect and had violated her right to equality.

The much-publicized Ontario court's finding came down in the summer of 1998, six months before the Supreme Court of Canada's decision in *Ewanchuk*. Sexual assault, consent, duty to warn, got a lot of ink that year. Toronto Jane Doe's case was an object lesson for police departments across the country.

\+ + +

Nov. 5, 2020—The Regina Police Service is issuing a public advisory about a man who is considered to be a high risk to reoffend sexually… [Steve] Ewanchuk is six feet tall and weighs about 200 pounds, with green eyes and brown hair.

—CBC News

After the Supreme Court of Canada reversed Ewanchuk's acquittal, *R v Ewanchuk* was sent back to the trial judge for sentencing. Judge Moore, undoubtedly not happy that his decision was so definitively and publicly overturned, thumbed his nose at the Supreme Court and sentenced Ewanchuk to a year in jail. He said he considered imposing a conditional sentence—no jail time, providing Ewanchuk obeyed prescribed conditions—but noted that "the public would not accept that." The Crown clearly agreed that the public would not accept a one-year sentence and appealed the sentence. The Alberta Court of Appeal—McClung was not sitting on the appeal—increased it to two years.

Ewanchuk was incorrigible.

Within weeks of his release, after serving his sentence for the assault of Edmonton Jane Doe, he was arrested again. This time, he was charged and convicted of three counts of sexual assault of an eight-year-old girl. Edmonton Judge Sterling Sanderman sentenced him to sixteen and a half years and let loose, calling Steve Ewanchuk "repulsive and loathsome" and "the most disgusting of human beings," and then declared him a "long-term offender," thus adding ten years of strict post-release supervision to his sentence. But when Ewanchuk was released, nowhere in Alberta would or could take on the strict supervision. Saskatchewan found a place for him, and that's how it came about that the Regina police issued a public safety warning in 2020.

During his sixteen-year jail sentence, Steve Ewanchuk had surgery for prostate and colon cancer and was stabbed multiple times by another inmate. As of 2021, he was living in Regina. His supervision order goes until 2028, by which time he will be seventy-eight.

Claire L'Heureux-Dubé retired from the Supreme Court of Canada at seventy-four in 2002 (the mandatory retirement age for Canadian Supreme Court judges is seventy-five). Four years ago, by then a woman in her nineties, she told *Maclean's* magazine that her judgement in *R v Ewanchuk* was her proudest moment on the bench.

5. The Cases That Refuse to Die

If we have a generation of girls who would rather support themselves than marry, and wives who would rather be breadwinners than mothers, nature must have made a dreadful mistake.

—*Grain Growers Guide*, 1909

The message left on Pat Barter's answering machine was simple enough, if a little odd: "I think you knew Stella Bliss fifty years ago. I would really like to talk to you about her. Could you call me—please?" Pat Barter was the last hope; no one else seemed to remember Stella Bliss. This woman whose case ended up redefining the "equality" of women in Canada seemed to have disappeared without a trace.

Barter had been president of SORWUC (Service, Office and Retail Workers Union of Canada), the feminist union that had backed Stella Bliss in her court challenge in the 70s. Surely she would remember Bliss. For decades, Pat Barter had been living in the little town of Powell River on the BC coast, and she was busy, still involved in projects. It was several days before she phoned back. The *Bliss* case was about Unemployment Insurance (UI) Maternity Benefits, as they were called at the time, and whether the denial of Stella Bliss's claim added up to discrimination. Important stuff, but Pat Barter could only dimly remember sitting in a makeshift courtroom in Vancouver when the Bliss case was appealed, watching the faces of the judges, listening to the arguments, and feeling discouraged.

Lynn Smith, then only three years out of law school, had the same visceral memory. "We did not feel encouraged," she says. Smith, together with Allan MacLean, was representing Bliss. "We got a stony reception. There were very few questions from the judges," she remembers, "never a good sign." They argued that the Unemployment Insurance Act discriminated against women, that denying Stella Bliss maternity benefits flew in the face of the Bill of Rights. The case went on for seven years, and this was early days. The argument seemed futile. "We thought it was a good idea to raise the issues, but it was a case, at the time, that people had doubts about." And she adds with the wisdom of hindsight, "Later it became so obvious."

Lynn Smith was even younger than her client, this woman with a newborn baby. She has a dim memory of Bliss as a tall young woman with long, reddish hair. Activist and union organizer Jean Rands also knew Stella Bliss. No longer in good health, Rands nonetheless remembers the long, flowered dresses she wore. Pat Barter can't remember the dresses or the hair. "I don't remember much about her at all," she says, looking out over the Pacific Ocean from Powell River. At the time of the hearing, Barter was in her twenties, and what sticks in her memory are the three "liver-spotted old white men"—judges of the Federal Court who were hearing the case. They ruled that Stella Bliss was not discriminated against as a woman when she was denied her unemployment benefits. After all, in the natural order of things, men and women were fundamentally different, they reasoned. By definition, they could not be equal. Half a century after that day in court, Pat Barter was still spluttering with rage.

Stella Bliss died long ago; her first lawyer, Allan MacLean, has also died; Lynn Smith, brought in for the appeals, only met Stella Bliss once or twice; Leslie Pal, who interviewed Bliss in the 80s, now lived and worked in Qatar and his back-of-the-envelope notes have disappeared. Stella Bliss was a shadow on the legal landscape. Like *Murdoch v Murdoch*, her case, *Bliss v Attorney General*, went all the way up to the Supreme Court. And like Irene Florence Murdoch, she lost. But it was what Stella Bliss started, again like Florence Murdoch, that pushed women's groups, activists, and ultimately the courts and government to change the law. The *Bliss* case led to stronger wording of the equality provisions in the 1982 Charter of Rights and Freedoms, a huge step forward in the pursuit of equality for women. When it all began, no one saw that coming.

Seldom do the risk takers, the defiant ones set out to change the law…
Bliss *was another of those cases.*

—Leslie A. Pal and F.L. Morton

***

Stella Bliss's life was complicated, her status in Canada was complicated. She was an immigrant. Born and brought up in the UK, she had lived and worked in Vancouver from 1965 to 1969. No one remembers why, but for some reason, she went back to the UK. Somewhere along the line, Stella Bliss met a young American. Was he one of the thousands of American draft dodgers who came to Canada? Maybe. Did they break up, and is that what sent her back to the UK? Perhaps. Then she changed her mind, and in 1975, she and her American boyfriend applied to come back to Canada, to immigrate and to "start an antique business," she said. To complicate things, they planned to return to the West Coast of Canada via New Orleans, his home. Before they left England, they were told that the paperwork was all in order, but when they got to New Orleans, there was no record of their immigration application. Destined to eat shrimp gumbo for eternity it seemed, they were trapped in Louisiana by Canadian bureaucracy.

Days turned into weeks of delay until finally in June of 1975, Stella, partly on the strength of a job offer from the company that had employed her when she lived in Vancouver earlier, got her immigration papers. It wasn't as easy for her boyfriend. The Vietnam draft had ended two years earlier, but there may have been some residual reluctance, on the part of Canadian immigration officials, to let young American men into the country. For whatever reason, he was issued only a three-month work permit. They were worried that he would be deported after that work permit expired, and so

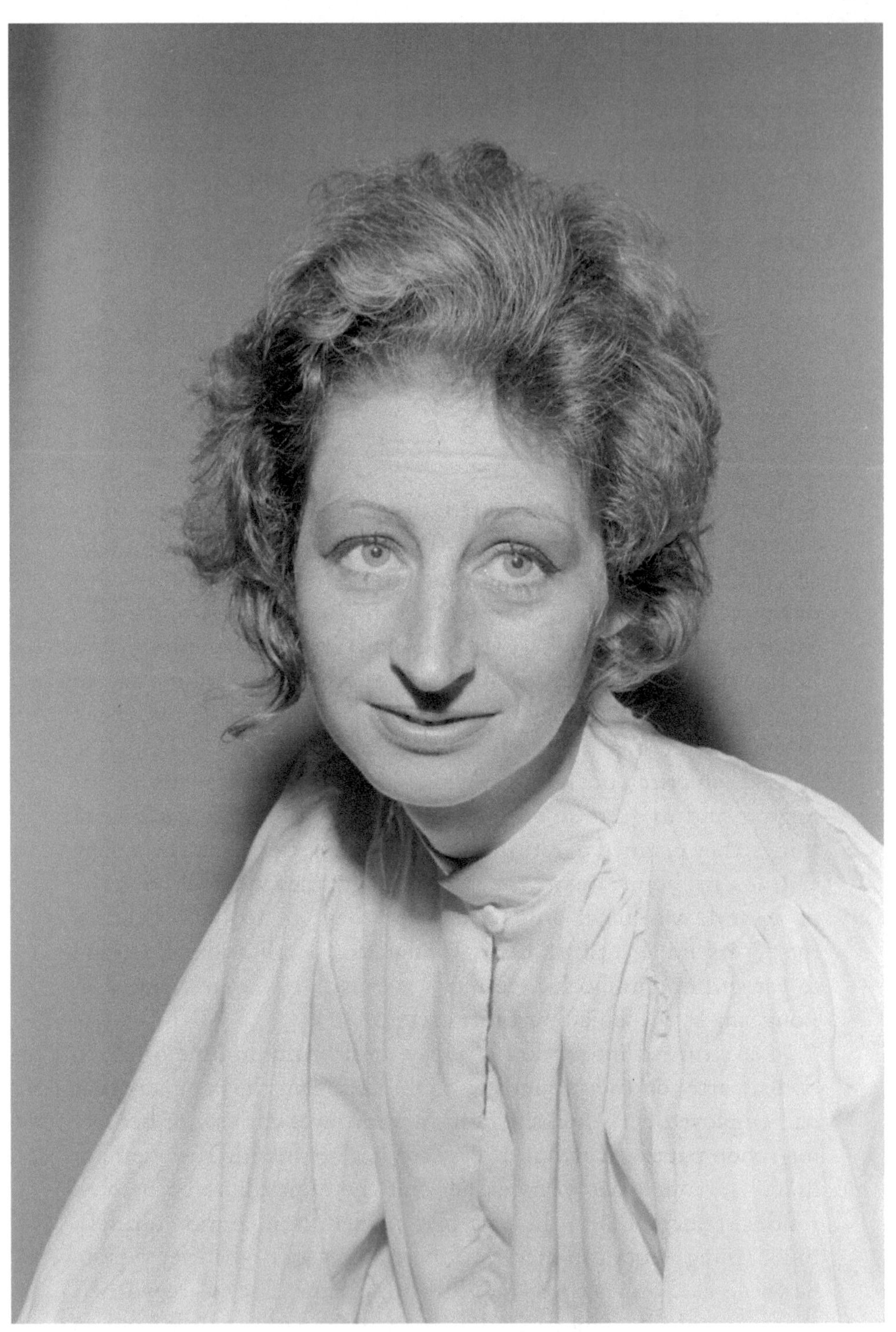

Stella Bliss, 1970s.

in August of 1975, they got married. It was a circuitous route into Canada, but they were in.

Finally, they could return to Vancouver, set up house, make a life. Canada was now their home. But because of the immigration delays, the job offer they had been counting on fell through. In 1975, unemployment in Canada was nearly 9%. Jobs were hard to find, and they had gone through their savings while they were waiting in New Orleans.

And they didn't know Stella was two months pregnant.

+++

Remarkably, she quickly found herself a job and on September 24, 1975, Stella Bliss began working for Brown Bros Ford as their leasing secretary. She realized that she was pregnant not long after. She was thirty-five and she wanted this baby, and she wanted—needed—this job. Pregnancy was an employment liability, and Stella Bliss knew it. She didn't tell Brown Bros and somehow, she managed to hide her growing belly through the fall and into the winter. In January of 1976, Brown Bros finally figured it out. She was seven months pregnant when they fired her.

In British Columbia, it had been illegal to fire a woman because she was pregnant for fifty-four years. Clearly, it still happened despite the fact that BC was progressive in its laws around employment and pregnancy. It was the first Canadian province to introduce maternity leave. That was back in 1921. It was unpaid leave, but it was a start. BC had also been the first to introduce legislation that gave mothers the same rights as fathers when it came to custody and care of children. Those reforms were attributed to Helen Gregory MacGill, the first female judge in BC (third in Canada after Emily Murphy and Alice Jamieson), and Mary Ellen Smith, BC's first woman MLA. That early Maternity Protection Act gave a woman limited leave before and after birth and thirty minutes twice a day to breastfeed her child. Impressive for the 1920s.

By the end of the 70s, over 60% of women between the ages of twenty and thirty were working outside the home. *Un*paid maternity leave wasn't good enough. In 1971, the federal government introduced *paid* maternity leave into the Unemployment Insurance Act. A pregnant woman could take fifteen weeks leave—paid at 66% of her regular salary—around the birth of her baby, provided she had worked and contributed twenty weeks of UI premiums.

Stella Bliss was unemployed because she was pregnant. Surely she was eligible for Unemployment Insurance Maternity Benefits? It sounded simple enough, but she was new to Canada and didn't know how things worked. She needed the help of her friends.

\+ + +

Existing unions have done nothing to organize female workers. Women must do it for themselves.

—Jean Rands

The 70s was a time of radicalization and action. According to Pat Barter, then president of the feminist Service, Office and Retail Workers Union of Canada, it was, in all likelihood, a woman named Jean Rands who advised Stella Bliss and told her what to do next. Rands was a union organizer, a woman with strong political convictions, and one of a coterie of women called the Vancouver Women's Caucus. Some were the same highly politicized young women, most in their early twenties, who had organized the Abortion Caravan, travelled across the country, and invaded Parliament demanding reform to the abortion laws. When they smuggled themselves into the galleries of the House of Commons and shut down government, they made the front page of every newspaper in Canada. The energy and boldness of the Vancouver Women's Caucus was remarkable.

There was an equally impassioned group within the Vancouver Women's Caucus dedicated to labour issues. When Stella Bliss arrived back in Vancouver in 1975, that group had successfully organized what became the Association of University and College Employees (AUCE), at the University of British Columbia. In its very first collective agreement, AUCE made history. They were the first union in Canada to negotiate fully paid maternity benefits: the government paid two thirds of a woman's salary and the employer agreed to top it up. Jean Rands was key to the creation of AUCE.

Likely acting on her advice, Stella Bliss applied for Unemployment Insurance maternity benefits. She was turned down and told she had to have been working *before* she became pregnant to be eligible. Stella Bliss had been waiting for her immigration papers when she got pregnant.

Next, she appealed her dismissal to the still relatively new BC Human Rights Commission (established in 1973). That was more successful. The Commission told Brown Bros that they had to take her back. The heavily pregnant Stella tottered back into the office, pushed her desk chair back a little farther, and started working again. The atmosphere could not have been pleasant. In the 70s, many pregnant women quit work as soon as they could, and car dealerships were a boys' club—men sold cars to men. Nearly fifty years later, of the fourteen Brown Bros "team members" listed on their website, only three were women.

Brown Bros clearly did not want this young woman, with her big belly, lumbering around the place, and on March 12, they fired her again. On March 16, she gave birth to her son. "Six days later," according to the Vancouver Status of Women, "she was cleared by her doctor as being ready to go back to work." Six days to recover from childbirth, make childcare arrangements, and be ready to get back on the bus to go to work, wherever that work might be. Stella Bliss, with her leaky breasts and hormones all awry, looked for another job, and—as a woman, according to her doctor, medically able and eager to work—she applied for regular UI benefits. She was turned down again. Because Stella Bliss had just had a baby, her claim was treated as one for maternity benefits (pregnancy, childbirth, and the weeks immediately after were all treated as "maternity leave" under the Unemployment Insurance Act). The act said that any woman who had given birth must wait out the six-week postdelivery period before being eligible for regular benefits. She was refused maternity benefits because she got pregnant too soon and denied regular benefits because she had a baby.

Stella Bliss was beginning to see that there was something bigger to prove here. With her baby boy in tow, she began to climb the ladder of appeals, and with every appeal, the case of Stella Bliss, an insignificant clerical worker at a BC car dealership, attracted more attention.

***

I do not feel that the expression…would be interpreted by the courts as to say we are making men and women equal, because men and women are not equal: they are different.

—Davie Fulton, Minister of Justice, 1957

Stella Bliss was no fool. She argued her own case in front of the Board of Referees, the first of four appeals. Unable to afford a lawyer, she had no choice. She had gone to talk to a law student, most likely at the student legal aid clinic at the University of British Columbia, and that's where the germ of the idea that seven years later carried the day was born. Stella Bliss, with her reddish hair and in one of her flowery dresses, stood up before the Board of Referees and argued that to deny her Unemployment Insurance benefits because she had a baby was discrimination on the grounds of sex, a violation of the principle of equality before the law, articulated in Canada's Bill of Rights.

The Bill of Rights had been on the books for fifteen years. It was a directive to the courts of fundamental equalities that must never be violated, or so Stella Bliss and most people thought. But her high-flown, principled argument cut no ice with the Board of Referees and in July of 1976, her appeal was denied. Stella Bliss was not naïve. "All is as expected," she wrote when the decision came down. She had only been back in Vancouver for a year. What a year it had been.

The next appeal was to the aptly named "Umpire." But to appeal to the Umpire, she needed either the consent of the Chair of the Board of Referees or the support of a union. The Chair of the Board said that "there was no principle of importance involved in the case" and turned her down flat. Stella Bliss went to the women she knew who were involved in those new women's grassroots

SORWUC LOCAL 7

service, office, & retail workers union of canada

ARE YOU

a mother
an office worker
a bankworker
a housewife
a waitress
a salesclerk
a homemaker
a volunteer worker

a woman interested in joining the struggle for our workplace rights?

GET INVOLVED!

call:
234-4726

write:
P.O. Box 4454
Station E
Ottawa
K1S 5B4

SORWUC is a union established on democratic principles, dedicated to organizing in those areas where women are concentrated. We are committed to the concerns of those whose work is paid and those whose work is unpaid.

SORWUC

Recruitment poster for Local 7 of SORWUC, 1982.

unions, AUCE and SORWUC. SORWUC represented daycare workers, the workers in a tuxedo rental store, and some banking and finance workers. It had been started in 1972 by twenty-four women. One astute Canadian labour relations board official said that SORWUC "is entirely different [from other unions] I think they see themselves differently too...as an instrument of social reform rather than a bread-and-butter union." He was right. Stella Bliss needed SORWUC. By this time, 1976, it had grown to forty-one locals and hundreds of members. They were grassroots feminists who were not content with the lack of attention traditional unions had paid to women workers. "Established union leadership...are not prepared to fight for women," said Rands. Maternity benefits was their kind of issue, and at its July meeting, SORWUC agreed to back Stella Bliss. She became a member-at-large, and with SORWUC behind her, took her appeal to the Umpire.

Not only did Bliss have the backing of a union but now she had a lawyer. That summer, she made her way to the Vancouver Community Legal Assistance Society, one of the first community legal clinics in the country. It provided free legal help to people like her who could not afford a lawyer. There, she met twenty-nine-year-old Allan MacLean, a freshly minted lawyer with a passionate commitment to human rights and labour issues. At first, MacLean was reluctant to take on the case. As Lynn Smith says, looking back to the 70s, there were doubts. How far would they get? This was going to be a Bill of Rights case, and MacLean knew that Bill of Rights challenges had not done well in the courts. It's a good bet that it was Jean Rands, a tenacious woman who seldom gave up, who talked MacLean into helping Bliss.

The 1960 Canadian Bill of Rights was a John Diefenbaker creation. Diefenbaker, a Saskatchewan criminal defence lawyer before he was elected to the House of Commons, was bound and determined that Canada should have a Bill of Rights. Its intent, broadly stated, was to ensure that government, at any level, could not pass laws that infringed on the rights of the individual. Exactly what those rights were was the problem. Saskatchewan passed Canada's first Bill of Rights in 1947. It prohibited discrimination on the grounds of "race, colour, creed or nationality"—not sex. None of the earliest

SORWUC picketers, Simon Fraser University, 1979.

provincial rights bills included sex discrimination. Equality rights for women were barely contemplated when discrimination was discussed. As the much-respected Dean of the University of Alberta Law School, W.F. Bowker, said in 1959, there was no need for any protection against sexual discrimination since "parliament had already removed unfair legislation from the statute books."

Sex did get added to grounds of prohibited discrimination in the federal Bill of Rights but what was meant by women's equality was something else again. Kamloops MP Davie Fulton, John Diefenbaker's Minister of Justice and the man responsible for shepherding the Bill of Rights through Parliament, was clear in what he thought women's equality meant. Or rather, what it didn't mean: "I do not feel that the expression ['the right to equality before the law and the protection of the law']...would be interpreted by the courts as to say we are making men and women equal, because men and women are not equal: they are different."

Scholars and legal pundits pulled their beards, talked about the natural difference between men and women, and tried to fathom the idea of gender equality. Difference became the justification for discrimination and inequality. The Bill of Rights was argued in thirty-five cases between 1960 and 1982. It succeeded in only five of those cases, and arguments alleging sexual discrimination did not win the day in any cases. No wonder Allan MacLean was reluctant to take on the case of Stella Bliss.

+++

There wasn't one clear day in Vancouver in November of 1976. The fog came in, and when rain occasionally gave way to drizzle, that was a good day. Vancouverites wore out their raincoats that November.

On the last day of the month, Stella Bliss shook out her umbrella, probably looked in the mirror, bemoaning her frizzy hair, and, leaving a trail of wet footprints, made her way to the front of the hearing room with Allan MacLean at her side. This was the hearing before the "Umpire," the second level of appeal. Pat Barter had outlined what SORWUC wanted to say in a letter to MacLean.

(The letter was unearthed years later by Leslie Pal and Ted Morton.) The Unemployment Insurance Act, Barter stated on behalf of SORWUC:

> discriminates between pregnant working women and all other working women, and...against all women by creating a special section of the Act which ignores the biological role of childbearing which is as much a part of any woman's life as is working itself.

The union was talking about the provision of the Act that said that a woman could not collect regular benefits eight weeks before her due date and six weeks after she gave birth.

Stella Bliss had worked enough weeks to qualify for ordinary unemployment insurance benefits but not enough for "unemployment caused by pregnancy." If she were a man, she could collect ordinary benefits, but because she was a woman with a baby, she could not. She must have felt like Alice when she stepped through the looking glass, a woman trying to make sense of nonsense.

Interest in the *Bliss* case was beginning to grow. There was an audience and press in the hearing room during the appeal before the Umpire. The *Vancouver Province* newspaper reported that SORWUC said it would appeal the decision if it went against Bliss and, in the tradition of militant Vancouver feminists, would lobby Parliament *vigorously* to change the legislation. The battle was on.

The Umpire, Judge Frank U. Collier of the Federal Court, delivered his decision in February 1977. He started with the basic tenet of unemployment insurance: "provided a claimant is capable of and available for work, entitlement is the rule."

The Umpire agreed that Stella Bliss was capable and available for work and so Frank Collier wrote,

> I am driven to the inescapable conclusion, that the impugned section [the section that said a woman could not collect benefits eight weeks before and six weeks after her child's birth], accidentally perhaps, authorizes discrimination by reason of sex, and as a consequence,

> abridges the right of equality of all claimants in respect of the Unemployment Insurance legislation.

To the delight of the women in Vancouver, Collier had decided in favour of Stella Bliss. It was a big decision that was about far more than one woman's UI benefits. The "impugned" section of the Unemployment Act, he had ruled, violated the Bill of Rights; it was bad law and should be thrown out. It was a ruling that could affect tens of thousands of women and cost the government and employers millions of dollars.

When the decision was faxed to Vancouver from Judge Collier's office in Ottawa—that's how they did it back then—Stella Bliss, Allan MacLean, and the SORWUC women enjoyed a few days of happiness. The Unemployment Insurance Commission announced that it would appeal. No one was surprised. Disappointed, but not surprised.

✦✦✦

May of 1977, the winter rain had been good for the plants. Rhododendrons were in full bloom, and the massive hedges that surround the grand houses on Oak and Granville were flourishing as a taxi from the airport whizzed by into the city. Three middle-aged men had their garment bags over their arms as they got out of that taxi and checked into the hotel. Inside those bags were the black robes with the gold-coloured facings worn by judges of the Federal Court of Appeal. The three men (there were no women appointed to the Federal Court until 1987, five years after the first woman was appointed to the Supreme Court of Canada), were in Vancouver to hear the third appeal of *Bliss v Attorney General*.

This was the hearing that Pat Barter remembers—a hotel meeting room converted into a courtroom with those three "liver-spotted white men" deciding whether Stella Bliss should receive a few hundred dollars of Unemployment Insurance benefits, and with it, the much bigger question: did the Act discriminate against her by reason of sex? Mr. Justice Louis Pratte, who wrote the court's decision, was fifty in 1977—not that old, but to a group of twenty-something women, library clerks, daycare workers, and waitresses, he and his two fellow judges must have seemed remote and disconnected from the reality they were judging.

Allan MacLean was waiting for Stella Bliss in the hearing room. He checked his watch. Waited a little longer, looked at his watch again. Was she going to miss her own hearing? It was a distinct possibility. As the months had gone by, Stella Bliss had pulled back from her case. She was worn out. Her little boy was fourteen months old, walking, getting into everything, needing more attention, and her marriage was failing. The pressure of the case was wearing both Stella and her husband down. Years later, when she talked to Leslie Pal and Ted Morton, Stella Bliss said she did not subscribe to the "hard-line" feminism or the left-wing politics of her supporters. As well, the publicity, the media attention, had become overwhelming. That day, May 19, she made it to the courthouse just in time.

This time around, Allan MacLean was joined by the Chair of the Vancouver Community Legal Assistance Society, Lynn Smith. Smith was a rarity. In 1977, there weren't many women lawyers in practice, let alone feminist lawyers. Smith stood out. She was working for a Vancouver firm that had given her the time to do the *Bliss* case pro bono—at no charge—for which she was grateful. Four years later, she would join the faculty at the UBC law school, becoming dean in 1991. Forty-five years after she argued the *Bliss* case, Lynn Smith was teaching it to her students. But no one could see that coming in 1977.

"That hearing," says Smith, "was quite something. They—the judges—came up with so many reasons to deny her claim: [Unemployment Insurance benefits] was a benefit not a penalty, therefore it did not count as discrimination"—a not uncommon determinant of discrimination at the time—"there was a valid federal objective for the legislation as a whole and on it went."

On June 2, only two weeks after the hearing, the fax came through from Ottawa with Justice Pratte's ruling. "If [Section] 46 treats unemployed pregnant women differently from other unemployed persons, be they male or female," he wrote, "it is, it seems to me, because they are pregnant and not because they are women."

Lynn Smith, Dean of Peter A. Allard School of Law, UBC, from 1991–1997, and judge of the Supreme Court of British Columbia from 1998–2012.

That statement, "because they are pregnant and not because they are women," was hard to fathom at the time; nearly half a century later it is laughable. The judgement went on to say that if Stella Bliss, first a pregnant woman and then a newly delivered mother, was "discriminated against it would not have been by reason of her sex."

Ten years later, the chief justice of the Supreme Court, Brian Dickson, would give voice to what must have been going through every woman's mind: "one can only ask, how could pregnancy discrimination be *anything other than* sex discrimination?"

But in 1977, the Federal Court of Appeal saw things differently. Men and women were equal but different. Equal in some otherworldly, strange dimension, but different when it came to eligibility for economic rewards like Unemployment Insurance benefits.

Now the question for MacLean, Smith, and Bliss was whether to go to a fourth appeal and take the case to the Supreme Court of Canada. The Unemployment Insurance Commission itself said that the decision affected 25,000 women every year. That was 25,000 reasons for MacLean and Smith to pack their bags and get on the plane.

+++

Vancouver Community Legal Assistance Society lawyers will take the case to Ottawa.... We hope to raise $3000 to cover the trip.... We are looking to women, unions, and community groups for support.

—Vancouver Status of Women, October 12, 1977

This would be no luxury trip. They would stay at the then-modest Lord Elgin Hotel, economizing where they could. There was the airfare to pay and expenses to be met. Money had to be raised. The Stella Bliss Appeal Fund began to slowly pull in donations. The lawyers, Smith and MacLean, were doing the appeal for nothing. So too was John Nelligan, an Ottawa-based, more senior lawyer and former president of the Canadian Civil Liberties Association. As Lynn Smith says of herself and MacLean, "We were both not long out of law school and normally fledglings don't go to the Supreme Court." Nelligan, known as a consummate courtroom orator, had appeared before the Supreme Court before. He would stand up in court and argue *Bliss*. Smith and MacLean would be his "juniors."

Before he asked for leave to appeal (by 1977, parties had to ask for permission or leave to appeal), Allan MacLean wrote to Walter Tarnopolsky, Canada's reigning civil rights expert, and asked: Did they have a chance? Was it worth raising the money, making the trip? Tarnopolsky's reply has not survived but he must have said yes, if for no other reasons than to put the issue of women's equality under the Bill of Rights before the Supreme Court.

According to Pal and Morton, by November the Vancouver Status of Women had only raised $400 of the $3,000 that they needed. Things looked grim, but the unions came through, and money started to come in from women in Quebec, Ottawa, and Manitoba. Tickets were booked, reservations made, written arguments submitted to the court. MacLean and Smith were ready. And what about Stella Bliss? There was no money for her to go to Ottawa, and she did not want to go. As publicity about the case had grown, she started getting more and more letters from women in similar situations across the county. She had been answering them all, but had had enough. The discussion around the case was becoming inevitably more legal, less human. Bliss was also feeling that she had become a symbol rather than an actor in her own story. She felt much like Florence Murdoch, that this case had very little to do with her anymore. But unlike Florence Murdoch, Stella Bliss did not become embittered. She was still willing to do publicity to support the case, but happy to stay in Vancouver.

Smith and MacLean left for Ottawa in June of 1978, ready to put the case of Stella Bliss before the Supreme Court.

⁂

"It was a very long walk to the Women Barristers room, I remember that." There's a hint of a smile in Lynn Smith's voice. It was her first time at the Supreme Court. The Women Barristers room, where the few women barristers changed, would have been an architectural afterthought, tucked away somewhere.

As they hoisted their robes and settled in front of the judges, Smith, MacLean, and Nelligan were faced with a new problem. Bora Laskin, by now the chief justice of the Supreme Court, the judge who had dissented in favour of Florence Murdoch in her bid for half of the Murdoch ranch, was ill. To maintain an odd number of judges and avoid a tied decision, another judge had to be removed. It was Mr. Justice Spence. Both Laskin and Spence had a history of favouring Bill of Rights challenges. What was already going to be an uphill battle had just turned into the ascent of Everest.

A few days earlier, Nelligan had talked to his Ottawa neighbour over the fence. "Mr. Diefenbaker," Nelligan called out, knowing how proud Diefenbaker was of his Bill of Rights, "we have a Bill of Rights case coming up at the Supreme Court in a few days." Diefenbaker, by then in his mid-eighties, reportedly nodded and gave Nelligan a thumbs-up. It made for a good story but that was it.

The judgement came down on October 31, 1978. Halloween. To no one's surprise, it went against Stella Bliss. The Supreme Court held that when the Canadian Bill of Rights talked of "equality before the law," it was to be interpreted as "equality of treatment in the administration and enforcement of law." What the judges were saying was that as long as Stella Bliss was treated the same way as any other pregnant woman, her rights had not been violated. The court held that the provisions defining eligibility for maternity benefits under the Act did not contravene the Bill of Rights, and that denial of benefits because of pregnancy did not discriminate on the basis of sex. Infuriating, exasperating—women's groups were beside themselves. The Honourable Justice Ritchie, born to a distinguished Nova Scotia family in the late Edwardian era, wrote the judgement. As if to add insult to injury, he said: "Any inequality between the sexes in this area is not created by legislation but by nature."

An old man's dry chuckle seemed to linger in the air.

◆◆◆

On the day of the Supreme Court hearing, John Nelligan finished his argument, packed up his big lawyer's briefcase, said goodbye to his colleagues, and walked back to his office on Metcalfe Street. There was not much enthusiasm in his step. He knew it did not look good. He and his Vancouver juniors did not see the case in quite the same way, but it was agreed, he had argued it well and, as it turned out, with a degree of personal conviction.

Many law firms in the 70s didn't hire young women lawyers, sometimes because they didn't think they were up to the job but, just as often, for fear of pregnancy. Maternity leave costs businesses money. Nelligan and his partner had recently hired two young female lawyers; that meant a quarter of the lawyers in his firm were women of child-bearing age. A frightening thought. Having just argued *Bliss*, maternity leave may have been in the back of his mind as he got off the elevator and nodded to his colleagues.

A little more than a year later, one of those young women lawyers was pregnant. Her baby bump could no longer be ignored but still, she had not asked, nor had anyone at the firm talked about mat leave. The firm was liberal, for the most part, in its attitudes, but there must have been some trepidation. One day, the second young woman lawyer, looking ahead to the prospect of her own babies, poked her head around her colleague's door and said, "So, what are we doing about maternity leave?" Together, they marched into John Nelligan's corner office. "Well?" they asked. Nothing more needed to be said. Nelligan looked at them both. "When we hired two nubile young women," he said, "we knew one day we would have to deal with this. We'll just keep paying you." Perhaps his views had been reinforced by what happened to Stella Bliss. (Several years later, when the same woman was pregnant with her third child, a colleague asked her in all seriousness, "Don't you ever think of the firm?")

The day the Supreme Court decision came down, Lynn Smith kept Stella Bliss company in Vancouver and stayed with her through the inevitable media interviews. "We sat together by a fountain," she recollects. "Funny what you remember." And she goes back to that day in her mind. "She was so disappointed. By then she was interested in alternative therapies and spiritualism but still she was so disappointed." Stella Bliss had had hope. Hope was, by then, nearly all she had. Her marriage was all but over, and she was not well. Her friends gradually lost track of her, and Stella Bliss faded away. The case did not.

The importance of the big issue, defining equality of the sexes, was becoming, as Smith said, "so obvious."

The Employment and Immigration Commission wrote an internal discussion paper in the aftermath of the decision. "It can be assumed," the paper read, "that the political ramifications of the court decision will be operationally more important than the decision itself." *Bliss* became a national cause. In Toronto, Maire Bradshaw of Parkdale Community Legal Services, that city's oldest and biggest legal clinic said it clearly: "This case may have been lost but we now know that there is support for the cause. We all have to take up from where Stella Bliss and her union left off. This is not the end; it is only the beginning."

+++

One of the minor consolations in this business is even the ones you lose sometimes refuse to die and have their effect for future litigants even though your client goes away dissatisfied. In my conversations with Doris Anderson, one time president of the Women's Advisory Council, I was convinced that part of their fervour in obtaining a special place for women's rights arose out of the shock they received on reading the Bliss *case.*

—John Nelligan to Allan MacLean, 1981

A little more than a month after the Supreme Court decision, Allan MacLean wrote to Bud Cullen, then Minister of Employment and Immigration, asking him to repeal the section that denied pregnant women regular unemployment benefits. Cullen responded telling MacLean that the general subject was "under study." He added, "As you are no doubt aware, these issues bear heavily on the cost on the private sector through the Unemployment Insurance Premium account."

The *Bliss* decision was widely known, it was definitive, yet the challenges to the Unemployment Insurance Act kept on coming. In Scarborough, Ontario, Anna Santos, an eighteen-year-old Portuguese-speaking woman who had arrived in Canada from the Azores in 1978, was denied her maternity benefits because she was one week short of the requisite insurable earnings. With the support of the Canadian Textile and Chemical Union, she appealed. She and the union argued: "We believe Section 30 to be discriminatory. It places discriminatory requirements on female claimants...and further it assumes ill will on the part of women entering the workforce." Santos had her baby on July 19. She was back at work at the McGregor Hosiery factory the day after Labour Day.

Laurell Ritchie, who argued the case on behalf of the union and Santos, said, "We knew we would lose the appeal but fought it anyway because we wanted to expose UI's discriminatory conditions for women." She made sure the media was there as they came out of the hearing. Anna Santos, through an interpreter, told the *Globe and Mail* newspaper that even if she lost, she was pursuing the case to help other women with future claims.

The Canadian Human Rights Commission had written a report about *Bliss*, which called for the repeal of the offending sections of the Unemployment Insurance Act and pointed out that maternity benefits claimants (i.e., women) had to work ten weeks longer than men claiming regular benefits. Laurell Ritchie submitted that report to the Umpire, Judge Lieff, in the Santos case. Clearly sympathetic, Lieff quoted from the *Bliss* case as if to say "my hands are tied." He then added,

> I admire the zeal and expedition with which the appellant [Anna Santos] proceeded to fit into the labour force and commend her for her attitude. Were the state of the law such as to permit me to exercise a discretion in her favour I might be persuaded to do so. However, I have no such power.

+++

It had become undeniable that women's equality rights under John Diefenbaker's Bill of Rights were not protected. The Bill of Rights, much heralded in the 60s, was labelled "a dead letter," "failed," "ineffective," and more. Women's groups, human rights lawyers, and politically sophisticated feminist leaders were looking for a stronger, more effective declaration of equality rights. Timing is everything. Their demands coincided with Prime Minister Pierre Trudeau's push to repatriate the constitution and to attach to it a new, more muscular declaration of human rights—what would become the Charter of Rights and Freedoms. As Pal and Morton point out, Section 15 of the new Charter, with its phrase "the equal benefit of law," came directly from the Stella Bliss case. At the time, it was the strongest guarantee of equality to be found in any modern democracy in the world.

It was not easy getting to this new guarantee of equality. Initially, the Charter wording proposed by Trudeau's government was essentially the same as the old Bill of Rights, but then came the Special Joint Committee of the Senate and House of Commons on the Constitution. In November and December of 1980, the committee heard from all the major women's groups.

Things did not get off to a good start. Alberta Senator Harry Hays, co-chair of the committee, welcomed the National Action Committee on the Status of Women (NAC) by saying, "Well, it is all fine and good for you girls to be here, but who is looking after the kids?" He opened his mouth wider to make room for the other foot and added, "I'm just wondering why we don't have a section in here about babies and children. All you girls will be out working and we're not going to have anybody to look after them."

In retrospect, seasoned feminists say that Senator Hays wasn't used to well-educated, articulate, professional women, and he did not know quite how to deal with them and their demands. The Canadian Advisory Council on the Status of Women demanded wording that "will provide such clear direction to judges that they cannot possibly misinterpret the intended content and meaning." The chair of the NAC pointed directly at the *Bliss* case. "In view of the Stella Bliss case especially, it is clear that more specific directions need to be given to the courts for the interpretation of equality." The language was strengthened. Section 15 now reads,

> Every individual is equal before and under the law and has the right to the equal protection and equal benefit of the law without discrimination and, in particular, without discrimination based on race, national or ethnic origin, colour, religion, sex, age, or mental or physical disability.

There was one more crucial addition to the new Charter of Rights and Freedoms. The provinces pressed for a "notwithstanding" clause that would permit either level of government to exempt legislation from the provisions of the Charter. Pierre Trudeau recognized that without the notwithstanding clause, the Charter would not be accepted. Feminists working on the Charter, however, were having none of a blanket exemption. They advocated for a notwithstanding clause of their own, intended to maintain equality: Section 28 specified that the rights of the Charter would be enjoyed equally by men and women *notwithstanding* other Charter provisions.

The day agreement was reached there was an exhausted celebratory yelp from feminist lawyers and strategists. Shoes were kicked off; someone opened another bottle of wine. It was quite a moment in Ottawa.

Meanwhile in the rest of the country, Anna Santos headed to the sock factory in Scarborough, the woman who replaced Stella Bliss at the Brown Bros car dealership in Vancouver got off the bus and sat down at her typewriter, and working women across the country got on with their lives. These constitutional reforms would only start to mean something when the language of the law filtered down to everyday reality. It didn't take long.

Brian Dickson, Chief Justice of the Supreme Court of Canada from 1984–1990.

+++

The year that the new Charter of Rights and Freedoms was proclaimed, 1982, was a big year for babies at the Safeway store in Brandon, Manitoba. Three part-time cashiers, Susan Brooks, Patricia Allen, and Patricia Dixon were all pregnant. All three women were denied benefits under their group disability insurance plan *because* they were pregnant.

It was déjà vu all over again. The Unemployment Insurance Act had changed, and they got their UI benefits of $133.47 a week, but Susan Brooks would have—should have, she said—got $188 weekly under her group insurance plan, and the numbers were similar for the other women. Their insurance plan denied pregnant women benefits for a period of seventeen weeks around the birth of their child. Like *Bliss, Brooks v Canada Safeway Ltd.* went all the way up to the Supreme Court. It took seven years. In 1989, ten years after *Bliss,* the court handed down its decision in favour of the women. The way in which the court interpreted the law had changed. The Supreme Court had also changed. Only two of the judges who heard the case of Stella Bliss (Brian Dickson and Jean Beetz) were still on the bench, and now the nine judges included two women: Bertha Wilson and Claire L'Heureux-Dubé.

Once again, Lynn Smith made the long walk to the Women Barristers changing room. This time, she was acting for Women's Legal Education and Advocacy Fund (LEAF), an organization formed following the proclamation of the Charter. Its mission was to take major women's rights cases forward, pro bono, and to intervene in existing cases, as they did in *Brooks*. "They let me redeem myself after Bliss," Smith chuckles, "and I was counsel. What was so impressive," she says, "was that Brian Dickson"—Dickson was now chief justice—"had completely changed his mind. A person who is able to change his mind and correct an error is a stronger person. I have great admiration for him." After a brief pause, she adds, "He also had Bertha to encourage him."

The judgement was a complete *volte-face*. "With the benefit of a decade of hindsight and ten years of experience with claims of human rights discrimination," wrote Chief Justice Dickson, "I am prepared to say that *Bliss* was wrongly decided or, in any event, that *Bliss* would not be decided now as it was decided then."

This is how he ended his judgement in *Brooks*:

> It is difficult to conceive that...discriminations based upon pregnancy could ever be regarded as other than discrimination based upon sex.... It is difficult to accept that the inequality to which Stella Bliss was subject was created by nature and therefore there was no discrimination; the better view, I now venture to think, is that the inequality was created by legislation.

For Stella Bliss, like Florence Murdoch, it was a matter of what might have been. The highest court in the land referred to her by name and said what happened to her was wrong, that she was discriminated against. That doesn't happen every day. But who knows if she ever heard or even read about the *Brooks* case, or if she felt redeemed. No one can remember where Stella Bliss was living or what she was doing by 1989. By then, her husband was long gone and had taken their son, now a teenager, with him to live in the United States. She had only eight years left to live. Stella Bliss was fifty-six when she died of brain cancer in 1997.

Stella Bliss, this rather ethereal, not particularly political young woman who no one remembers, was the woman behind the redefinition of equality in Canada's Charter of Rights and Freedoms. That would be worth inscribing on her tombstone.

6. Bake Sales and a Wild Meat Dinner

When I think about Lizzie, I often think who would be the famous five today? The famous five only fought for women like them—white and able-bodied. The famous five "won" their case on the back of Indigenous sex workers.

—Naomi Sayers

When Jeannette Corbiere Lavell, the woman behind what became known as the Indigenous Persons case, started her march to the Supreme Court of Canada in 1970, she didn't know anything about Lizzie Cyr. It's a safe bet that fifty-plus years ago, almost no one, Indigenous or not, had ever heard of Lizzie Cyr.

In the early years of the twentieth century, there were those two women magistrates in Alberta: Emily Murphy in Edmonton, and Alice Jamieson in Calgary. Jamieson was the widow of a previous Calgary mayor, a woman described as "active in club life." Emily Murphy beat her into the history books as the "first woman magistrate in the British Empire" by a mere six months. They were two upper-middle-class, Protestant, white women with social power and a zeal for their particular version of women's justice. Neither had any legal training. With Jamieson's appointment, Alberta congratulated itself in being in the "vanguard of progress in recognizing the importance of women in judicial life."

Alice Jamieson was less than a year into her job in May of 1917 when twenty-nine-year-old Lizzie Cyr came up before her. The court clerk read the charge: "Vagrancy," a much-used euphemism for prostitution. Cyr's lawyer, John McKinley Cameron, was an eccentric man—there are always one or two hanging around courthouses—who was known to sleep with his dogs in the hayloft and show up in court wearing rubber boots. Cameron stood up and addressed the court: "I want to object that your Honour has no power or jurisdiction to try this case."

"Call your witness," said Jamieson to the prosecutor, ignoring Cameron's objection, and the prosecutor called Cyr's alleged client, John James Ryan. Ryan, it rapidly became evident, was angry because Cyr had given him a dose of gonorrhea. At least, that's what he said. Or had he given it to her? Cameron postulated that in what became a very graphic cross-examination with references to Ryan's "running penis." Was Cameron deliberately trying to throw Alice Jamieson off her game, to embarrass her? She was becoming irritated.

Next came the arresting officer. Lizzie Cyr, he testified, had admitted to taking her fee, $10. Cameron then asked him, "You don't know whether she gave him gonorrhea?" Jamieson, perhaps

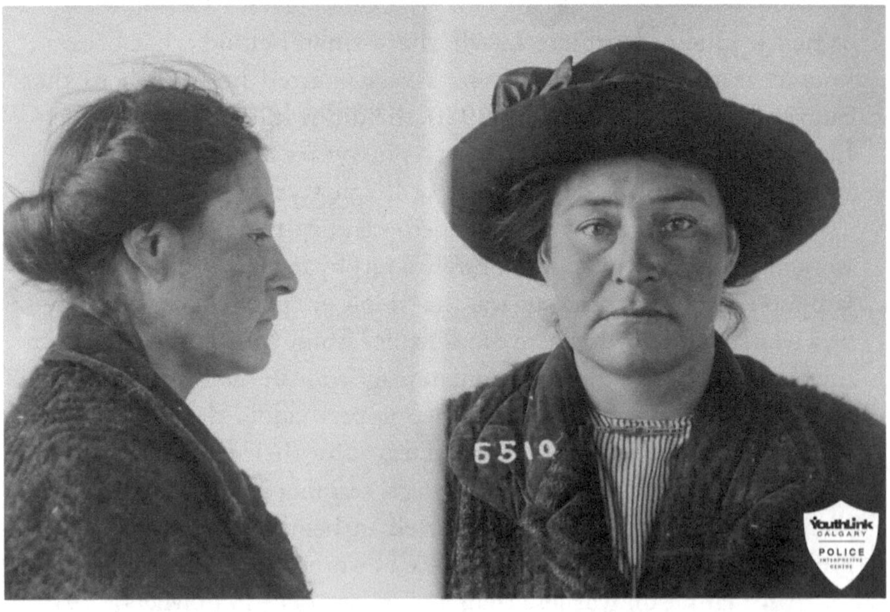

Lizzie Cyr, 1917.

anticipating more testimony about John Ryan's "running penis," had had enough: "Lizzie Cyr, I sentence you to six months hard labour." And that was that. Cyr was led away. Cameron protested that his client had no chance to defend herself and reiterated that this "non-person," Alice Jamieson, had no jurisdiction to try the case.

Some days later, Her Honour wrote to her fellow magistrate, Emily Murphy. "One of the lawyers here is threatening to put me out of office claiming no woman can be a Police magistrate—so you see what I am up against—I will let you know what comes from it." Murphy had been similarly challenged, but she was convinced there was more going on. She, along with Nellie McClung and the rest of the Famous Five, had two constant causes: women's suffrage and prohibition. Most of the women's suffrage leaders were card-carrying members of the Women's Christian Temperance Union and had led the push for prohibition, which began in Alberta less than a year before Lizzie Cyr's conviction. Emily Murphy was vehemently anti-liquor and very vocal. On May 26, 1917, she forwarded Jamieson's letter to an Alberta court official and added,

> It would seem the action to remove the women magistrates were a concerted one and doubtless originated with the liquor interests. At any rate, so far as I am concerned, it is on a liquor case that my competency is to be argued out.

Nothing more was heard of Murphy's theory that the liquor companies were behind the push to get women off the judicial bench.

When John Cameron appealed Lizzie Cyr's conviction to the Alberta Court of Appeal, he argued that "the said Mrs. Alice J. Jamieson has never been legally appointed Police Magistrate in the Province of Alberta...and is incompetent and incapable of holding the said appointment." The Court of Appeal, led by Justice Stuart, looked at American cases (there were no Canadian precedents), and ruled that, "[by] reason and good sense...this Court ought to declare that in this Province...there is at common law no legal disqualification for holding public office...arising from any distinction of sex." Both women continued to sit as police magistrates in Alberta.

Alice Jamieson, second woman magistrate of the British Empire.

The real loser was Lizzie Cyr. She was a Métis woman with two convictions for drunkenness as well as vagrancy, and Alberta was intent on a moral cleanup. Put that together with ongoing racist attitudes toward Métis and First Nations people, and Lizzie Cyr didn't stand a chance. Six months hard labour—Alice Jamieson had given her the maximum sentence for vagrancy.

More than a hundred years later, Indigenous lawyer, activist, and former sex trade worker Naomi Sayers put her position out there, bold and loud: the Famous Five, socially well-positioned white women, had built their case on the back of an Indigenous woman. Lizzie Cyr, Sayers and others maintain, was the person behind the Persons Case. Women—white women—triumphed, but what about the dignity and recognition of Indigenous women?

That's what Jeannette Corbiere Lavell's case was all about—dignity, equality, and the Status of Indigenous women. What Corbiere began led to a series of cases and to a group of Indigenous women who became known as the Famous Six.

+++

A clever, confident, and beautiful young woman, Jeannette Corbiere was nonetheless a little nervous when she arrived in Toronto. It was the early 60s and this was her first big adventure. "I was born on Manitoulin Island in 1942," she says. "On the reserve." The reserve was the Manitoulin Island Unceded Indian Reserve (today, it's the Wiikemkoong Unceded Territory), and Jeannette Corbiere was a Status Anishinaabe (Ojibwe) woman. The reserve on Manitoulin in Lake Huron was her home, her community. Under the Indian Act, she had the right to live on the reserve, to share in band resources and, as of 1951 when the Act was changed to allow women to vote for the band council and chief, to have a voice in her community. She was a young woman venturing out from her prescribed place in the world, her community, secure in the knowledge that she could always come home. Less than ten years later, she married the man she loved, David Lavell. He was white. More importantly, he was *not* First Nations, not a registered Indian under the Act. Her life, her identity, changed. Jeannette Corbiere lost her status and everything that went with it. The federal government told her she couldn't live on the reserve, had no say in Band affairs, no right to a share in whatever money the band generated—all of this because she was a status *woman* who had "married out."

When the first Indian Act was passed in 1875, an Indian was "any male person of Indian blood." When the Act was amended seventy-six years later, "blood" was replaced by "status." The word "male" didn't change. For a woman, being born a Status or Registered Indian under the Act wasn't enough for the federal government. As of 1951, Section 12 (1)(b) of the Indian Act said, "a woman who married a person who is not an Indian...[is] not entitled to be registered." When a Status Indian woman married a white man or any man who was not a Status Indian, she lost her status. When a Status Indian man married a non-Indigenous woman, the opposite happened.

He kept his status and his new wife, whatever her race, and their children gained status. The concept echoed nineteenth-century attitudes in white Canada; a woman's identity was absorbed by her husband when she married.

Jeannette Corbiere came from a well-respected family: her mother was one of the first women on the reserve who was active in business, and her Anishinaabemowin-speaking father ran a grocery store. But there wasn't much future on Manitoulin for a young woman. "I had my education, my grade 12 and I didn't want to get married on the reserve." Laughing, Jeannette Corbiere adds, "Most of the young men were relatives, anyway." Looking back at the age of eighty-one, she goes on, "So I went to Toronto and got involved with other young people. Mohawks, Cree, they were all there for education and for work."

She worked as a secretary in an insurance company for a year. "That was dull," she says. "Then I went to the Friendship Centre." The Canadian Indian Friendship Centre in downtown Toronto was new. (In 1972, it was renamed the Native Canadian Centre of Toronto.) This was the place for those young people to gather, more than 6,000 came by in the first year. By 1964–65, the number was up to 10,000. The Friendship Centre initially offered social programs, translation services, hospital and prison visits, and legal services. There were too many young First Nations kids getting into trouble. Jeannette Corbiere was quick and she was smart. "I knew the [Anishinaabe] language and got my first job as a court worker. I got on the job training about the legal system." She was also attractive. Beauty pageants were still big in the 60s, and in 1965, Jeannette Corbiere was asked to enter the Indian Princess contest. She won. It was all coming together for her.

Corbiere was an admirer of Wilfred Pelletier, author, philosopher, and future teacher at Carleton University who was also from her reserve. She was part of the group that set up what became the Nishnawbe Institute, one of the earliest attempts to explore and teach First Nations history and culture. Corbiere's circle of contacts was expanding, and in 1968, she was invited to join the field staff of the Company of Young Canadians. The CYC was a Canadian government program that recruited hundreds of young people from across the country and trained them in what was politely called "social animation," otherwise known as political disruption and organizing the downtrodden. CYC projects pulled together early environmentalists, anti-poverty and political activists, and young Indigenous leaders. Corbiere worked out of Winnipeg, travelling to Alberta, northern Saskatchewan, and BC. "We were thinking about human rights and becoming more aware of our own history," she explains. "Our lives had been so controlled. There was nothing to do in our communities. There were more and more young people [who] wanted to come out and explore and see what there was available. At that time, it was so invigorating, so exciting," she adds, thinking back. "Anything seemed possible."

By the time she came back to Toronto, Jeannette Corbiere was nearly thirty and knew a lot more about the world, but she was still single. In the 1960s, women were typically married by the time they were twenty-one. "My father was teasing me, 'When are you going to get married?' he would say. 'I'll find you someone.'" He didn't have to. Jeannette Corbiere met David Lavell, a musician, at a Toronto coffee house. He performed. They listened to music and talked about social change and started living together.

"Marriage? I had not been thinking about marriage," and when she did, she didn't think there was a problem. David Lavell was a white man. "I had cousins who had married non-Indian men and everything seemed to be going fine for them."

+++

Toronto was erupting in political protest. Loudest and most militant were the demonstrations against the war in Vietnam. There were rallies in support of decriminalizing abortion, and LGBTQ groups, primarily gay and lesbian, began to organize. Greenpeace, which practiced its own brand of environmental creative confrontation, was founded in 1971. Defiance was the tenor of the times.

Corbiere and Lavell were in the thick of it all. They lived at Rochdale College, an eighteen-storey concrete tower in the centre of the city that has been described as "Toronto's great hippie experiment in free education and communal living." At a time when communal living was everywhere and alternative education was thriving, Rochdale was the largest experiment of its sort in North America. Eighteen floors of idealism destined to go horribly wrong. It opened in 1968.

"We were there from the beginning, and we had the seventeenth floor for our people. We were always there thinking about our culture and our history." This was the beginning of the Nishnawbe Institute. There were ten-day training programs in "cross-cultural communication" from the Indigenous perspective. "'Reconciliation' today," Jeannette Corbiere says, "but we were doing it in the 60s."

By the early 70s, with over eight hundred young people crammed into a concrete tower, Rochdale's communal idealism overflowed into chaos, anarchy, and a lot of drugs.

Only a few city blocks away from Rochdale was Yorkville. Today, Yorkville is all elegant designer boutiques, perfectly staged little restaurants, and very expensive high rises—a place that bespeaks fashion and money. Fifty years ago, Yorkville was full of draft dodgers, hippies, and political activists. That activism extended to the burgeoning Indigenous movement. As Harold Cardinal, whom Corbiere had worked with in Alberta, said,

> We can and we have watched [B]lack riots in the United States, and we can and we have pondered their lessons.... Our people have seen the methods used by other groups in similar situations, and we have measured their successes—and failures. We are learning from others about the forces that can be assembled in a democratic society to protect oppressed minorities.

At twenty-three, Cardinal was already president of the Indian Association of Alberta.

Once back in Toronto, Jeannette Corbiere returned to work at the Native Friendship Centre, this time as the Youth Coordinator. She hired a freshly minted lawyer, Clayton Ruby, to give rights workshops to the young people who dropped into the centre. Ruby was, to quote *The Canadian Jewish News*, "a smart-ass kid who drove his teachers crazy" and "was kicked out of synagogue for being a disrespectful miscreant." He was also much loved and admired by his contemporaries and would become one of the country's most respected human rights lawyers. In the late 60s and early 70s, Ruby and his partner, Paul Copeland, were handing out free legal advice on the sidewalks outside a Yorkville convenience store to anyone who needed it. He said back then, "If change is going to come, I am convinced it will have to be from the streets, not from the courts." They wrote *Law, Law, Law*, a guide to Canadian civil rights. It sold more than ten thousand copies in the first six months. *Law, Law, Law* was floating around Rochdale College and so was Clayton Ruby. Not surprisingly, when Jeannette Corbiere realized that by marrying a white man she had a problem, she turned to Ruby.

She and David Lavell had gotten married in April of 1970. "The Chief's daughter had married a non-status Indian. It didn't seem to be a big deal. I didn't think about the legalities." The year went on, her son was born, and at the beginning of December, an institutional envelope arrived in the Corbiere-Lavell Rochdale mailbox. "My mum," says Jeannette Corbiere's daughter, Dawn Memee Lavell-Harvard, with a smile, "wasn't much for opening her mail." There was too much going on all around them. When she did pick up that envelope and slit it open, she unfolded a letter from the Registrar of Status Indians in Ottawa. Because she, Jeannette Vivien Corbiere Lavell had married a non-status man, the letter said, she had been struck off the Indian Registry.

> When I got that letter, then it hit home. Oh my God, this is true. I hadn't thought about the implications, how it would affect me personally. David and I talked. I knew Clayton and we went and saw him. It was a Thursday night, and we went and saw him at his place on Prince Arthur Avenue and showed him the letter. He looked at the date and said, "Tomorrow is the last day you can do anything." He looked at me and said, "Do you want to do something about this?" I thought, I don't like this...not being part of my community. I don't want to be excluded. "Okay. But I don't have any money." "Don't worry," he said, and he did it pro bono.

+++

A hundred kilometres west of Toronto, another First Nations woman had gathered her courage and said enough is enough. Her name was Yvonne Bedard. Corbiere Lavell was an activist: she wanted to regain her Status rights, to be able to go back to her reserve and to be part of her community. She had a career, a place to live in the city, a marriage, and people to support her. Yvonne Bedard had none of that. She was an Onondaga woman from the Six Nations of the Grand River. Losing her status meant ostracism and homelessness for herself and her children.

Bedard was in her thirties when she came back to the Six Nations reserve. She had moved off the reserve when she married a non-status man in 1964. The marriage failed and in 1970, the same year that Jeannette Corbiere married David Lavell in Toronto, Yvonne Bedard brought her two children "home" to live in the house on the reserve that her mother had bequeathed her. After she moved in, the entrenched band council, many of whom had been in power for at least a decade, passed a resolution giving her six months to move out. She and her children were no longer Status Indians under the Indian Act, and they had no right to live on reserve. Yvonne Bedard thought she had come safely home, but now she was by herself, fighting her own band council. Family came through. Bedard transferred her interest in the house to her brother who let his sister and her children live in what had been their mother's house, rent free. In September 1971, council asked the district supervisor (the government agent) to serve Yvonne Bedard with documents to "quit the reserve." It was a telling sign of division in the Indigenous community and growing antipathy toward any women who defied the established order.

Corbiere Lavell knew nothing of Bedard's fight for months. The two cases zigzagged up the line of appeal. It was decades before the two women finally met.

Corbiere Lavell's case came up first. In the summer of 1971, York County Court Judge Grossberg heard her request for a judicial review of the letter striking her off the register of Status Indians. Clayton Ruby made the same Bill of Rights argument that would be made on behalf of Stella Bliss's claim for maternity benefits—that the law—in this case, the Indian Act—discriminated on the grounds of sex and contravened Canada's Bill of Rights by failing to treat men and women equally.

Ruby went on to show the court what striking Corbiere Lavell and hundreds of thousands of other women off the registry meant. Loss of status meant loss of connection to her community and her reserve, and loss of her culture. Judge Grossberg did not see the problem.

> [W]ith no disrespect to her, [I] am unable to accept her assertion that she cannot retain her Indian culture, heritage, and customs and inculcate these in her child or children if she so desires.

Her case went forward at the height of what was known as the Sixties Scoop, which, despite its name, went on until the 1980s. The thinking was that Indigenous children would be better off taken from their families and adopted and raised by white families, and assimilated into white Canadian culture. Corbiere Lavell recalled years later that the judge suggested she was better off as a non-Status Indian. "I should be happy to no longer legally be an Indian," he said to her, "and glad that marriage to David took me away from the terrible reserves." And then he added, "You want to have your cake and eat it too." She remembers the tone of the remark, but she had never heard the phrase before.

Neither Corbiere Lavell nor Ruby gave up easily. Clayton Ruby appealed the case to the Federal Court of Appeal. Given the history of the equality provisions of the Bill of Rights in the courts, it was a major surprise when Mr. Justice Arthur Thurlow ruled in their favour. Formerly a Nova Scotia Liberal politician and a judge best known for his decisions in maritime law, Thurlow agreed that the relevant section of the Indian Act flew in the face of the Bill of Rights. A man did not lose status if he married a non-Status Indian woman; women did lose status if they married out, and that amounted to "discrimination by reason of sex within the meaning of the Canadian Bill of Rights." Mr. Justice Thurlow said, "the consequences of the marriage of an Indian woman to a person who is not an Indian are worse for her than...for other Indians of her band who marry persons who are not Indians." A decision of the Federal Court of Appeal had an impact.

As was the case with *Bliss*, what had been seen as just one woman's problem was being recognized for the point of principle that it embodied.

Corbiere Lavell might not have been aware of Yvonne Bedard and her case. But Bedard's lawyers were following *Canada v Lavell* and jumped on the decision. In December 1971, when the *Bedard* case came before Mr. Justice Osler of the Ontario High Court, he looked to Arthur Thurlow's Federal Court decision and declared that because the marrying-out rule in the Indian Act contravened Canada's Bill of Rights, it was invalid; inoperative. Therefore, Yvonne Bedard did not lose her status and what really mattered to her—she could not be evicted by her band council.

It was one particular remark made by the Ontario judge in the *Bedard* case that set alarm bells ringing in Ottawa. Judge Osler said that his ruling might mean that "virtually the entire [Indian] Act must be held to be inoperable." Indigenous organizations like the National Indian Brotherhood were incensed. The Brotherhood's view was that the courts were making incursions on Indian self-determination. The federal government saw major political problems on the horizon, if this decision was not nipped in the bud.

\+\+\+

The ruling in the *Lavell* case at the Federal Court was the first victory against sex discrimination under the Indian Act. Up till then, cases alleging sex discrimination in the Act had not been brought before the courts. Indigenous women had very little power. They had only been eligible to vote in band council elections since 1951, and there were few women chiefs. Several Indigenous women's organizations were starting to come together, although they did not necessarily agree on priorities. Corbiere Lavell was one of the founders of the Ontario Native Women's Association in 1971.

Jeannette Corbiere Lavell, 2020.

In Quebec, one woman broke into a wide grin when she heard about Jeannette Corbiere Lavell and Yvonne Bedard. She herself was already a legend, but she was smiling because these two women were taking things further than she had dared. Mary Two-Axe Earley was a Kanien'kehá:ka (Mohawk) woman from the Kahnawà:ke Reserve across the Saint Lawrence River from Montreal. She was thirty years older than Corbiere Lavell, from a different generation. Mary Two-Axe had left her reserve in the 1920s, settled in New York state, and became one of the seven hundred Haudenosaunee who created the Little Caughnawaga neighbourhood in Brooklyn. Little Caughnawaga was home to the legendary Mohawk Skywalkers, the high ironworkers who built New York City's bridges and skyscrapers. It was such a deeply rooted community that the local Presbyterian Minister gave his sermons in the Mohawk language. When she was living in New York, Mary Two-Axe married out. Her husband, Edward Earley, was an Irish American electrical engineer. In 1966, she was back in Canada visiting a friend and clan sister who had also married out when that friend had a heart attack and died in her arms. Two-Axe Earley, by then fifty-five, was convinced that the stress of losing her property rights and her connection with her reserve had contributed to the death of her clan sister. Mary Two-Axe took on the cause of Indigenous women's rights but she never took her case to court.

The next year, at the invitation of Quebec feminist leader Thérèse Casgrain, Mary Two-Axe and thirty other women travelled from the Kahnawà:ke Reserve to Ottawa to present a brief to the Royal Commission on the Status of Women. They were pressured by their band leadership not to go. It was the first time Indigenous women's issues were on the agenda of mainstream white feminist organizations. The Royal Commission on the Status of Women recommended that First Nations women who married out should retain their status. "Mary was trying to do it behind the scenes," Corbiere Lavell says. She remembers Mary Two-Axe with great affection:

> She was very quiet—a huggable, beautiful woman. She knew what she wanted, "to be buried on my

Mary Two-Axe Earley, October 17, 1979, receiving the Governor General's Award in Commemoration of the Persons Case from Governor General Edward Schreyer.

> reserve," she said. "I'm not allowed." We used to laugh and tease her. She was so likeable, so passionate about who she was—a Mohawk. And Mohawks are matrilineal. Losing her status meant even more to her.

As Jeannette Corbiere Lavell appealed her case, Mary Two-Axe quietly supported her. So did the Chief of the Wiikwemkoong band; his daughter was in the same situation. Others went against her. Some, Corbiere Lavell says, resented the media attention she was getting. Her brother would not stand with her, and she remembers death threats from one high profile Mohawk leader. Most notably, the Native Women's Association of Canada only weighed in on her side after the court case was resolved.

For most Indigenous organizations, the paramount issue was Indigenous sovereignty. There did not seem to be room to discuss anything else. "There was a deafening silence about the injustice of sex discrimination," wrote Genevieve Painter of Concordia University in her PhD dissertation. When there was a mention of the Indian Act and women's loss of Status, "[it] also omitted the impact on Indigenous women's lives and the commitment of Indigenous women to Indigenous self-determination." Nearly all major Indigenous organizations came out against Corbiere Lavell and Bedard as their constitutional challenges went forward.

The battle was on in the courts. Jeannette Corbiere, one young First Nation woman confident in her heritage and steeped in the radical atmosphere of the times, together with her equally young and principled lawyer, were disturbing the political plans of both the federal government and the major male-led Indigenous organizations across the country.

+++

Since its inception in 1971, Indian Rights for Indian Women (IRIW) has been one of the few native organizations prepared to deal with…the rights of Indian women to live, die, and be buried on their reserves.

—Indian Rights for Indian Women

By December of 1972, the federal government had launched an appeal of the Federal Court of Appeal's decision to the Supreme Court of Canada. There was too much at stake politically to let things lie. The *Bedard* and *Lavell* cases were combined and would be heard together. Jean Chrétien, then Minister of Indian Affairs and Northern Development, was quoted in the *Globe and Mail* as saying he was "willing to help any Indian group wishing to appeal to the Supreme Court of Canada to reverse…the Federal Court of Appeal" decision in *Lavell*. The federal government invited leaders of Indigenous organizations to Ottawa for a conference; the dates conveniently coincided with the Supreme Court hearing. Chiefs were flown in from across the country.

If any of the women wanted to watch things unfold at the Supreme Court of Canada, they had to pay their own way to Ottawa.

"We had to fundraise, to get our train tickets." Decades later, Jeannette Corbiere is still angry, but she laughs at the memory. "We had bake sales at the Friendship Centre, I was still working there. And one of the things we did in the fall, we had a wild meat dinner, wild rice, and many of our traditional foods—muskrat, moose, deer, fish. The Department of Natural Resources even gave us a deer. I had to do the organizing and I ended up cooking." And she laughs again. "You do what has to be done."

They raised enough money for the train tickets but had no idea where they would stay in Ottawa. Corbiere Lavell's friend from back home, Yvonne McCrae, the Wiikwemkoong wife of Thunder Bay Member of Parliament Paul McCrae, rented a room in the Chateau Laurier hotel. The Corbieres piled in. The Elders got the bed, and she slept on the floor. The rest of the women camped out in various church halls.

+++

On February 22, 1973, the nine Supreme Court judges looked down from the bench, ready to hear the arguments. In front of them were nineteen black-robed lawyers—nineteen. Facing the judges on one side of the courtroom were four lawyers acting for the attorney general of Canada and two more acting for the Six Nations Council; on the other side were Clayton Ruby for Corbiere Lavell (this was Ruby's first appearance before the Supreme Court) and a lawyer acting for Yvonne Bedard. (Bedard had not made the trip to Ottawa. She and Corbiere Lavell had yet to meet.)

Behind them, shuffling for space, were another eleven lawyers, appearing for the fifteen "interveners"—groups or individuals whom the court has agreed have an interest in the issues and can contribute some extra knowledge. Those interveners, as they are listed in the court documents, included eleven regional First Nations associations, the Native Council of Canada, Yvonne Bedard's Six Nations Band of Indians of the County of Brant, and the Treaty Voice of Alberta. They all argued that this was no way to change the Indian Act, that Indigenous people and organizations should make major decisions—not federally appointed judges. The Treaty Voice of Alberta added an argument that went back to the nineteenth century: that Indian status *should* come down through the male line to protect the institution of family in society and that "the customs of the Indian people are exactly the provisions set out in the Indian Act. An Indian maiden who married a brave from another band left her band for the band of her husband."

At most Supreme Court hearings, lawyers' voices bounce off the walls of the cavernous, nearly always almost empty courtroom. Not this time. The place was packed. "There must have been a hundred chiefs. All there in their regalia." Jeannette Corbiere remembers Chiefs and the women's supporters fighting for space in the gallery. When a delegation of women from the Indian Rights for Indian Women—her supporters—arrived outside the Supreme Court building, one woman recalled, "There were men who were swearing at us outright. 'Bitches,' they said. That's how we were treated." Police escorted them to their seats. The National Indian Brotherhood accused the women of being selfish and "anti-Indian" because they were fighting against the law that, as they saw it, guaranteed Indigenous self-determination. (The NIB was restructured and renamed the Assembly of First Nations in 1982.) As Jeannette Corbiere Lavell and her daughter, Dawn, look back on that day, they both remember thinking, "An awful lot of chiefs had white wives and what if the court declared that anyone, man or woman, who married non-Natives should lose their status?"

Among the cluster of lawyers representing the interveners were two women. They acted for an unusual coalition: the Alberta chapter of Indian Rights for Indian Women plus the University Women's Club of Toronto, University Women Graduates, and the North Toronto Business and Professional Women's Club Inc.—three very white, middle-class women's groups. New alliances were being forged.

The legal arguments for Jeannette Corbiere Lavell and Yvonne Bedard were straightforward. The Indian Act treated the marriages of men and women to non-Status Indians differently. This amounted to sexual discrimination, Clayton Ruby and the lawyer for Yvonne Bedard argued, contrary to the Bill of Rights. Ruby was hanging his hat on the only successful case involving the Bill of Rights and the Indian Act: *R v Drybones*. Joseph Drybones was an Indigenous man who was convicted of being intoxicated while off reserve, contravening Section 94 of the Indian Act. (He lived in the Northwest Territories where there are no reserves.) In 1969, the Supreme Court held that yes, he was discriminated against on the grounds of race; the same penalty would not have been imposed on a non-Indigenous man. The section of the Indian Act dealing with liquor was declared invalid.

But sex discrimination was something else again.

When the Supreme Court judgement came down at the end of the summer of 1973, Jeannette Corbiere Lavell and Yvonne Bedard lost by one vote. It's difficult to understand today, but five judges saw no discrimination in the marrying-out rule. Four judges would have allowed the women's appeal.

Corbiere Lavell and her supporters were deeply upset. Clayton Ruby was more than upset. "I don't think he could believe it." Jeannette Corbiere Lavell shakes her head. "He was flabbergasted. Not long after, Clay went to California." To lick his wounds? "And got another degree," a Master of Laws from the University of California at Berkeley.

The legal decision in *Lavell* has been described as "confused, inconsistent, and undirected." A split decision makes for weak law, and almost every judge in *Attorney General of Canada v Lavell* had different reasons for their decision. The thousands of women who had lost their status (between 1958 and 1960 alone, almost five thousand women were struck off the Indian Registry primarily because they had married out) were no further ahead. Moreover, the court had not clarified what "sex discrimination" meant under the Bill of Rights.

When Corbiere left the Supreme Court that day, she left disillusioned. Not with the decision—that would not be issued until months later—but with the demeanor of the court. "I was looking at the esteemed judges, and I couldn't believe that they were judges. They were asleep—snoring. It really disappointed me to think about justice and the court."

Ultimately, as in the *Bliss* case, it was the 1982 Charter of Rights and Freedoms that led to change. When the Charter was introduced, there was a three-year delay while government combed through all the legislation and identified equality issues. Mary Two-Axe and others had been lobbying hard. In 1985, government recognized that changes had to be made in the Indian Act to address discrimination and introduced Bill C-31. It reinstated 117,000 First Nations women and gave their children Indian status.

The first woman to regain her status was Mary Two-Axe Earley. She was a revered figure. The Chief of Staff to David Crombie, Minister of Indian Affairs and Northern Development, recognized a good photo opportunity when he saw one, and sent a ministerial car to the Kahnawà:ke reserve to drive her to Ontario for the ceremony. Jeannette Corbiere Lavell and her three children, all born before 1985 and Bill C-31, were among the 117,000 now listed on the federal Indian Register. Still, some bands fought reinstatement. The Sawridge Band in Alberta, a band with only fifty members, launched its own constitutional challenge. The Sawridge had done well. There was oil money and more than $125 million in trust funds and the inevitable suggestion was that the Chief and the band did not want to share the wealth.

Jeannette Corbiere Lavell became president of the Ontario Native Women's Association and continued to be involved with Indigenous women's organizations. She was recognized as the first of the Indigenous Famous Six; Yvonne Bedard, the second.

The third was Sandra Lovelace Nicholas of the Tobique First Nation in New Brunswick. She left for the United States to work as a carpenter in the 1960s, married out, and lost her status. When she returned in the 70s, she and her son were denied housing, education, and healthcare. Undeterred, they pitched a tent on the reserve. In 1977, Lovelace Nicholas and other women occupied the band office for four months. She launched her own court case (*Lovelace v Canada*, 1977–81) and, in 1981, petitioned the United Nations Human Rights Committee, which ruled that Canada was in breach of the International Covenant on Civil and Political Rights.

The process of remedying gender discrimination in the Indian Act went on for decades. Sharon McIvor, a lawyer and member of the Lower Nicola Indian Band in BC, was

The Indigenous Famous Six, April 17, 2018, the day they were honoured by the Senate. L–R: In blankets, Lynn Gehl, Sharon McIvor, Sandra Lovelace Nicholas, Yvonne Bedard, and Jeannette Corbiere Lavell (missing Lillian Dyck).

number four. She took the issue further. Under Bill C-31, she could pass her status on to her children but not her grandchildren, whereas a man in the same position could. *McIvor v Canada* was heard in the BC Supreme Court in 2006. It had taken seventeen years to come to trial. The court found in her favour, and the federal government did not appeal. There were more court cases and amendments to the Indian Act spurred on by two other Indigenous women, Lillian Dyck, number five, and Dr. Lynn Gehl, number six. The Famous Six.

In 2018, forty-eight years after Jeannette Corbiere married David Lavell, she, Bedard, Lovelace Nicholas, McIvor, Dyck, and Gehl were honoured by the Senate.

The Famous Five women: Murphy, McClung, Edwards, Parlby, and McKinney—fought for the right to be recognized as "persons" and sit in the Senate. Women's groups from across the country lobbied to make Emily Murphy the first woman senator but that did not happen. Was she too much of a troublemaker? Probably.

Rather, in 1930, it was Cairine Wilson, a comfortably well-off Anglophone from Montreal and a strong supporter of Mackenzie King's Liberal government, who became Canada's first woman senator.

The first Indigenous woman was appointed to the Senate sixty-seven years later. She was Thelma Chalifoux. Like Lizzie Cyr, Thelma Chalifoux was a Métis woman from Alberta.

7. Le seul choix

On July 17, 1989…a male Quebec judge told us that our bodies would never belong to us. That there were two classes of individuals: free men and women.

—Marie-Eve Sevigny

They met at a Radio Shack in Montreal in November 1988. He must have smiled at her, maybe answered a question when she couldn't find a salesman, helped her a little, smiled again. Perhaps they went for a drink. She was barely twenty, a waitress new to the city. He was five years older, a big man, tall, 1.9 metres, six foot three, with a moustache. He had a habit of biting his lower lip; you can see it in some of the photographs. He seemed nice enough.

That's how it always starts.

Chantale Daigle (she is Chantal Daigle in court documents, Chantale Daigle in French-language newspaper stories and on the cover of her book) might have been a young, small-town girl—she was from Chibougamau, eight hours north of Montreal, population eight thousand—but she knew her own mind. What helped her survive all that was to come was her family. They stuck by her. She lived with Jean-Guy Tremblay, that tall man with a moustache, for five months, and it turned out he was not so nice. *Quelle surprise*. She got pregnant. One night, he knocked her to the ground and said that he would "bring her into line once and for all." No, he was not so nice.

"I am not going to stay." She said it to herself at first. "I do not want this relationship or the baby of this relationship." When she told Tremblay that she was leaving and she was going to have an abortion, he went to court to try to stop her. The self-proclaimed pro-life movement was there to encourage and support him. But this "little woman in a red dress with a Peter Pan collar," as someone described her, stood her ground.

It was a little more than a year earlier that the Supreme Court had ruled in *R v Morgentaler* that the criminalization of abortion, which had been an offence since Canada's first criminal code in 1892, violated a woman's right to security of the person under the Charter of Rights. Chief Justice Brian Dickson described it as "a profound interference with a woman's body."

The *Morgentaler* decision was, in the view of many, the most important Supreme Court decision when it came to a woman's autonomy. There had been decades of lobbying, of violent opposition. Doctors who provided abortions had been jailed and shot at, thousands of women had died from illegal backstreet abortions, and thousands of unwanted babies were born. Women can remember where they were and what they were doing when they heard the news of the *Morgentaler* decision. (I was driving past Casa Loma in Toronto.) But just as quickly, it became clear that this was one battle in a longer, larger war. Brian Mulroney's Progressive Conservative government threatened to bring in new legislation prohibiting abortion. Nor did decriminalization guarantee a woman's *right* to abortion. There were big legal questions hanging in the air: Was a foetus a person? Could the father of a foetus veto an abortion? Could anyone?

When Tremblay took Daigle to court to try to stop her abortion, women in Quebec took to the streets like never before. In Montreal, ten thousand women marched through the rain in support of Chantale Daigle. Ten thousand.

+++

I cannot think of anyone more entitled to the court's protection...than a husband.... [I]t is difficult to think of anyone who could have an interest equal to that of a husband in the pregnancy of his wife.

—Mr. Justice Robert Reid, Ontario Supreme Court, 1984

It started not in Quebec but in Ontario with another couple, Gregory Murphy and Barbara Dodd, a week or so before the Chantale Daigle Affair—as it became known—began to unfold.

Abortion was on people's minds. It had been a key issue in the 1988 federal election: *Morgentaler* was decided in January, the election took place in November. The debate became increasingly heated as the year progressed. In the 70s, in the early years of the push to decriminalize abortion, the pro-choice forces had the upper hand. They were better organized, more motivated, and had a great many noisy, angry young women on their side, backed up by their equally angry if not so noisy mothers, aunts, and grandmothers. As Henry Morgentaler established his abortion clinics, first in Montreal and later in Toronto and Winnipeg, the pro-choice faction became more defiant. Morgentaler said publicly in 1973 that he had conducted more than five thousand abortions. The other side, vehemently opposed to abortion and with the force and funds of conservative religious organizations behind them, regrouped and fought back. Morgentaler was charged repeatedly in Quebec; despite what appeared to be unassailable evidence, juries acquitted him more than once. In 1976, the Parti Québécois justice minister declared the sections of the Criminal Code dealing with abortion unenforceable. Quebec stopped going after Morgentaler. His legal battles switched to Ontario. In 1988, after a series of charges, acquittals, and appeals, the Supreme Court of Canada issued its definitive ruling that the criminalization of abortion violated a woman's Charter rights. It was not over. In the spring of 1989, there were demonstrations, altercations between pro and anti-choice groups outside abortion clinics almost every week.

Morgentaler, abortion, Montreal; Toronto, abortion, deeply held beliefs, demonstrations, abortion; violence, attacks, abortion. The words, the placards, the name calling—it was all swirling around as Chantale Daigle and Jean-Guy Tremblay and the Ontario couple,

Barbara Dodd and Gregory Murphy, grew up. In 1989, they were all in their early 20s. Tremblay and Daigle had been living together since January. By March, Chantale Daigle was pregnant. Eight or nine weeks later, so was Barbara Dodd. Neither woman was happy about it. Dodd was dealing with additional challenges: she was a woman with 90% hearing loss and she struggled with literacy, factors that would prove decisive in the weeks to come.

Toward the end of June, Dodd told Greg Murphy that she was pregnant and that she was going to have an abortion. It was not what Murphy wanted to hear. He maintained later that it was a planned pregnancy, although it was never clear how long they had "been together." Murphy called a leading anti-abortion organization, Campaign Life, and was put in touch with lawyer Angela Costigan. Costigan moved quickly and got a temporary injunction preventing Barbara Dodd getting an abortion.

In his affidavit in support of the injunction, Murphy swore that he was the father of the unborn child and added, not that anyone asked him, that he was from an "intellectually superior" family. There were reports from Costigan that this was Campaign Life's twelfth attempt to assert the rights of a father over a foetus in the courts. This was the case that the organization had been waiting for. Not surprisingly, the injunction and Gregory Murphy's crusade hit the papers. When women campaigned to decriminalize abortion, they marched wearing signs around their waist that said, "This Uterus is Not Government Property." "Post-Morgentaler men," as Murphy and Tremblay have been called, seemed to be saying, "No, it's mine."

Six hours down the highway in Montreal, Chantale Daigle had decided she would leave Jean-Guy Tremblay and she, too, would have an abortion. Chantale Daigle stated in an affidavit, "I do not wish to have a child at the present time in light of my age, my social situation as a single person and my moral values as I want to provide for a child in a serene stable family environment in which there is no violence."

In the 1980s, not much was said publicly about domestic abuse. It was seen as a mark of shame that somehow reflected more on the woman than the man. Daigle just didn't talk about Tremblay's behaviour. Later on, she said that Tremblay had become increasingly "possessive" as the pregnancy had progressed, and their relationship was full of "violence and fear." When she made her decision to leave and to have an abortion, she was eighteen weeks into her pregnancy and fully aware that she had to move quickly. In Quebec, twenty weeks was the cut off for legal abortion. She made the appointment.

Tremblay, the story has it, received a call at the garage where he worked telling him that in Ontario, Greg Murphy had successfully blocked his girlfriend's efforts to abort "his child." If Murphy could do it, he thought, so could he. Tremblay applied to the court in Montreal and on July 7, like Murphy, he obtained a temporary injunction against his former girlfriend. Daigle was on her way to the abortion appointment in Sherbrooke an hour and forty minutes east of Montreal when she was told that there was a court injunction against her. If she kept that appointment, she would be in contempt of court and could face a $50,000 fine and two years in jail. She turned around and went back to Montreal.

On that same day, July 7—every day counts in this story—there was a new twist in the Toronto case. The headline in the *Toronto Star* read "A Second Father Appears." A man named Christen Mucciacito had come forward claiming that Barbara Dodd was carrying *his* child, not Gregory Murphy's. Dodd did not deny Mucciacito's claim. They had been seeing each other regularly.

Barbara Dodd was profoundly isolated. There was her hearing loss and she had no one to explain what was going on. She did not have a lawyer to represent her at the injunction hearing.

When the case hit the papers, Clayton Ruby—the same Clay Ruby who represented Jeannette Corbiere—stepped forward and became Dodd's lawyer. He said of the injunction and the way it was handled: "This is the way you treat a slave, not an independent human being." He appealed the temporary injunction to the Ontario Court of Appeal, and introduced evidence that when Barbara Dodd was served with the initial court documents (by the lawyer Angela Costigan herself rather than a professional process server), nothing was explained in sign language. Dodd had no idea what the documents said because she could not read well nor could she hear what Costigan was telling her as she handed her the documents. The Court of Appeal held that on that basis alone, the

Clay Ruby

injunction was invalid. Abortion rights organizations rallied, and the Canadian Hearing Society held a triumphant press conference. But the case of Barbara Dodd and Gregory Murphy did not tackle the big questions. The Ontario court did not have to decide on Gregory Murphy's claim of a father's right to protect the foetus or whether a foetus had rights.

Barbara Dodd had her abortion on Tuesday, July 11. Lawyer Angela Costigan asked for the remains of the aborted fetus so that Gregory Murphy could give it a "proper burial." The request was refused. Nonetheless, Murphy et al., held a well-publicized "memorial" next door to the Morgentaler clinic.

+++

In Quebec, Jean-Guy Tremblay moved to get his temporary injunction made permanent. This time, the hearing took place in Val-d'Or, not far from Chibougamau, Chantale Daigle's hometown. Like Barbara Dodd, Daigle did not have a lawyer. But she knew enough to apply for Legal Aid, the government-funded plan to ensure that anyone with serious legal problems who could not afford a lawyer did not go into court unrepresented. Daigle made the eight-hour drive north from Montreal, got her legal aid certificate, and found her lawyer: Daniel Bédard, the newest hire at "le clan Cliche," a well-known firm in Val-d'Or. Thirty years later, the firm still advertises its involvement in "l'affaire Chantale Daigle." Bédard, barely out of law school, found himself swimming in deep and uncharted waters.

On Monday, July 17, Chantale Daigle, composed and dignified in a white blazer and dark skirt, walked into the Val-d'Or palais de justice. The night before, she had appeared on Radio Canada's *Téléjournal*, where she said very clearly, "It's my decision. It's up to me to do what I want best with my body." The entire province knew who Chantale Daigle was and her position. She also told the television audience that "a pro-life" lawyer had offered her $25,000 to "keep the child," to not have an abortion.

The case was called and Daniel Bédard, her lawyer, stood up, faced the court, and argued that since the Supreme Court had decriminalized abortion, it was a woman's Charter right to govern her own body. Jean-Guy Tremblay's lawyer answered, "Women's rights have limits." The Quebec Superior Court agreed—women's rights have limits—and made the temporary injunction permanent. Chantale Daigle was now the only woman in Quebec forbidden to have an abortion.

Seldom has a case moved so fast. Three days later, her appeal was heard by five judges of the Quebec Court of Appeal. Tremblay's lawyer expanded his argument and maintained first that his client, the father, had a legal right and duty to protect his unborn child and second that the foetus was a person with legal rights under the Quebec Charter of Human Rights and Freedoms. It took the Quebec Court of Appeal six days to come to a decision. To Daigle, it must have felt like an eternity, knowing as she did that time was as big an enemy as Tremblay. That twenty-week deadline for a legal abortion was looming, by some calculations, it had passed when the decision came down. Two of the judges would have allowed the appeal but three agreed with Tremblay's argument, that a father has rights in the foetus and that more fundamentally, a foetus is a person. "It is not an inanimate object nor the property of anyone, but a living human entity distinct from the mother...and has the right to life and protection from those who conceived it."

"I won my case," crowed Tremblay. "I am expecting the child at this time."

The Quebec Court of Appeal had ruled that the rights of the foetus and the father trumped the rights of the mother. Writing in the newspaper *Le Devoir* thirty years later, noted Quebec journalist and feminist Francine Pelletier said,

> It was not just the *right to abortion* that was threatened, the whole question of gender equality was also raised. For twenty-five years now, the emancipation of women has been going well, transforming the laws and the public square in its image, and now a headwind has been rising, relayed by our highest judicial authorities.

Days after the Quebec Court of Appeal decision, Pelletier was among those ten thousand women who took to the streets of Montreal. She called it "one of the most important demonstrations in the history of Quebec, and the most important in the history of abortion."

In Ontario, the saga of Barbara Dodd and Gregory Murphy was not over. Within days of having her abortion, Dodd knocked on Murphy's door and said that she regretted her decision and had been duped into having the abortion. Years later, Dodd became involved in advocacy for the rights of deaf or partially deaf people and developed her own voice. (In 2008, she won an action in front of the Ontario Human Rights Commission over the absence of a visual fire alarm in a hotel.) But on July 31, 1989, the cover headline of *Maclean's* magazine read, "Barbara Dodd's Change of Heart." Campaign Life held a press conference

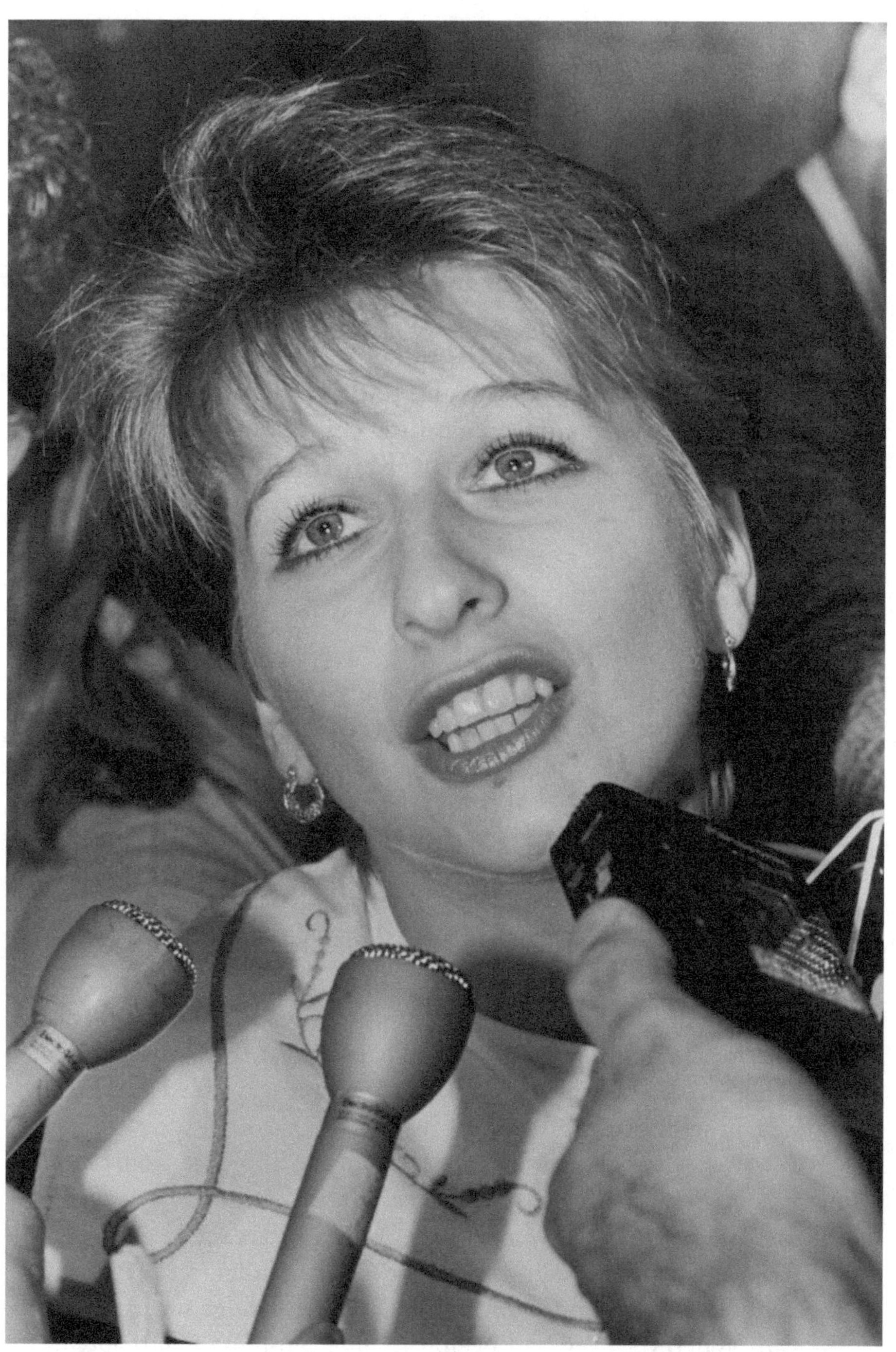

Chantale Daigle speaking with reporters, 1989.

announcing that Dodd and Murphy were together again and were heading for Quebec to plead with Chantale Daigle not to have an abortion.

Daigle was not about to change her mind. The Montreal newspaper *La Presse* ran interviews with Jean-Guy Tremblay's relatives. They were not flattering, with the *coup de grâce* coming from his mother, who described her son as "irresponsible, violent, and a liar." Chantale Daigle appealed the Quebec Court of Appeal decision to the Supreme Court. Public opinion was behind her. Tremblay was on the defensive and told the *Globe and Mail* that he was "sick and tired of people calling [him] a wife-beater and a criminal," and he added that he never hit Daigle "hard enough to leave marks."

⁂

August 8, 1989, the day the Supreme Court of Canada heard *Tremblay v Daigle*, became known as one of the most dramatic days in the history of the court. It can—and usually does—take years for a case to wend its way through the various levels of appeal before it lands on the doorstep of the Supreme Court. Just ask Stella Bliss (three years), or Irene Florence Murdoch (five years). In the case of *Tremblay v Daigle*, it was barely a month between Jean-Guy Tremblay's first application for an injunction to the Supreme Court of Canada's ruling.

If Chantale Daigle's appeal to the Supreme Court of Canada was going to mean anything, then it had to happen fast. The court was on its summer recess. Chief Justice Brian Dickson scrambled as a chief justice had seldom scrambled before.

Beverley McLachlin, only appointed to the Supreme Court four months earlier, was in Switzerland vacationing with her son when the message reached her—be back in Ottawa and ready to go in two days' time. Antonio Lamer, the senior Quebec judge on the court, was manoeuvring his boat under the Brooklyn Bridge when he got the call. Wherever they had been, the nine Supreme Court judges were all back in Ottawa on August 8, robed and ready.

Out on the lawn in front of the great grey Supreme Court building, demonstrators with strollers, stuffed animals, and a sign that read, "gifts for Chantale and Jean-Guy's baby," positioned themselves for the TV cameras. A strong press contingent strained to hear and identify the players as they made their way into court. This was another case where the gallery would be full; all the interest groups were there. Daigle herself, like most of the women whose legal battles wound up at the Supreme Court, was not about to put herself through the media circus. She, everyone assumed, had given up and stayed home. By now she was past the twentieth week of her pregnancy.

Young Daniel Bédard found himself in front of the highest court in the land. He must have taken a few deep breaths as he arranged then rearranged his books and papers on the table at the front of the courtroom, waiting for the judges to file in. Among the interveners sitting behind him were lawyers for the attorney general of Canada and the attorney general of Quebec. The arguments would, everyone knew, dig deep into constitutional and jurisdictional issues. Quebec and the federal government would be pitted against each other. The spotlight, however, clearly shone on the foetal rights issue and who, if anyone, could veto a woman's decision to have an abortion.

Marie Tison, writing for *La Presse*, reported that Bédard led off with "a solid plea." At the lunch break, the journalists scrummed the president of Campagne Québec-Vie, Gilles Grondin, a retired diplomat and the man "leading the charge" to ban abortion in Quebec. Then just after two p.m., as they were scheduled to resume, Daniel Bédard, "looking distraught," wrote Tison, stood up to address the court. He announced, "his voice unsure," that his client had had an abortion the week before in Boston.

"The bombshell hit after lunch...." Madame Justice Beverley McLachlin, viewing events from the bench, took up the story. "I saw the tide of red anger creep up Chief Justice Dickson's face.... To say the chief justice was displeased and all the other justices upset is only to say what became clear later in court." What Bédard had announced could be seen, in the language of the court, as "lack of candour" or "abuse of process," one step short of lying to the court. No wonder Bédard was nervous. He explained that he had been unable

Beverley McLachlin on the bench for the *Daigle* case. She was the Chief Justice of the Supreme Court of Canada from 2000–2017.

to reach his client for the last few days and was previously unaware of what she had done. McLachlin, writing after she retired from the bench, described Daigle's conduct as "more panicked than contemptuous, less a slap in the face of justice than the action of a woman running out of time."

The chief justice called a recess and the nine judges met "backstage." Given that the abortion had already happened, should the hearing continue? Henri Kélada, the lawyer now acting for Tremblay, said it was a private matter; it's over and done with. Daniel Bédard argued no, the same could, and almost inevitably would, happen to another woman and the issue should be decided. Besides, there was the matter of the contempt of court charge hanging over Chantale Daigle's head. Hurried phone calls were made by lawyers for the many interveners back to their clients for "instructions." The lawyers for the attorney general of Canada privately suggested to their political masters—stay out of the way, let's get this decided.

The court ruled that the case would continue. The central legal question had to be determined: Does the law, viewed objectively, recognize foetal rights? Arguments were brief and it only took the nine judges an hour to agree that only a woman can decide whether to carry her pregnancy to term; that a foetus has no legal personality, and the father has no veto. The injunction against Chantale Daigle was lifted and with it the contempt of court charge. Abortion was the woman's decision and her decision alone. Seldom had a matter so weighty been determined so quickly. (That same day, the *Chicago Tribune* reported that Chantale Daigle had her abortion in Boston a week before the Supreme Court hearing and that it was paid for by the Montreal Women's Health Centre.)

The pack of journalists circled Jean-Guy Tremblay at the end of the day. "Do you still love her?" someone asked. Tremblay, reported Tison for *La Presse*, was enraged. "How can you ask me that? She just killed my child." Tison wrote that the journalists were "stunned by his aggression."

Jean-Guy Tremblay left Quebec and resurfaced in Alberta a few years later where he racked up fourteen convictions for beating, stalking, and choking women. In 2000, he was designated a long-term offender by Alberta Queens Bench Judge Scott Brooker. Expert witnesses, including psychiatrists, described him variously as psychopathic, narcissistic, paranoid, aggressive, and predatory. He refused treatment in prison "because he said that would be"—according to a Corrections Services supervisor—"tantamount to admitting wrongdoing." In 2006, Tremblay was convicted by Ontario Superior Court Judge Andromache Karakatsanis of criminal harassment of another woman. (Karakatsanis was appointed to the Supreme Court of Canada in 2016.) After his release from prison, Tremblay was under court order to live in a halfway house until 2016. In 2011, *Le Journal de Québec* reported, "*Jean-Guy Tremblay, un multirécidiviste en matière de violence conjugale, s'est marié.*" This multi-recidivist in domestic violence got married. A year later, Quebec City police picked him up after another domestic violence complaint.

✦✦✦

It made all of us grow without wanting to.

—Chantale Daigle

The Supreme Court gave its oral judgement from the bench, something that doesn't happen often, the day of the hearing. It was the middle of November when the written judgement was issued. This time, Chantale Daigle was front and centre. What she said at the press conference was simple and straightforward: "I was not pro-abortion. I was 100% pro-choice. Journalists wanted to make the case too spectacular.... It stopped being a debate about a woman wanting an abortion. Suddenly everyone was pro-Chantale or pro-Jean-Guy." Twenty-one and branded by many as an evil, wicked woman, she faced the press and the public, said what she had to say, and then Chantale Daigle went back to Chibougamau.

The next year, she released a book titled *Le seul choix, le mien,* and after that, she changed her name, got married, had four children, and lived, as far as anyone knows, a "normal" life. She has raised her head only once since. In 2022, a production company made a six-hour miniseries that retold her story. Too many young women, the producers said, did not know about Chantale Daigle. She quietly endorsed the project. *Disobey: The Chantale Daigle Affair* streamed in March of 2023. It came hard on the heels of the United States Supreme Court decision to overturn *Roe v Wade* and with it, fifty years of American women's right to abortion.

Older women said to their juniors, "The fight is never over."

As for the law, the case of *Tremblay v Daigle* held that a foetus is not a person and that only a woman has the right to decide whether or not to continue with a pregnancy. But there are always more questions. Two years after *Daigle,* two self-taught midwives assisted in a home birth in Vancouver. It was a difficult delivery. The baby's head had emerged when contractions stopped. After twenty minutes an ambulance was called, and once at the hospital, the baby was delivered but showed no signs of life. The two midwives were charged with negligence causing death and bodily harm to the mother. But was this a foetus or a baby, and if a foetus was not a person, then how could these midwives have caused its death?

Women's Legal Education and Action Fund (LEAF) once again intervened. They argued that in the midst of the attention previously given to father's rights and in all the discussion of the legal status of a foetus, it was the woman who got short shrift and who lost her equality under the Charter of Rights. LEAF asked the court to enhance women's equality "by ensuring that the status of the foetus is not considered apart from the woman who carried it."

LEAF went on to point out that had there been more women shaping the law over the course of history, the right words might have been found to describe the relationship between a woman and the foetus she carried. The law was only beginning to come to terms with issues that are unique to women. To return to the words of Madame Justice Bertha Wilson, as more women entered the legal profession, "Perhaps they [would] succeed in infusing the law with an understanding of what it means to be fully human."

8. The Uplifted Knife

As time went on, I lost everything; my confidence, self-esteem, my pride—with time, I even lost the ability to care or to feel. Bill took everything from me, a bit at a time, until there was nothing left but a shell.

—Jane Hurshman

Wendy Annand sits herself down in the big, old recliner and leans back. The chair slides away, the footrest lifts up, and much to her relief, she is lying almost flat. She sighs; finally, the pain in her back is manageable. She is by the window in the living room of her old friend Dianne Crowell's house on the road to Lunenburg. Crowell comes in from the kitchen with a tray of tea and kicks her oxygen line out of the way as she goes. Age takes its toll. There they are, two grey-haired women, among the last caretakers of the memory of Jane Hurshman.

It is a grey spring day in Nova Scotia, with patches of snow still on the ground. Annand has just come from the dentist. She had been Jane Hurshman's parole officer, and they became friends. It's 2023, more than thirty years since Jane Hurshman died. "If we knew then what we know now about trauma and what it does"—Annand takes a swallow of her tea before she finishes her sentence—"I never would have let her do what she did—all that talking about what had happened. But we didn't know."

It was a solitary gunshot that killed her, but was it suicide or was she shot by someone else? What did Wendy Annand believe? The question didn't have to be asked. It hung in the air.

The Halifax police investigated and decided it was suicide. Some still think she was killed—vengeance for killing Billy Stafford. Or she was shot to shut her up, to stop her talking about the beatings and convincing women that there was a way out. Billy Stafford beat her for five years, the whole time she lived with him. He beat her with the metal tube of the vacuum cleaner, a belt, a stick, whatever was at hand; he beat her into unconsciousness, and he went after the kids. He boasted to the neighbourhood how he'd thrown a man overboard when they were at sea fishing, and no one doubted him. They knew that he had it in 'im. One day, he drove straight at a woman who was pushing a stroller across the street, and when she threatened to report him, he shot a bullet through the window of her house. Then he laughed, what Jane Hurshman called his "evil laugh." Billy Stafford would tell anyone who crossed his path that he had been sent by the devil. He wouldn't let anyone bring a Bible into the house.

In 1982, Jane Hurshman shot him with his own shotgun, blasted his head off while he was passed out in his pickup truck. The local RCMP sergeant said, after they arrested her, "She deserves a medal. She probably saved a couple of our officers' lives.... I'm sure we would have gone out there one day and he would have shot one of us."

There was no doubt that she pulled the trigger, but the jury in the little town of Liverpool on Nova Scotia's south shore acquitted her on the grounds of self-defence. The Crown appealed, the case was retried, and she served two months for manslaughter.

But unlike Florence Murdoch and Chantale Daigle and Stella Bliss, who kept to themselves after their go-round with the legal system, Jane Hurshman, whose entire life had been about surviving violence, did not hide herself away. She spoke out, talked about wife beating to groups of women, to lawyers, judges, to the national media. She advocated for women in shelters. She put herself out there; it was the 70s, no one had done that before. Jane Hurshman did not live to see it, nor would she have had much time for the legal argle-bargle, but she laid the groundwork for what became known as the battered woman defence to murder, a redefinition of self-defence.

+++

The beatings, men slapping their wives around, were nothing new. It's just that it took a very long time before it was considered worth talking about. It was progress, a starting point in a perverse way, when in 1826, Chief Justice William Campbell in Kingston, Ontario, set out the common law position in Canada. A man had "a right to chastise his wife moderately," he pronounced. For the wife to be justified in hitting back or, perish the thought, leaving her husband, "the chastisement must be such as to put her life in jeopardy." And then, bruised and bloodied, to keep a roof over her head and look after the kids, she had to find a way to make a living. Of course, women didn't complain. There was too much at stake, the man was head of the house; she took him for better or worse.

In the nineteenth century, long before there were women's shelters or legal protection, there were charitable organizations to protect women as there were to protect animals (principally white Anglo women; women of other ethnicities and races had to find their own protection). A woman had no legal right to complain, he had the right to "chastise her moderately," yet the morally upright Victorians displayed compassion and sheltered a beaten horse or a kicked dog, and eventually, as an act of charity, an abused woman. The Society for the Protection of Women and Children from Aggravated Assaults was set up in London in 1857. In 1878, Massachusetts had the Society for the Prevention of Cruelty to Children; in 1881, the Society for the Protection of Women and Children was established in Montreal. The year before, Halifax had added the protection of women and children to the animals it looked after through its Society for the Prevention of Cruelty.

The first priority for the women served by the Halifax Society was money, the means of survival. Beatings were almost incidental. Halifax middle-class matrons weren't keen on sticking their noses into failed marriages; they were much more comfortable looking after stray

Jane Hurshman with her parole officer and friend, Wendy Annand.

dogs and cats. Family violence, particularly middle-class violence, was a private matter too embarrassing to be mentioned. The working-class clients of the Society, however, were assertive. The women more often reported husbands to the courts for non-support, not violence, which the law of the time countenanced. They brought the beatings to the anti-cruelty Society, and relied on the Society rather than the police to take things to court if and when it was possible.

The anti-cruelty societies—and as time went on, the social service organizations and their limited help—were part of city life. But Jane Hurshman was born in Brooklyn, Nova Scotia, three hours or more down the south shore from Halifax. She lived in "rural isolation." The only jobs in Brooklyn were fishing or working in the sawmills for the men, and next to nothing for women. In 1949, when Jane Hurshman was born, there were no role models in backwoods Nova Scotia to show her how to build a different life.

In the late 1940s, the Korean war was brewing, the Canadian army was recruiting, and Jane Hurshman's father, Morris, like so many men in the Maritimes, signed up. The army promised a stable income if not a stable address. Over the years, the family lived in New Brunswick, Winnipeg, Truro, then Germany, and back to Canada. As a child, Jane was an "army brat": Brave, Resilient, Adaptable, and Tough. When she went to school, she did well, but she did not go to school that often.

She was sixteen when she got pregnant.

+++

Milford took care of everything. His sister loaned me a blue dress. Milfie bought me some flowers and my aunt Judy, and her new husband stood for us.

—Jane Hurshman

Jane Hurshman's childhood was erratic, both geographically and emotionally. Morris Hurshman was an alcoholic, a mean alcoholic. As a little girl, she watched as he smashed her mother across the room and drank himself into a stupor. She would spirit her sisters away when the fighting began. That was how life was, so she didn't think it was particularly out of the ordinary when it turned out that her new husband, Milford Whynot, was her father's equal and then some.

There she was at sixteen, in her borrowed blue wedding dress, weighing in at ninety-eight pounds, and pregnant. She and Milford moved in with his grandparents. When she went into labour, Milfie Whynot dropped his wife and her suitcase at the nursing station and went drinking. She had a son. He started "fooling around," his drinking escalated, and he smacked her around. He developed his own particular way of frightening her. Brian Vallée, a journalist and a man with six sisters, was the first person to tell the story of Jane Hurshman (Vallée's book, *Life with Billy,* was published in 1986). She told Vallée about Milfie, about how he used to throw knives at her. He would tell her to sit in the rocking chair and rock, and he would practise his aim. God help her if she changed the rhythm of the rocking.

Her first baby boy was shortly followed by another. Life with Milfie Whynot got worse, and one winter's night when the youngest was three, Jane Hurshman stuffed their clothes into green garbage bags, loaded the children and whatever she could grab into the car, and drove. For a small province, there is a great deal of unpopulated woodland in Nova Scotia. Drive ten miles inland and picturesque coastline gives way to scrubby trees and long, deserted roads. Somewhere along one of those stretches of dark emptiness, her car broke down. She piled the bags full of clothes on the boys to keep them warm, left the car on the side of the road, and shivering in her cheap winter coat and broken-down boots, walked to the closest house. They took her and the boys in for the night.

She wasn't going back to Milfie Whynot, but he took the boys. When Jane Hurshman applied for benefits, the welfare officer shrugged and said, "You don't have any dependents. We can't help you." She was on her own. She had lost her children. She also had little confidence, no family to help her, and no job. Milfie Whynot had a friend, Billy Stafford. She decided that Billy Stafford was her way forward, her knight in shining armour. They had sex, it was her idea. It was the fastest way to divorce Milfie.

Out of the frying pan into the fire.

+++

Bangs Falls, Nova Scotia, as Vallée described it, was like something out of a Ma and Pa Kettle movie from the 1940s. Ma and Pa Kettle were hillbillies. Hollywood hillbillies. The movies were comedies, full of "country charm," with a ramshackle farm and rambunctious children. There was nothing charming, comic, or pleasantly ramshackle about Bangs Falls. Still isn't. A single-lane dirt road—potholed and, in the spring, muddy—runs beside the Medway River which flows southeast into the North Atlantic ocean thirty kilometres away. In the spring of 2023, there were piles of wood and garbage dumped along the road. A twenty-year-old lime-green Chevvy sat abandoned in the trees, and a rusted-out excavator was forever parked next to a house with a frayed Newfoundland flag hanging loosely from its roof. The only work to be had is with the local sawmill further up the road. Bangs Falls is where Billy Stafford brought Jane Hurshman in the late 1970s. She set up house, cooked on a hot plate, and hauled water from a well, one bucket at a time.

William Lamonte Stafford, to give Billy his full name, was a gone-to-seed giant of a man—tall and weighing more than two hundred and fifty pounds. He was eight years older than her. What Jane Hurshman didn't know was that he had a common-law wife who had escaped and gone out west, and that before her, he had been married to Pauline. They had five children together. One night, Billy Stafford had been drinking. Pauline was pregnant again, and he began to beat her about the head. Her face was bloodied and bruised. There was snow on the ground outside but wearing only her nightgown and her slippers, Pauline Stafford ran to the nearest house. They took her to the hospital. Assault charges were laid against Billy Stafford but dropped when he signed a peace bond. Then he headed out fishing, came back, and, she testified at Jane Hurshman's murder trial, tried to drown her.

"He was nice one minute and crazy the next," she told the court. He liked to bite her—bite her so hard that she had scars. "I just more or less stayed hid in the house. I was not allowed to do anything to stop getting pregnant." She went on, "He would line [the kids] up on the stairs and put lit cigarettes in their mouths and wait till they burnt down and then force them to eat the stubs. He was like a mad dog; he'd actually froth at the mouth when he came after me."

Pauline Stafford's family eventually got her and the kids out and she went to live with her cousin in Ottawa.

Now it was Jane Hurshman's turn.

Bangs Falls was depressing enough in 2023, but in the late 70s, the road was worse, the bridge across the Medway River more slippery, the road darker. Keeping an eye out for deer, Jane would slither up the River Road at night on her way home from her job at a care home in Liverpool. She was the one with an income. Billy Stafford had been blacklisted from the fishing boats ever since the man-overboard incident. Everyone figured he was making money dealing dope.

By the fall of 1976, Jane Hurshman was pregnant again. She'd been advised not to have any more children, but Stafford threw her birth control pills in the garbage. It was not an easy pregnancy, and she became incontinent. He would holler at her, "It ain't bad enough you're big as a barrel, now you have to be like a dog and go around pissing on everything. Fuck you, I ain't taking you anywhere until you have that kid." Darren was born in the spring of 1977, and she had her tubes tied. They weren't married, but the hospital required her "husband's" signature on the form. "Fuck that," he said. "You expect me to sign for an operation that makes you no good anymore." She forged his signature.

And she carried on. Reliable, cheerful Jane Hurshman.

Her work colleagues said she often had bruises or a black eye. At home, Billy Stafford knocked her unconscious, fired bullets in her direction, sexually degraded her. She was hypervigilant, walked on eggshells, afraid for her little boy, for herself, for anyone who lived nearby. Stafford carried a gun in the truck. Everyone was scared of him, including the police. The RCMP officer in charge of the Liverpool detachment told his men, "If you go out to the Stafford place, go armed."

The situation with her family had improved. Her mother had become ill, and it scared Morris Hurshman so much that he stopped drinking. Now she did have some family support. But if she even hinted to Billy that she might leave, he upped the ante. He would kill her family, he told her, if she left. She believed him. By now her older son, Allen, was also living with them. Billy Stafford didn't have any time for Allen, but it was the baby he really went after. He would shovel food into the small child's mouth and when Darren threw up, he made the child eat everything in the bowl including the vomit. That, wrote Brian Vallée, was the detail that hit home with the jury.

Jane Hurshman was outside, gardening, the day things blew up. Billy Stafford was lying on the bed with the little boy. To get her attention, he fired the rifle out the window. "Get in here, old woman," came the voice. "You've got a mess to clean up." Darren was lying in a pool of blood and excrement. Stafford had broken off a mop handle and beaten the child. He was quivering, his little body was covered with welts. Jane started to cry. Billy Stafford punched her in the face. "Get this fucking mess cleaned up. We're going out." She cleaned up. Then he came at her with the metal tube of the vacuum cleaner. They did eventually "go out" to friends to play cards. By the end of the evening, he was drunk and stoned, and as she drove them home, he was ranting about Margaret Joudrey, their card-playing neighbour who lived in a trailer down the hill. Jane Hurshman said later, "She'd been like a mother to me." Margaret Joudrey had no illusions about Billy Stafford. When they played cards, she always had a gun on the table. "If that fool ever comes down here causing trouble, he won't be walking back," she told Hurshman. As they drove home that night, Billy Stafford looked back at the lights in Joudrey's trailer. "When Margaret turns her lights off down there tonight, it'll be lights off for her, for good!" and he gave his "evil laugh." "I got five gallons of gas in town today, and I'm going to dump it all 'round that fucking trailer and watch 'em burn. They'll never get out. They won't have a chance. And I'll deal with that son of yours at the same time."

She said nothing, they were nearly home. There were rules about everything—when she drove them anywhere, she was not allowed to get out of the truck until he told her she could. Men like Billy Stafford, psychiatrists say, demand not just obedience but complete surrender.

It was late when Jane Hurshman drove them up the hill and pulled in by the house. She turned off the ignition and sat in the truck in the dark. It didn't take long before Billy Stafford passed out. She told the court at her trial what happened next: "I sat there and sat there and the words, everything he had said started sinking in. What he was going to do...and I just said to hell with it. I'm not going to live like this anymore."

Her son Allen brought her the gun. She told him to go back in the house. When she heard the door close, she went to the open window of the truck, turned her head away, and pulled the trigger.

+++

Wives don't have the right to take the lives of their husbands.

—Justice Merlin Nunn

The beatings, the attack with the metal pipe, the welts on the baby—those are the things that the Nova Scotia appeal court ruled should never have been admitted into evidence. They were context, not evidence of self-defence; they merely served to create sympathy for the defendant. It was difficult, to put it mildly, to convince Canada's justice system that women like Jane Hurshman, and later Angelique Lyn Lavallee, and so many more, have legally defensible grounds to kill their partner.

Jane Hurshman moved fast the night she killed Billy Stafford. Allen brought her clean clothes, friends dumped the gun in the Medway River, then she drove the truck with the headless Billy Stafford beside her and parked it on a side road. Her father drove her the seven miles back to the house.

It didn't take long for the RCMP to find the truck and the body and decide this was no suicide—where was the gun? Staff Sergeant Peter Williamson arrived and looked in the truck. "I admit," he said later, "I thought to myself it couldn't have happened to a better guy." The RCMP drove back to the house and told her, "I'm sorry to say but your husband is dead." She fainted.

Jane Hurshman was taken in for questioning. She confessed within twelve hours and was charged with first degree murder. If the Crown, the prosecution, could prove she had *planned* to kill Billy Stafford, then murder it was and she was facing life in prison.

✦✦✦

In 1911, Angelina Napolitano, an illiterate Italian woman from somewhere outside Naples, took an axe to her husband Pietro and killed him. In the early years of the century, the Napolitanos had crossed the Atlantic to New York City where they lived for seven years. They then moved to Canada and became part of the community of Italians who settled in Sault Ste. Marie, with its steel mills and employment opportunities. Angelina, Pietro, and their four children lived in a too-small, top-floor apartment. The opportunities were there, but Pietro couldn't quite seize them. He wanted to build a house, but he didn't have the money. Frustrated, feeling like a failure, he took it out on Angelina. In November of 1910, Pietro Napoliano stabbed his wife in the face, neck, and chest with his pocket knife. She recovered. He also told her to go out and prostitute herself and supplement the family income. She was pregnant with their fifth child. On Easter Sunday of 1911, he came home from night shift at the mill, rounded on her, and threatened to kill her and the baby she was carrying if she did not "be a bad woman," in her words, and earn the money they needed by the time he woke up. Then he passed out. Just like Jane Hurshman eighty years later, Angelina Napolitano had had enough. She found a weapon, not a gun but the family axe, and went after him. When the neighbour discovered her covered with blood, she said she had butchered a pig. Then she sat down and waited quietly for the police to come and arrest her.

The trial lasted three hours. Angelina Napolitano barely spoke English. There was no translator. Her court-appointed lawyer, a man named Uriah McFadden, piecing things together, told the judge and the jury that the beatings, the stabbings, the threats to her children, had shocked her so badly that she acted in self-defence, anticipating a murderous rage when her husband woke up. It was a valiant effort on McFadden's part, but in 1911 (and for almost another eighty years thereafter), it was an argument that would not fly. Judge Byron Moffatt

Angelina Napolitano, age 29, from a newspaper drawing, 1911.

Britton said no, this was not self-defence, and asked how could it be when the stabbing had happened months earlier? There was no imminent threat. "If anyone injured six months ago could give that as justification or excuse for slaying a person, it would be complete anarchy."

Angelina Napolitano, distraught and with no idea what was going on around her, was found guilty. In 1911, a murder conviction meant the hangman's noose. (Canada hanged its murderers until 1962. The death penalty was not completely removed from the books until 1998.)

Sault Ste. Marie was a small town that was seldom noticed by the rest of the world. It was more than eight hundred kilometres from Toronto, the closest Canadian city, but the story of Angelina Napolitano went viral by the standards of the day. Before they became lawyers, Uriah McFadden and his brother had owned the local newspaper. They had media connections, and like any good defence lawyer, Uriah McFadden knew the value of publicity. The brothers used their connections and made sure the story circulated. Opinion in Sault Ste. Marie was divided—Angelina was, after all, a foreigner, a "hot-blooded foreigner," as Italians were labelled. Her behaviour was not proper. But feminists far and wide were outraged. They saw what she did as self-defence, the only thing possible for a woman in her situation. An American doctor, Alexander Aalto, even offered to be hanged in her place reportedly saying, "It would only be fair to Mrs. Napolitano for a man to give his life for her, inasmuch as her life is in peril on account of a man's persecution of her, and because men condemned her." The British suffrage journal *Common Cause* said both the law and the way it was applied were "bad," for "they are exclusively masculine."

Canada had no compunction in executing convicted murderers, but *pregnant* convicted murderers were something else again. (There was a common view that pregnancy made a woman "temporarily insane," therefore, she could not be guilty.) Angelina Napolitano's execution was delayed until after she gave birth. Petitions for clemency came in from all over the world, and three months after she was convicted, her sentence was commuted to life in prison. The baby was born in prison but died a few weeks later. Her other children had been "taken into care," whatever that meant in 1911. She tried to contact them—no one knows if she succeeded. Napolitano served eleven years in the Kingston penitentiary, was released on parole, and died of peritonitis ten years later.

Angelina Napolitano's conviction provoked an outcry, but the law did not change. Self-defence in 1911 meant defending yourself against an imminent threat, a threat of immediate and serious physical harm. It was not considered self-defence for a frightened woman to take a weapon to a comatose man. And that's how things stood in 1982 when Jane Hurshman's murder trial started in the tiny, white courthouse in Liverpool, Nova Scotia.

+++

"I really liked Jane. She was always so natural, with a bright shining disposition." Wendy Annand smiles at the memory from the recliner.

"Knowing a bit of...the horrors that she'd been through and seeing what a positive outlook she had on life—it was just a treat." Across the room, Dianne Crowell reaches into the cardboard box that she had hauled out of the storage room. The box is full of newspaper clippings and tapes about Jane Hurshman, letters that she wrote, account books for the Jane Hurshman Memorial Fund, long wound up. Crowell had held on to all of it for thirty years.

Things moved quickly after Billy Stafford's body was discovered, and Jane Hurshman was charged with murder. She needed a lawyer. Because she was facing a serious charge and had no money, Hurshman in Nova Scotia, like Chantale Daigle in Quebec, was eligible for Legal Aid. But Legal Aid offers minimal compensation to lawyers. High-powered, experienced courtroom lawyers generally will not take on Legal Aid clients. Jane Hurshman got lucky. Alan Ferrier was thirty-one, and for one so young, he had handled a remarkable number of serious criminal cases. He knew what he was doing, and more importantly, she trusted him.

Ferrier tried to plea bargain, to convince the Crown to settle for the lesser charge of manslaughter, and in return, she would plead guilty. There was no dispute about who pulled the trigger, and it would eliminate the expense and, for Jane Hurshman, the trauma of a trial. But the Crown was having none of it. The charge was murder, and they weren't budging.

The trial lasted nineteen days, nearly four weeks. Ferrier called forty-six witnesses, witnesses to Stafford's behaviour: the random gunshots, the threats, punches to whoever might be passing by. Witnesses to her bruises and the abuse she suffered and, this was new territory, witnesses who could testify to the impact of five years of assaults, verbal and emotional abuse, and threats to her children. What Alan Ferrier did in defence of Jane Hurshman laid the foundation for an expanded understanding of self-defence.

She was out on bail and wasn't going anywhere; on the contrary, when Jane Hurshman was released from jail, she and two of her boys moved back to the house in Bangs Falls. Bleak and depressing it might be, but it was her home. Cynthia Wine, a nationally known journalist then living in Port Medway, visited her in Bangs Falls. "The house looked like a hillbilly shack from the outside," said Wine, "but inside—it was spotless, meticulously taken care of. That was Jane."

Every day, Jane Hurshman drove down the washed-out road to the little courthouse in Liverpool and listened as the string of witnesses talked about her life and the lives of her children. A child psychiatrist testified, not surprisingly, that Darren, the baby, was an abused child and then spoke about "battered woman's syndrome," a term that had been coined only three years earlier. Another psychiatrist, Dr. Carole Abbot, took it further and testified that "[Jane Hurshman] could never predict when he [Billy Stafford] was going to react.... It's this unpredictability that made it difficult for her to feel that she could do anything to control the situation." A psychologist testified that Stafford's threats to the children meant that she could not escape, "and I don't think she had much doubt that there was a very, very high chance of her husband carrying through his threats. She knew he had the ability to do that and had made the plans to do it."

An awareness of domestic abuse was starting to grow in the country. Awareness. "Understanding" was a step too far. Less than two months after Jane Hurshman shot Billy Stafford, the New Democratic member of Parliament for Vancouver East, Margaret Mitchell, stood up in the House of Commons and told the House that one in ten women were regularly beaten by their husbands. Her fellow MPs guffawed—"I don't beat my wife. Do you George?"—and their laughter echoed round the chamber.

Jane Hurshman, unlike Irene Florence Murdoch or Chantale Daigle or Stella Bliss, had decided that she wanted to talk about what happened to her to try to change awareness to understanding. Unlike most women, she wasn't ashamed of what had happened to her. But first, she had to get through the trial.

+++

Jane Hurshman never tried to avoid responsibility for Billy Stafford's death. The question was whether it was legally justified self-defence. What "imminent threat," the prosecution asked, did Billy Stafford pose while passed out in his truck? And if things were as bad at home as witnesses on her behalf and she had testified, why didn't she leave? That was always the sticking point. Jane Hurshman had known there was a women's shelter in Halifax, two hours away. But, she said, "If I'd have left, there would have been a lot more people killed than Bill." She had to protect her children. "Self-defence" was a legal concept that had been in existence for nearly a thousand years and was part of Canada's first Criminal Code. It had been honed by men thinking in terms that made sense to them, about fights between more or less equally matched combatants. It did not seem to have occurred to jurists that a hundred-pound woman would, first, see threat differently and would, must, defend herself and her children differently. And should have the right to do so.

The little Liverpool courthouse, built before Canada was a country, was packed every day. Everyone knew Jane Hurshman and Billy Stafford; the witnesses were their neighbours. What would they say? Margaret Joudrey, who was "like a mother to Jane," changed her tune. To her it was best not to mess with the established social order.

"She got me mixed up in this and there's no need of it."

Alan Ferrier asked her, "And your idea is that when there's a man, he should be the head of the household?"

And Joudrey answered, "That's right."

The RCMP officers were more sympathetic to Jane Hurshman. "That man had threatened many of our members, and...we went into the house and checked his guns and each of the guns were loaded and hanging on the wall."

"And you weren't really surprised to hear all of the personal abuse that Mrs. Stafford had undergone?" asked Ferrier. "No, not in the least," was the response.

And on it went. After four weeks of testimony, the Crown turned to the jury and summed up, "We may sympathize...no one is questioning that she had one hell of a life with this man. But the law is the law."

The jury, following seven and a half hours of "instruction" from the judge, retired to deliberate. One day passed, then a second, and finally they filed back into the courtroom. They were having none of "the law is the law." When the foreman announced the "Not Guilty" verdict, the packed courtroom rose as one and burst into applause. There was no doubt what the town felt. But this was not a movie. Happy endings are not guaranteed.

Alan Ferrier told Jane Hurshman to enjoy it for the moment. The Crown, he predicted, would appeal. And they did.

"Battered women don't have a license to blow the heads off the men who abuse them just because Jane Stafford got off," Ferrier told the reporters. "You simply won't find many situations in which a jury will say it was okay for a person to kill someone. This was a special case. And I think the verdict does show that our system of punishments isn't flexible enough to take into consideration abuse like this."

+++

The Crown got its pound of flesh but at what cost to our judicial system? ... There are those of us who felt that the jury was the pillar of our judicial system.... We know now that this is not so.... What did the Crown really accomplish through this exercise? Did they prove to the citizens of Queen's County that Ms. Stafford committed a crime against our society? Did they show society that she deserved to be punished?

—*Liverpool Advocate*

A growing number of people in Liverpool and beyond were angry with the Crown for rejecting the people's, the jury's, decision. As in the Quebec *Morgentaler* trials (he was acquitted by a jury three times), even when they seem to fly in the face of logic, jury decisions send a very strong grassroots message.

Nonetheless, the appeal went ahead. In its judgement, the Nova Scotia Court of Appeal said, "In my opinion no person has the right in anticipation of an assault that may or may not happen, to apply force to prevent the imaginary assault. The jury should not have been permitted to consider a possible assault as a justification of her deed." The trial judge, the Court of Appeal was saying, was too liberal in his instructions to the jury. It overturned the acquittal and ordered a new trial. Strangely, it did not seem to bother Jane Hurshman.

Right from the beginning, "She was prepared to go to jail for a couple of years," said Ferrier, "but the Attorney General's office evidently did not want to be seen to be engaging in plea bargaining on a murder trial. They let the jury decide. Now they're not too pleased with what the jury decided."

This time, the Crown was prepared to bargain. The charge was reduced to manslaughter. Jane Hurshman entered a guilty plea and was sentenced to six months in prison. In sentencing her, Justice Nunn of the Nova Scotia Supreme Court said: "There must be deterrence in the law. Wives don't have the right to take the lives of their husbands."

As she waited for the legal process to play out, Jane Hurshman had started to rebuild her life. She had signed up for a nurse's aide course, and while in prison, she was allowed to continue her course in Halifax. Every night, she scrambled to get back across the bridge to Dartmouth in time to meet her curfew. The toll booth attendants watched for her and made sure she got through in time. Everyone liked Jane Hurshman. She was paroled after two months, and on the day she was released, the prison gatekeeper called out to her over the speaker, "Goodbye, Jane. Be happy."

+++

I can say that for the first time that things are looking good. I survived hell and feel that I am a different person.

—Jane Hurshman, 1984

It was what Jane Hurshman did after she was released from prison that ultimately led to change. She talked about what happened to her, about domestic abuse. She was on parole for the next four months, and on probation for two years after that. All of that time, she was under the supervision of Wendy Annand, the woman with the bad back in the recliner in the little house on the way to Lunenburg. "She became more confident although her personality did not change." Annand takes another sip of her tea, pauses a moment, and goes on. "Her ability to analyze was amazing. She picked things up almost by osmosis. She wouldn't sit down and read a feminist tome on wife battering and she wouldn't necessarily label her ideas, but just by being around people who held certain views, they came out that way."

Annand, the probation and parole officer, recognized that she had a rare client in Jane Hurshman. Most of the people she supervised were men. She matched them cuss word for cuss word and kept them on the straight and narrow. Then there was Jane. It was Annand's job to supervise her, assess the appropriateness of what she was up to, and say no to anything that was not contributing to her rehabilitation. Annand had become involved in the justice system through another of those activist-oriented federal government youth programs of the early 70s. Back then, she wanted to change the world. She still did. Wendy Annand was completely behind Hurshman's efforts to put "domestic abuse" on the table, to talk about it publicly. Nobody realized in the 1980s that "talking about it" might not be a good thing for the woman; no one knew what the long-term effects of relentless abuse could be, how it could continue to eat at a person, or how to effectively "treat" this kind of post-traumatic stress. PTSD had only become a psychiatric diagnosis in 1980.

Early on, Annand organized a gathering of judges, lawyers, and police officers in Lunenburg. "I asked her [Jane] to come and do a presentation—she loved it." It was the first time that Jane Hurshman had ever spoken in public about anything let alone about what she had gone through, and for the majority of these officers of the law and the court, it was the first time they had met a woman who could talk about domestic abuse from her own experience and with intelligence. "No one has the right to take another's life but I'm never sorry that Billy is dead," she told them.

She spent time with women at Bryony House, the women's shelter in Dartmouth. She got a job as a nurse's aide, got her kids back, and started therapy. She wanted to talk to people, most of all to convince other women that there was a way out. That was the hard part. When she was asked "Do you get used to speaking in public?" she answered, "Every time I do [it], it brings back all the bad memories. You do it because you want to make a change—to stop the violence."

Jane Hurshman publicized domestic abuse and increased awareness like no one else could have. There was a strange moment when she appeared on CBC's *The Fifth Estate*. The sound technician clipped the microphone to her shirt and did a sound check. He came back shaking his head. "There's this loud thumping sound," he said. And he checked the microphone. There was no problem with the equipment; it was her heart, beating faster and louder, overwhelming her efforts to keep everything under control. Jane Hurshman spoke well, and she spoke often. Too often. Those who knew her talked about a glazed look that came over her during those speeches. But no one knew enough to recognize what it was doing to her.

There was physical pain as well as emotional, a knot in her chest. She was unable to sleep or eat. "I feel guilty," she told Brian Vallée. "I was still frightened and scared. I kept going, fighting to hold on to the rational me, trying to let everything sink in. Bill was really dead. Maybe now there would be peace. It wasn't over—it's still not over. It keeps coming back at me."

In 1985, she was about to address a women's conference in Lunenburg when she was approached by Harry How, then chief judge of the Provincial Court of Nova Scotia. How had been attorney general when Jane Hurshman was on trial. According to Vallée,

> He apologized for granting an appeal in her case, but said he had no choice. How explained that she did not kill in response to "sudden provocation," since Stafford was asleep, and the law did not recognize "slow burn" or cumulative provocation; he also said that self-defence covered only an immediate confrontation. Then, How said, "Now Jane—off the record—I want to say, that cocksucker should have been shot a long time ago."

Should she feel guilty for not having acted sooner?

Law professor Elizabeth Sheehy, in her book *Defending Battered Women on Trial,* points out that Jane Hurshman was criticized by the court for choosing the wrong solution to her domestic "problem."

Why hadn't she left, gone to a shelter? Gone to the police? But as Sheehy writes,

> Attorney General How, arguably one of the most powerful men in the province, claimed that he had no choice.... The state justified its response by reference to "the law" and its principles when a jury of her peers understood all too clearly that "the law" had nothing to offer Hurshman.

Sheehy puts the case of Jane Hurshman as "before the beginning." Then came Angelique Lyn Lavallee.

+++

The gravity, indeed, the tragedy of domestic violence can hardly be overstated.... Far from protecting women from it, the law historically sanctioned the abuse of women within marriage as an aspect of the husband's ownership of his wife and his "right" to chastise her.

—Madame Justice Bertha Wilson

R v Lavallee was the case where the courts recognized that what was then called "battered wife syndrome"—the cumulative effect of sustained abuse, of what amounts to captivity and PTSD—changed the definition of "self-defence."

In Nova Scotia in the summer of 1986, Jane Hurshman was out of prison, putting her life in order, and talking to other women who had been through something like she had. Several thousand kilometres away in Winnipeg, at the end of that summer, there was a party, a loud, boozy party at the house where twenty-two-year-old Lyn Lavallee lived with Kevin "Rooster" Rust. Things got out of hand as they often did. Kevin was drunk, mad at Lavallee, and going after her. This is how she described what happened in the statement she gave to the Winnipeg police later that night:

> I went upstairs and hid in my closet from Kevin. I was so scared.... My window was open and I could hear Kevin asking questions about what I was doing and what I was saying. Next thing I know he was coming up the stairs for me. He came into my bedroom and said "Wench, where are you?" and he turned on my light and he said, "Your purse is on the floor" and he kicked it. OK then he turned, and he saw me in the closet. He wanted me to come out but I didn't want to come out because I was scared. I was so scared.

According to the police statement, she started to cry, stopped after a minute or two, and went on,

> [Kevin] grabbed me by the arm right there. There's a bruise on my face also where he slapped me...he yelled at me, then he pushed me and I pushed him back and he hit me twice on the right hand side of my head. I was scared. All I thought about was all the other times he used to beat me, I was scared, I was shaking as usual. The rest is a blank.
>
> All I remember is he gave me the gun and a shot was fired through my screen.... And I was going to shoot myself. I pointed it to myself, I was so upset...and I was sitting on the bed and he started going like this with his finger.

The police statement indicated that she made "a shaking motion with an index finger,"

> [He] said something like "You're my old lady and you do as you're told...wait till everybody leaves, you'll get it then.... Either kill me or I'll get you...." He kind of smiled and then he turned around. I shot him but I aimed out. I thought I aimed above him and a piece of his head went that way.

She shot and killed Kevin Rust. Lyn Lavallee, like Jane Hurshman, was charged with murder. Rust was not "passed out" or "asleep" but he was walking away from her. There was no "imminent threat" but as with Hurshman and Stafford, there was a history.

The two cases, *Hurshman* and *Lavallee*, trod a similar judicial path.

At trial, the jury in Liverpool found Jane Hurshman not guilty on the grounds of self-defence; the jury in Winnipeg found Lyn Lavallee not guilty; but the appeal courts in both provinces said no, this was not self-defence as we know it and sent the cases back for retrial. Lavallee's lawyer, Greg Brodsky, was ready to argue that it was time to think of self-defence differently, as had Alan Ferrier at trial. Brodsky took it up a notch and obtained leave to appeal to the Supreme Court of Canada where *R v Lavallee* was heard in 1990. Jane Hurshman had been tried for the murder of Billy Stafford in 1982; eight years had passed. Attitudes were shifting.

By 1990, Bertha Wilson was well-ensconced and well-respected by her fellow judges. By then she was not the only woman on the court—Claire L'Heureux-Dubé had joined her. That same year, Wilson had been asked to talk to lawyers and students at York University. She asked a question many had been contemplating: "Will Women Judges Really Make a Difference?" She told her audience that when she was appointed to the Supreme Court, she received many congratulatory letters saying, "this will be the beginning of a new era for women. So why was I not rejoicing?" she asked herself.

> I had the sense of being doomed to failure, not because of any excess of humility on my part or any desire to shirk the responsibility of the office, but because I knew from hard experience that the law does not work that way. Change in the law comes slowly and incrementally; that is its nature. It responds to changes in society; it seldom initiates them. And while I was prepared—and, indeed, as a woman judge, anxious—to respond to these changes, I wondered to what extent I would be constrained in my attempts to do so by the nature of judicial office itself.

She told her audience that, realistically, there could never be such a thing as complete judicial neutrality and she cited several American studies:

> These studies confirm that male judges tend to adhere to traditional values and beliefs about the natures of men and women and their proper roles in society. The studies show overwhelming evidence that gender-based myths, biases, and stereotypes are deeply embedded in the attitudes of many male judges, as well as in the law itself.

And given that "the judiciary has been very substantially male," some areas of law reflected a "distinctly male perspective." Wilson continued, "some aspects of the criminal law…cry out for change and in this day and age, are nothing short of ludicrous." It was a steel fist in a velvet glove, strong stuff from a sitting Supreme Court judge.

Bertha Wilson was on the bench for *R v Lavallee*. "[I] thought to myself," she said, "now here was a chance to give some leadership to what I said in my speech." The court accepted Brodsky's argument that, in a case like *Lavallee*, self-defence should be thought of differently, and it was Wilson who wrote the judgement of the court. Later, she said, "the biggest mystery of all my judgements was how [*Lavallee*] ended up as a unanimous judgement when they all thought I was mad to think there was anything that could even be said."

She knew that redefining self-defence in a case like *Lavallee*, where the issue was ongoing domestic abuse, was going to be difficult for not only her fellow judges but also everyday citizens to accept.

> The average member of the public (or of the jury) can be forgiven for asking: Why would a woman put up with this kind of treatment? Why should she continue to live with such a man? How could she love a partner who beat her to the point of requiring hospitalization? We would expect the woman to pack her bags and go. Where is her self-respect? Why does she not cut loose

> and make a new life for herself? Such is the reaction of the average person confronted with the so-called "battered wife syndrome." We need help to understand it and help is available from trained professionals.

Bertha Wilson cautioned that most people—lawyers and judges in particular—think they understand human nature. Not so. The Supreme Court found that expert evidence, the evidence of psychiatrists and psychologists, is essential in understanding what was going on in the mind of a Lyn Lavallee or a Jane Hurshman. Wilson wrote, "expert testimony may also assist the jury in assessing the reasonableness of her belief that killing her batterer was the only way to

Bertha Wilson, Supreme Court of Canada judge from 1982–1991.

save her own life." How else was it possible, she asked, "for the jury to pass judgement on the fact that a battered woman stayed in the relationship. Still less is it entitled to conclude that she forfeited her right to self-defence for having done so."

It was only in the previous few years that domestic abuse had even begun to be talked about. Was Bertha Wilson thinking about Jane Hurshman's appearance on *The Fifth Estate*? Or Margaret Mitchell's statement in the House of Commons and how she was mocked? Perhaps.

Madame Justice Wilson not only accepted expert evidence on battered wife syndrome, and reinstated Angelique Lyn Lavallee's acquittal, she also referred to a 1977 American case, *State v Wanrow*, the first American case that accepted a broader definition of self-defence. Wilson quoted Washington State Supreme Court Justice Utter who, in *Wanrow*, referred to America's "long and unfortunate history of sex discrimination." And went on,

> Until such time as the effects of that history are eradicated, care must be taken to assure that our self-defence instructions afford women the right to have their conduct judged in light of the individual physical handicaps which are the product of sex discrimination.

Gone was the requirement that the threat must be "imminent," there need not be, she wrote, a "clenched fist" or "an uplifted knife."

More than once, Bertha Wilson referred specifically to Jane Hurshman and *R v Whynot* as it was referred to in court records (Jane Hurshman still legally bore the name of her first husband, Milford Whynot). She swatted away the judgement of the Nova Scotia Court of Appeal, particularly its requirement that a battered woman must wait until the physical assault is "underway" before she decides what to do. That would, said Madame Justice Bertha Wilson, "in the words of an American court, be tantamount to sentencing her to 'murder by installment.'"

Angelique Lyn Lavallee was acquitted, and, as a by-product of that judgement, Jane Hurshman was all but exonerated.

+++

Dianne Crowell leafs through the box of memorabilia beside her chair. "Jane kept working," Crowell says, "and she looked after the boys and she didn't stop talking about abuse." Crowell finds a photograph in the box. It's a picture of Jane Hurshman and her final partner on their wedding day. Wendy Annand chimes in from across the room, "Jane always wanted a man in her life." Her final man was Joel Corkum, a mechanic eight years her junior. They met in 1990, were engaged a few months later, and within a year, they were married. It was her fairy tale wedding. This time she got married in a "proper" church—the Lutheran church, the middle of the three churches reflected in the waters of Mahone Bay on every postcard of the town. There she was in another blue wedding dress, smiling as she went down the aisle quietly cheered on by Wendy Annand and all her friends. She looked happy.

The next time those wedding guests gathered in that church would be for Jane Hurshman's funeral. She began to receive death threats in the late 80s when Brian Vallée's book *Life with Billy* came out. The threats were taken seriously, and for a few weeks, she was under twenty-four-hour RCMP protection. No individual was ever identified. Many people, women as well as men, did not want to hear what she had to say, including Margaret Joudrey, the neighbour whom Billy Stafford threatened to burn out. Joudrey went after Jane Hurshman and her public appearances.

> She'd go in front of all them women...and oh my God. I seen her on TV, and she'd tell them women about abuse and all this shit, and it's hard to tell what kind of hell she made for them and their husbands by telling the kind of stuff that she was telling them. It would just cause them more trouble at home.

Wendy Annand and a group of Queens and Lunenburg County women, with the support of Hurshman, set up a transition house for women in the summer of 1985. They asked Queens County council for $6,300. Council turned them down. One councillor, according to the

Jane Hurshman with Joel Corkum in 1991.

Queens County Advance, was of the view that a shelter "entices women to leave their home and family." Too many women leave their husbands for no reason, he said. They "simply need their backsides kicked."

Jane Hurshman, Joel Corkum, now her husband, and two of the boys moved to Halifax. Jane kept working the night shift at the nearby rehabilitation centre, counselling other women, making submissions, and testifying before domestic abuse inquiries. A lot of people were counting on her. Too many. She was told by her friends to slow down, back off.

Then there was the shoplifting. The arrests had begun when she was living with Billy Stafford. She tried various forms of treatment for kleptomania—medicines, psychotherapy, and hypnosis, but she could not get it under control. Initially, she talked about that too. "When I mess up—as in shoplifting," she wrote to a Halifax newspaper, "it is because I cannot believe that I deserve to be happy, or that I am worthy of good things or good people around me." But as time went on, she became increasingly embarrassed and ashamed, and began to hide the problem from her family. A hearing for a fifth shoplifting charge was coming up in March of 1992. This time, she knew she could be looking at more than a suspended sentence. Once again, she was failing to manage her life.

The threats had not gone away. There were phone calls and letters telling her if she didn't stop talking about the abuse of women, she would be stopped. Dianne Crowell hands over a letter from that box of memorabilia. At the beginning of February, in her very neat schoolgirl handwriting, Jane Hurshman had written to a friend:

> Since the beginning of the new year I have been receiving some threatening phone calls and notes and we have reported it to the RCMP—all to no avail and I talked to the RCMP about it today in hopes that that we can find out something. It gets creepy thinking it is someone out there and I don't know who it is or why he wants to hurt me. Life continues on anyway!

She made light of it all, but her life was unravelling. This time, there were no black eyes and bruises. The injuries were psychological and, it turned out, insurmountable. Early in the morning of February 23, 1992, a couple was walking along the Halifax waterfront. They came across a deserted blue Ford. Looking closer, the man saw a woman in the front seat. There was a gunshot wound to her chest. Jane Hurshman was dead.

There was evidence that she had bought a gun, contacted someone she knew, and tried to make the death look like murder. She had taken out a life insurance policy, wanting to leave something for her boys. The suicide finding nullified the insurance and her children got next to nothing. No one wanted to believe that Jane Hurshman had given up, that she couldn't hold it all together anymore. She was the symbol of hope, proof that things could work out. But they hadn't.

Her friends gathered again at the Lutheran church in Mahone Bay for Jane Hurshman's funeral. They were overwhelmed. Numb.

Wendy Annand shakes her head. "I cannot remember a thing about that day," and there is silence in the little living room.

"One way or another," she says eventually, "what happened with Billy killed her."

+++

NOVA SCOTIA REDUX

Over time she lost contact with the reality of how destructive the relationship had become.

—Report of Nova Scotia Mass Casualty Commission

Nearly forty years later, Nova Scotia had a much bigger public tragedy to deal with. The Nova Scotia weather forecast for the weekend of April 18, 2020, was not good; heavy snow, high winds. Nova Scotia had been through late winter storms before. People could have dealt with that.

What they woke up to on Monday morning was far worse than any storm. A Nova Scotia man, a prosperous professional from Portapique on the north side of the Minas Basin, had set fire to a dozen buildings and shot and killed twenty-two people. It was the worst mass shooting in Canadian history.

In the aftermath of the shootings, the blame was focused on the RCMP and what was seen as their deadly bungling of Gabriel Wortman's rampage. No one paid much attention to how and why it all began. Then came the seven-volume, three-thousand-page report of the Mass Casualty Commission released at the end of March 2023. The worst mass shooting in Canadian history, the Commission concluded, had its roots in domestic and child abuse. The events of that weekend started with Wortman's attack on the woman he lived with, Lisa Banfield. That Saturday night, Wortman soaked the floor with gasoline, then he dragged Lisa Banfield by the hair through the house—she kept slipping because the floor was so wet. He slammed her down on the ground, fracturing a rib and several vertebrae. Then he handcuffed her and fired his gun on either side of her, dragged her to his replica RCMP cruiser, and locked her in the back seat. When he went back to the house, she stripped the skin from her hand pulling off the handcuffs. Despite the fractured ribs and broken back, she managed to dive through a gap in the plexiglass barrier separating the back from the front seat of the car, got out, and ran. Lisa Banfield cowered in the woods all night, watching buildings go up in flames, listening to the gunshots.

In her initial interviews with the police, Banfield reportedly said she felt guilty for running away. As her lawyer, James Lockyer, said at a later press conference, "I know she says to herself, 'if I hadn't run and got away, would I have saved twenty-two lives?' And of course she says that to herself, and always will. The probable answer is that it would have been twenty-three lives and not twenty-two, but she's never going to believe that."

The Mass Casualty Commission report reads: "Self-blame by the long-time partners of abusers is not uncommon...we believe it is important to recognize that she is a survivor of the mass casualty, and she has also been failed by many people and institutions in its aftermath."

Like Jane Hurshman, Banfield was frightened and afraid to leave her partner. Wortman threatened to kill her family as Billy Stafford had threatened to kill Jane Hurshman's children. Hurshman received death threats for speaking out; Lisa Banfield was subject to the wrath of the families of some of the victims because she had not stopped Wortman.

The women who run Nova Scotia women's shelters and sexual assault centres testified before the inquiry: "She's not responsible for the actions of her abusive partner," said Kaitlin Geiger-Bardswich of Women's Shelters Canada.

"She's not an extension of him, but because she survived, she has been scapegoated by a lot of different people," Geiger-Bardswich went on, "for reasons that people don't understand, [they are] asking, just as they had asked Jane Hurshman, 'Why didn't she leave?' 'Why didn't she call the police?'"

The RCMP charged Lisa Banfield and two members of her family with supplying Wortman with ammunition. Erin Breen, the lawyer representing three sexual assault and justice centres and

LEAF, was furious, saying that Banfield had been charged for what was "survival behaviour." Just as Jane Hurshman's murder charge had been the result of "survival behaviour" in 1982. "The real concern is that it would have a chilling effect on other survivors from going to police," Breen told *Chatelaine* magazine. "If people are afraid to come forward with their stories because they're afraid they're going to get charged, it's a reason why they continue to keep the violence private." The charges against Banfield were eventually withdrawn.

Self-defence had been redefined by the Supreme Court of Canada in the Hurshman era with the case of Lyn Lavallee, but this new understanding of self-defence has not been embraced by the courts. An Alberta woman, Helen Naslund, killed her husband, a man who had been beating her and waving a loaded gun at her and her son for nearly thirty years. In 2020, twenty-seven years after the Supreme Court's findings in *Lavallee,* Naslund was found guilty of manslaughter and sentenced to eighteen years, one of the longest manslaughter sentences ever handed down. During Naslund's trial, her lawyer had not mentioned the abuse, had not raised self-defence. The judge called Helen Naslund's attack on her husband "a callous, cowardly act on a vulnerable victim in his own home." Petitions with 18,000 signatures led to a review of her case by the Alberta Court of Appeal, which cut her sentence in half.

The language and understanding of domestic assault have changed and expanded to include what is labelled "coercive control"—isolation, surveillance, financial control—the manipulative behaviour that makes it psychologically impossible for women to leave. In October 2023, Quebec Superior Court Judge Marie-France Vincent, added "judicial violence" to the list. In Montreal, a wife petitioned to divorce her husband, a law professor. That divorce case, said Vincent, took "an unimaginable turn due to the behaviour of the defendant." *La Presse* reported the "judicial violence" described by the judge included more than forty-five hours in court, "dozens and dozens of orders," an attempt to have the wife's lawyer declared incompetent, a civil action against her and her lawyer (for $273,000), six appearances before the Court of Appeal, more than one thousand emails from the husband to the wife's lawyer, and two requests for recusal of the judge assigned to the case. In 2015, an Ottawa Valley inquest into the killings of three women, former partners of the man who murdered them, recommended that coercive control be added to the Criminal Code. The federal justice minister said he would consider it. The UK introduced legislation on coercive control in 2015 with disappointing results. It is difficult to prove.

Of the 130 recommendations contained in the Nova Scotia Mass Casualty Commission report, 75 were about policing. The report also talked about an "epidemic" of domestic violence and the red flags in Wortman's relationship with women that were ignored. The majority of the recommendations around domestic abuse centred on prevention and protection.

There was one "legal" recommendation. If prevention and social programs don't work, if there is violence, then, the report said, the law must protect women. If women in situations, like Jane Hurshman and Lyn Lavallee and Helen Naslund, attack their husbands, then the Mass Casualty inquiry recommended that, "The federal government amend the Criminal Code to recognize that reasonable resistance violence by the victim of a pattern of coercive and controlling behaviour is self-defence."

9. No Dark Spots

[She is] not a woman who happens to be [B]lack or a [B]lack person who happens to be female but a [B]lack woman.

—Mary Ross Hendriks

Viola Desmond is a Canadian icon. There she is, demure and sad, her makeup and her hair perfect, looking at you from the face side of a Canadian ten-dollar bill. There are Viola Desmond murals in Halifax, at high schools in the Toronto suburbs, a street named Viola Desmond Way in Montreal, a musical written about her in Richmond, BC, and more art hanging on the outside wall of what used to be the Roseland movie theatre (now a law firm) in New Glasgow, Nova Scotia.

Desmond is the Black Nova Scotian woman who, in 1946, refused to move from the downstairs whites-only section of the Roseland Theatre. It was a prime example of Canada's "unofficial" racism; Nova Scotia did not make racial segregation in a public facility "illegal" until 1959. The theatre owner, a three-term mayor, had his own segregation policy; many businesses did. Everyone in New Glasgow understood that white people sat downstairs, Black people sat upstairs, but Viola Desmond was just passing through town; what did she know? The ticket seller told her, "I'm not permitted to sell downstairs tickets to *you* people," and that did it. When she wouldn't sit upstairs, Desmond was removed, bodily, from the movie theatre. She spent the night in jail and was fined for non-payment of Nova Scotia's entertainment tax. She owed one cent.

The case of Viola Desmond was all but unknown for more than half a century until, in 2003, her seventy-three-year-old sister, Wanda Robson, began telling the story. First Nova Scotia, then the country tried to make amends. In 2010, Viola Desmond was pardoned for her offence and a chair in social justice was set up in her name at Cape Breton University. A Viola Desmond stamp was issued in 2012 and a Heritage Minute created for television. Six years later, Desmond became the first woman to be featured on a Canadian banknote and, in the same year, was designated a National Historic Person. The nation was embarrassed, we had betrayed our image. We were supposed to be the good guys.

Of course, we weren't. Witness: historic and ongoing discrimination—social, cultural, legal—against Indigenous people; the internment of Canadians of Japanese descent during World War II; the head tax on Chinese immigrants; the 1914 *Komagata Maru* incident when Canada wouldn't let 352 hopeful immigrants from India off the boat in Vancouver; or when more than 900 Jewish refugees were denied entry in 1939. The list goes on.

The story of Viola Desmond has little, if anything, to do with women's rights in Canada. But Desmond was a good candidate for icon-hood when it came to racial discrimination. She was a well-turned-out, well-mannered Black woman, owner of the Desmond School of Beauty Culture in Halifax. And she was no activist. She fought back and tried to have her penny-conviction set aside, but she wasn't one to shout, make speeches, or go on civil rights marches. Her sister, years later, said that to distract herself during her night in jail, she did not brood or scheme, rather she sat up straight and organized her purse.

Nor was she the first Black woman to be kicked out of a Canadian movie theatre. Carrie Best, who came from New Glasgow, was a constant activist, campaigning for civil rights for decades. Best and her son were removed from the whites-only section of the Roseland five years before Viola Desmond. She sued the theatre and lost. A 1939 Supreme Court of Canada case, the Fred Christie case out of Montreal, ruled that a business owner could serve or exclude who they wanted on the grounds of freedom of commerce.

Earlier still, in 1922, Lulu Anderson was barred from the Metropolitan Theatre in Edmonton. She also sued, and the *Edmonton Journal* reported that racialized people's "rights under the British flag were being tested." Tested and defeated. Not much more is known about the Lulu Anderson case, the government of Alberta destroyed all case files from 1921 to 1949. More than a decade earlier, the *Edmonton Evening Journal* published an interview with C.E. Simmonds, a Conservative politician from Lethbridge. The headline read, "We Want No Dark Spots in Alberta," and it fed a campaign to keep Black immigrants out of Alberta.

Viola Desmond, Carrie Best, and Lulu Anderson were educated, middle-class Black women who were prepared to go to court to argue for the same rights as white men and women. They got nowhere. The law surrounding racial discrimination did not effectively change until the dawn of the human rights era.

Movie theatres were tough territory for Black women and men in Alberta and Nova Scotia. It was the same in the most southerly slice of Ontario. Ten years into the twenty-first century, Harrow (near Windsor) was a hamlet of less than three thousand people, the

Canada's last segregated school, S.S. #11 near Harrow, Ontario, 1965.

majority of them white—the official count puts the Black population at seventy. Back in the days of the Underground Railroad, the mid-1800s, enough Black people had arrived and stayed in Harrow that there were segregated movie theatres and restaurants and schools. And they stayed segregated. Harrow's Blacks-only school, the last in Canada, didn't close until 1965. Racheal Baylis, a young Black woman when her story unfolded, came from Harrow. She was born in 1975. Segregated schools, movie houses, restaurants, and the attitudes that went with them were very much part of her family's past and, it turned out, her future.

\+ + +

My name is Racheal Dawn Baylis-Flannery, I am a 24-year-old recently married secretary, for a Physiotherapy office in Amherstburg, Ontario. I am writing because I am in a situation in which I don't know what to do.

—Racheal Baylis to the Ontario College of Physiotherapists

Racheal Baylis-Flannery, as she was in 2000, was at the end of her rope. She was working as the receptionist for a physiotherapist named Walter DeWilde who would not leave her alone, and she had no idea where to turn. Racheal Baylis was another everyday young woman who wound up in an unfathomable mess not of her own making. She described herself as Black and Métis, although, her mother says, "She hated racial labels." Her mother, Janet Crosby, is a Pentecostal minister, and Racheal grew up in a religious household. By all accounts, she was a quiet and reserved young woman. In a family photograph, she looks up shyly at the camera with a gentle half-smile.

Reserved but also principled and determined. "A thoroughly decent young woman," Raj Dhir, the lawyer who argued her case for the Ontario Human Rights Commission, called her. In 2003, the Commission dealt with more than 2,400 complaints. The case of *Baylis-Flannery v DeWilde* was one of the most consequential. Her complaints against Walter DeWilde included sexual and racial harassment. What was new was recognition that those complaints could and in this instance, did, intertwine to create a new and distinct form of discrimination. The *Baylis-Flannery* case was about "intersectionality," a term coined by Black American law professor Kimberlé Crenshaw in the late 80s. It was a term that Racheal Baylis in all likelihood barely knew or cared about, but one that was beginning to make inroads among Black feminists and human rights advocates of colour in Canada and slowly, very slowly, in the Canadian legal system. Intersectionality has since grown to include not only race and gender but race and gender is what *Baylis-Flannery v DeWilde* was all about. The Ontario Human Rights Tribunal adjudicator who heard the case, Mary Ross Hendriks, put it plainly: "the law must acknowledge that she is not a woman who happens to be [B]lack or a [B]lack person who happens to be female but a [B]lack woman."

+++

In the fall of 1999, life was looking good for Racheal Baylis. Full of change. She was twenty-four and about to get married, that was exciting enough, and then there was the possibility of this new job. Not just a job but something that could be the beginning of a career. She had been working for Walmart for $9 an hour since she graduated from high school, and she wanted more. Working for a physiotherapist meant learning how to update patients' charts, how to file workers' compensation and insurance claims, learning medical terms. It also meant a new wardrobe—a new look. True, it paid less, only $8 an hour, but there was a promise of a raise to $12 within sixty days. Her cousin Stephanie Vasildimitrakis had the job for the past two years and was leaving. She told her cousin that, from time to time, Walter DeWilde "gets on my nerves" and "irritates" her. Racheal Baylis figured she could deal with that.

There might have been a moment of apprehension, a fear that she wouldn't get the job because she was Black, and this was a semi-professional job working for a white man. Would he automatically rule her out? It must have occurred to her. This was 1999, the Civil Rights

Racheal Baylis

Movement had been on fire in the US for decades. Martin Luther King had given his first "I have a dream" speech across the border in Detroit before she was born. In Canada, things were different. It would be another four years before Wanda Robson began to champion the story of her sister Viola Desmond. "But Racheal," says her mother, Janet Crosby, "was political, aware of civil rights." She may have said to herself, "My cousin Stephanie is a young Black woman, kind of pretty like me, and DeWilde didn't seem to have a problem with her. And besides, I have rights." She handed cousin Stephanie her résumé and asked her to pass it on and put in a good word with Mr. DeWilde. Getting married, maybe a new job. Happy days.

There were a good number of applicants and, she found out later, several with better qualifications, but something swung things her way. She got the job and started at the end of October 1999. Her wedding was only ten days later. Racheal Baylis-Flannery floated along in a dream for another two or three weeks. It didn't take any longer before she realized that Walter DeWilde not only didn't have a problem in hiring young Black women, but he relished having them close to him. He had a salacious appetite for young Black women, for touching, for fantasizing, for humiliating.

"I am European," he kept telling her with a dismissive shrug. DeWilde was married with grown-up children, a man in his sixties. He had been brought up in Africa in the 1940s and then educated in Ghent, Belgium. He came from a different time and place. As Racheal Baylis sat at her desk, he would come by and touch her hands, her arms—letting his hands linger a little too long. She flashed her shiny new wedding ring and reminded him that she was married. He asked her what her sex life was like. Then, she testified, he would rub her upper legs, her shoulders. When she told him he was "too touchy," he laughed it off and told her again, "I'm European and we're touchy people."

He said to her how much he "liked being with young [B]lack girls." He liked "your big butts," "your lips," and "the way you're shaped. You move differently." He left books about Africa on her desk with the pages open to photographs of naked Black women and would point to their breasts saying, "look how they're hanging."

Then he asked her out to dinner in Detroit and told her how much he liked a particular Detroit strip club and a dancer named Malina and he would imitate the way Malina danced. It embarrassed her. Malina was her cousin Stephanie's sister-in-law, which made it worse. One day, DeWilde traced the neckline of Racheal's V-neck blouse with his finger. He showed her pornographic magazines. Another day he grabbed her face and tried to kiss her, and then as she was sitting in her chair, he straddled her. She stood up, crying. He began humming and walked back to his office.

By the time the Christmas party came around, she begged people to come. "I didn't want to be there with him by myself." She couldn't sleep and began having severe stomach pains. By this time, Racheal Baylis told the Human Rights Tribunal, "I hated my job with a passion." The stomach pains escalated to vomiting and she was seeing her doctor regularly. Then DeWilde began coming round to her house at night when her husband was out. She would turn out the lights. Racheal Baylis did not know what to do; quitting her job wasn't an option, and like most people, she didn't have a clue how the justice system worked, where to go, who to talk to. She only knew that she needed advice.

She called the Sexual Assault Trauma Centre, then a lawyer she found in the phone book, and friends and relatives for advice. It was a big family, and she had a brother-in-law who was a police officer. He told her to document what she could, to try to tape conversations, to call the Ontario Human Rights Commission and he threw in some practical, if inappropriate advice—to slap DeWilde next time he came too close. She, wisely, did not slap him but she did call the Human Rights Commission.

+++

It's February now and every morning I leave the house to go to work 10 minutes early. I sit in the car for 5 minutes and pray that God give me the strength to make it through the day. It feels like I'm on edge of going insane, I don't talk to my husband about this no longer because I fear what he may do.... I plead to you to understand how I'm feeling, I don't want to start trouble with him, I fear that if I do, he'll push me even harder. I would quit this job but me and my husband are hardly making it now. I beg of you to advise me on what to do.

—Racheal Baylis-Flannery to the College of Physiotherapists of Ontario

1999 turned into 2000, and nothing changed. Racheal Baylis poured her heart out in that long letter to the College of Physiotherapists of Ontario, the body that regulated professional conduct. The College, when it replied more than a month later, merely advised her of the necessary steps to make a formal complaint. It did reprimand DeWilde for drinking on the job.

Racheal Baylis-Flannery told the Tribunal that her depression became "overwhelming." Yet rather than capitulate, she stood up to DeWilde. More than twenty years later, her mother, Janet Crosby laughs softly over the phone, sighs a little, and says, "Yes, yes. That's my girl. It was in her nature to say what she felt. She was always like that—never backed down." And Racheal told DeWilde, "some of the things you do around the office really need to stop." He needed to cease his "touching, and don't disrespect my personal space." He answered, "Why do you people get like that?"

She changed the way she dressed. A couple of years earlier, halfway across the country, Edmonton Jane Doe was told by the court that she was sending a "yes message" to a man accused of sexual assault when she wore shorts to a job interview. Now, Racheal Baylis-Flannery tried to send a "no message." She wore bulky sweaters, nothing shape-revealing, and no makeup. She pulled her hair back and stopped wearing nail polish. "I didn't want him to look at me," she testified. That didn't work either. In March, after talking to relatives and friends one more time, she sat down, took out a pen, and wrote Walter DeWilde a letter: "I have told you time and time again to refrain from touching me in any...indecent or disrespectful way. You have crossed a line by your actions." And she itemized her objections: the touching, talking about his own sex life, asking about hers, visiting her at home, and finished by saying, "You need to understand you make my workplace stressful and very emotional.... So I am talking to you. If you ever make me feel uncomfortable or if you come to me in any disrespectful way, I will take legal action."

Two weeks later, on March 17, 2000, Walter DeWilde fired her.

Before the day was out, she had gone to the police station and told them all about Walter DeWilde. He was charged with sexual assault. But unbeknownst to her, the Crown agreed to a plea bargain and DeWilde entered a guilty plea to common assault. A conviction for sexual assault would have placed him on the National Sex Offender Registry for at least ten years and in all likelihood, cost him his job. Instead, he was sentenced to twelve months' probation.

In the meantime, the complaints Racheal Baylis-Flannery had filed with the Ontario Human Rights Commission were making their way through the system.

⁂

I remember the way that she tried to talk to him, to deal with everything. She did everything right.

—Raj Dhir, Counsel for the Ontario Human Rights Commission

When Raj Dhir met Racheal Baylis in 2003 she had no job, any thought of a "career" had disappeared, and she was scrambling for money.

After DeWilde fired her, she did find a job at another clinic but she kept running into people she had known at DeWilde's. She quit. The couple still needed her income, so reluctantly, she moved on to factory work. The factory closed and by then, she was seven months pregnant. When her baby was a few weeks old, she got a job at a Becker's convenience store. "The first time I met her she had her baby, her daughter with her," remembers Dhir. Her time with DeWilde and the uncertain employment had also put pressure on the marriage. "When I met her for the hearing," Dhir went on, "she was in the process of separating."

However, he said, her good nature shone through and she had an almost innocent belief that the Human Rights Commission and her Christian faith could, and would, make things right. "That was

Raj Dhir

the feeling I got when I met her, she was good natured and a spiritual person. I wanted to succeed for her, to help her. I wanted that innocence to come out."

The complaints that Racheal Baylis had made to the Commission had been investigated and come to the top of the pile ready to be adjudicated by the Tribunal. Raj Dhir was not only struck by Racheal Baylis's fundamental decency, but he also saw in this case an opportunity to push the law in a new direction that would recognize the combination of both sexual and racial discrimination, this new concept of intersectionality. (Dhir went on in his career with the Ontario Human Rights Commission to lead the inquiry into anti-Black racism by the Toronto Police Service.) But it was one thing for an American law professor to introduce intersectionality into academic discussion, quite another for Canadian courts to figure out what to do with it.

The Supreme Court of Canada had touched on intersectionality, not always by name, in several cases in the 90s and, for the most part, had made little of it. Other human rights tribunals had begun to consider it. It was a burgeoning concept, and the Ontario Human Rights Commission had published a discussion paper, "An Intersectional Approach to Discrimination," two years before Dhir met Racheal Baylis. "[That paper] is what triggered me to make the connection between this theoretical policy...and what was in front of me, what was happening to Racheal Baylis. This was a possibility to expand the law."

Dhir amended the complaints the Commission had filed on behalf of Baylis. Nearly half the complaints received by the Commission in that period included two or more grounds of discrimination. Yet, more often than not, only one was pursued. It was simply easier that way. Dhir went in and asked for permission to change Baylis's complaints to both racial and sexual harassment and discrimination, to combine the two. It was recognition that two grounds of prohibited discrimination could affect one person. To Dhir, it was important to see Racheal Baylis as she was—a Black woman—not to only tick one box. She had, it was now alleged, been both sexually and racially discriminated against. Dhir had laid the groundwork. Racheal Baylis understood, he remembers, that her case could be precedent-setting.

Before things moved to a hearing, in an effort to avoid confrontation and to come to an amicable agreement, there was mediation. In 2000, 40% of Tribunal cases were settled through mediation. It was a warm day in May. Everyone was assembled around a table—the closest DeWilde and Racheal Baylis had been to each other in four years—to try to work things through. She was, Dhir remembers, nervous, but the balding DeWilde somehow did not seem to understand what all the fuss was about. He had laughed things off when Baylis complained about his behaviour in the office. Now he had a lawyer, Ken Marley, to explain things, but as Dhir remembers, "We were not able to resolve things in part because I don't think he understood what was being alleged." It was as if he was still thinking, "So what? I'm European. We're touchy people."

\+\+\+

Over the summer of 2003, Walter DeWilde must had begun to understand what he was facing—which is not to say he understood that he might have done anything wrong.

He was on probation for assault, and the college was monitoring him. DeWilde realized he was in trouble. At the end of June, he quietly resigned from the College of Physiotherapists and effectively gave up his career. His criminal conviction did not automatically disqualify him from practising, a negative finding by the Human Rights Tribunal for sexual harassment in all likelihood would. Now without an income, he must have also blanched at the legal fees that were mounting up. Walter DeWilde was in a deep hole.

As the date for the hearing drew closer, Kenneth Marley, his lawyer, was having difficulty getting in touch with his client. He had spoken to DeWilde in May after the failed mediation and given him the dates for the hearing, but since the end of July, nothing. There was no answer at his home phone number, and when he called the office, he was told that DeWilde had closed up shop. Marley had no instructions from his client nor, equally if not more importantly, did he have a retainer. At the end of September, Kenneth Marley straightened his tie, smoothed his neatly trimmed beard, and went before the Tribunal requesting that he be "removed from the record."

Raj Dhir wasn't particularly worried. Walter DeWilde would not be the first respondent to appear before the Human Rights Tribunal of Ontario without a lawyer. "He had fully participated in the process up till then." September slid into October.

+++

It was Thanksgiving weekend. Raj Dhir, Racheal Baylis, and Mary Ross Hendriks—lawyer, claimant, and adjudicator—each sat down at home to their version of Thanksgiving dinner. The province was bubbling after the landslide victory of the Liberals ten days earlier and the end of eight years of Mike Harris's Progressive Conservative government with its cutbacks and restrictions on social programs. There was a new expansiveness in the air.

Tuesday morning, October 14, Dhir and Baylis were prepped and ready for the hearing in Room B of the Windsor Public Library, with Mary Ross Hendriks presiding. But where Walter DeWilde should have been, there was an empty chair. The clock ticked on. Dhir remembers, "We were still under the impression that he would show up."

But he didn't. DeWilde was a no-show, he had done a bunk. When the "accused" is not in the room, or more recently, on the screen, to face the charges, no court or tribunal will plunge ahead without making sure that he or she had every opportunity to defend themselves, that DeWilde, in this case, knew to show up. Hearing both sides of the story is fundamentally important. Mary Ross Hendriks satisfied herself that DeWilde knew the dates of the hearing, that he knew what was at stake, and that there was no good reason why he wasn't there, and she decided that the hearing could go ahead.

Racheal Baylis took the stand. In her judgement, Hendriks described her as a "forthright witness" and found her testimony "credible." As the story unfolded, it became clear that this wasn't the first time DeWilde had preyed on an employee. Racheal Baylis's cousin,

Stephanie Vasildimitrakis, testified that DeWilde not only "irritated" her and "got on her nerves," as she had told young Racheal, but he had also rubbed Stephanie's shoulders, showed her photographs of naked Black women, done many of the things to her that he had done to Racheal Baylis. Stephanie Vasildimitrakis told the Tribunal that he sang her a song "about a little [B]lack boy who sat in the rain and got washed white." Then she said that DeWilde asked her to find a pornographic website on the computer and he tried to get her to sit on his lap. It was the same pattern of behaviour. Perhaps out of fear or embarrassment, like many women, Stephanie Vasildimitrakis never filed a complaint of any sort.

The massage therapist who shared space with DeWilde backed Racheal Baylis up and testified that she seemed "very quiet and passive" and "frightened" when they worked together. Her doctor looked at her clinical notes and told the Tribunal that Racheal Baylis had come to see her in March of 2000 suffering from stress and anxiety; that she "was queasy" and "suffering from nausea." Dr. Jezdic had her tested for gastric ulcers and was clear that all of her physical symptoms came on after she began working for DeWilde.

Mary Ross Hendriks took two months to write her decision. She could, as Commission Counsel Dhir put it, have treated the case in a "cursory" fashion. She did not. "I was grateful for the fullness of her decision," he added. He had put various academic papers, secondary sources, before the Tribunal—intersectionality did, after all, spring from academic theory—and had argued strenuously that this was not a "single-axis" allegation. Ross Hendriks grappled with the big issue: "[R]eliance on a single-axis analysis where multiple grounds are found," she wrote, "tends to minimize or even obliterate the impact of racial discrimination on women of colour who have been discriminated against on other grounds rather than recognize the possibility of the compound discrimination." Ross Hendriks found that DeWilde had,

> sexually and racially harassed [Racheal Baylis] because she is a young Black woman that he, as her employer, could assert economic power and control over.

> He repeatedly diminished her because of his racist assumptions about the sexuality of Black women.

Ross Hendriks released her decision on December 16, 2003. She awarded Racheal Baylis damages of $48,384. It was a breathtaking amount. Damages at the Tribunal seldom rose above $20,000.

There they were—Raj Dhir, the lawyer, and twenty-seven-year-old Racheal Baylis, nine days before Christmas, feeling just a little thrilled. It had been a job well done. Thinking about Baylis, Dhir remembers that she talked about her future. "She had plans to go the US, to Detroit, and was thinking about modelling." She was ready to move on. "I had the sense that the whole world was in front of her and I remember thinking—it's going to be okay. This is behind her now and she had an idea where she was going to go next."

+++

More often than not, disadvantage arises from the way in which society treats particular individuals, rather than from any characteristic inherent in those individuals.

—Claire L'Heureux-Dubé

When the Supreme Court had begun to think about intersectionality in the 1990s, the red-robed judges couldn't get their heads around the idea. As the Ontario Human Rights Commission said in its policy paper, "When decision-makers, as eminent as the Supreme Court, are struggling to apply a multiple grounds analysis, it is not surprising that human rights commissions are also having difficulty." Human rights had traditionally been approached from a different point of view. This was a new way of thinking.

In 1985, a Toronto man named Brian Mossop, who worked for the federal government as a translator, took a day off to go to his partner's, Ken Popert, father's funeral. When he filed his timecard, he claimed a day of "bereavement" leave. Under his union's collective agreement, he was entitled to bereavement leave for a death in the immediate family. No, said the HR department, his same-sex partner's father was not Mossop's "immediate" family. Brian Mossop filed a grievance then a complaint with the Canadian Human Rights Tribunal.

In the early 90s, when the case reached the Tribunal, sexual orientation was not one of the prohibited grounds of discrimination under the Canadian Human Rights Act. (Sexual orientation had been recognized in the Human Rights acts of several provinces.) Mossop instead argued that he had been discriminated against on the grounds of "family status." Was a same-sex couple a family? That was the question. The adjudicator, Elizabeth Atcheson, in what has been described as a "cautious and carefully reasoned

Elizabeth Atcheson

judgement," ruled in Mossop's favour. She wrote, "the Tribunal agrees with the complainant that terms [family] should not be confined to their historical roots, but must be tested in today's world, against an understanding of how people are living and how language reflects reality."

Lived experience, "how people are living," became key phrases in changing the approach to human rights cases. It was an approach that made room for the weight of history and the force of social realities. Atcheson's decision was seen as the thin edge of the wedge in recognizing sexual orientation as a prohibited ground of discrimination at the federal level. It was also a brave decision that made some nervous because of its potential political ramifications. It boiled down to whether the country was ready to accept LGBTQ+ rights. Atcheson's appointment to the Tribunal was not renewed for a second term.

To no one's surprise, the case was appealed first to the Federal Court and then to the Supreme Court of Canada. The Tribunal decision was overruled in a split decision, which deftly postponed the real issue. The human rights gates had been opened a little wider only to slam back into place. Sexual orientation was not included as a prohibited ground of discrimination in the Canadian Human Rights Act until three years later. It was Madame Justice Claire L'Heureux-Dubé who wrote the judgement for the three dissenting judges in the Supreme Court decision. She plunged into the question of overlapping and interesting grounds of discrimination.

> It is increasingly recognized that categories of discrimination may overlap, and that individuals may suffer historical exclusion on the basis of both race and gender, age and physical handicap, or some other combination. The situation of individuals who confront multiple grounds of disadvantage is particularly complex.

It was the beginning of a move away from the "water-tight" grounds of discrimination and a recognition of a "lived experience."

Twenty years after Racheal Baylis took her complaints to the Ontario Human Rights Tribunal, intersectionality was recognized and applied by the Ontario Superior Court. It had taken that long. Seven families known as "lost Canadians" applied to have a section of the Citizenship Act declared unconstitutional by the court. The Citizenship Act said that because these seven Canadian couples had been born outside Canada, they could not pass their citizenship on to their children who were also born abroad. Ontario Superior Court Judge Jasmine Akbarali said that not only did the Act discriminate on the grounds of national origin, a prohibited ground of discrimination, but she said, "women are particularly impacted because of the intersection of their country of birth and their sex." She gave an example: Dan Warelis and Emma Kenyon, one of the seven born-abroad-Canadian couples, had a "stateless" baby in Hong Kong. For that baby to be Canadian, as the law stood, Emma Kenyon would have had to go back to Canada to give birth.

> It was Ms. Kenyon who would have had to miss work to travel to Canada. It was Ms. Kenyon whose health would have been at risk due to not having a physician. It was Ms. Kenyon's bodily integrity at issue. It was Ms. Kenyon who would have been responsible for uninsured health care costs.

Thus, said Judge Akbarali, the "burdens" of the second-generation cut-off, as it was called, "were felt differently, and more keenly, by Ms. Kenyon because the discrimination based on her country of birth had different impacts on her because of her sex."

Judge Akbarali also got in a dig at the Supreme Court. Thirty years after intersectionality and "lived experience" were first discussed, it had yet to "set out a method...for adjudicating intersectional discrimination claims." Human rights tribunals across the country dealing with thousands of intersectional claims every year had to work it out as they went along.

In 2005, two years after Racheal Baylis made her case in the Windsor Public Library, the BC Human Rights Tribunal heard from Gladys Radek, a middle-aged Indigenous woman whose leg had been amputated. She alleged that when she was thrown out of a downtown mall, she was discriminated against on the grounds of race, colour, ancestry, and disability, a multiplicity of intersecting grounds. Tribunal Member Lindsay Lyster, who was hearing the case, said, "These grounds cannot be separated out and parsed on an individual basis.... It is Ms. Radek who went through the events of that day, not a number of disembodied and distinct grounds."

Gladys Radek was awarded $15,000, a handsome amount, which she said she was going to share with the Native Housing Society. Racheal Baylis had been awarded much more two years earlier, but she was still waiting for her money.

+++

Raj Dhir had stayed in touch with Racheal Baylis after the hearing. He was doing everything he could to collect the money from DeWilde, but the reality could no longer be denied. Walter DeWilde was well and truly gone, taking whatever assets he had with him. "I always felt bad because Racheal—with all that she had been through, was not able to get damages. She never collected. At some point, I do think we learned that [DeWilde] had left the country."

There was no forgotten bank account, no real estate to sell—nothing. DeWilde had, in all likelihood, made use of his EU passport, slipped across the US border, and gone back to Europe. "Talking to her a year or two after, she was proud of the outcome but she recognized it was a pyrrhic victory."

Racheal Baylis did not build a big career as a model in the US. She stayed in the Windsor area doing a variety of jobs. Her mother remembers her working with paramedics, then campaigning for a Black man running to be mayor of Windsor. The Baylis family are chronicled in the Amherstburg Freedom Museum. "If you have that fight, you can do anything, that's what Racheal said," says her mother, Janet Crosby. Racheal Baylis's idealism ultimately didn't bear fruit. She won her case, but not only did she never see a cent of the compensation she was awarded, but also her health never recovered.

She developed Crohn's disease, and was forty-six when she died in the spring of 2022.

The BC Tribunal referred to *Baylis-Flannery v DeWilde* when it was considering the case of Gladys Radek, something that pleased Raj Dhir, but the Baylis case did not have the legal rewards he had hoped for. "We had done something good here," he says, "done something big. The decision really grappled with the issue in a unique way. I thought it would get more traction."

10. "A right to my own story."

"We can come back next week and pull a list together." The blonde woman closed her notepad and started to get up. Her friend pushed her chair back, and everyone wriggled into their coats in the cramped office. The two women had come downtown to help fundraise for a small Toronto classical music organization. It was the late 1980s.

"What about Monday?" asked the blonde woman. She had an English accent and was louder than her friend. "We can't do anything on Saturday."

"Monday would be fine." The woman who needed them to help fundraise smiled encouragingly, and the blonde woman kept on talking.

"Kaarina and I are picketing on Saturday." She laughed, wanting to be asked more.

Picketing? They were flight attendants. No one was on strike. "Picketing?"

"There's a group of us. We're all in the same boat, you know.... These guys, these fathers, they're not paying for their kids, not making their support payments. So, we're picketing their houses. The courts are useless so we're doing it ourselves."

They eventually gave their little group a name—Mothers Against Fathers in Arrears—MAFIA. More laughter from the blonde woman as she gathered her things. "Saturday, we are going to Kaarina's guy, the father of her son, to picket there."

"We're walking up and down in front of his house," Kaarina Pakka, in her very slightly accented English, spoke for the first time. That day, she looked tired. "We carry signs and we shout." Now, she is more solemn. "He can afford to pay for his son. But he will not." The little boy, Mika, was still a baby.

"Afford it!" added the other one, her voice rising. "He is rich, rich, rich. You should see the house. It's a mansion and he hasn't been paying. Mika is his son, he should pay, and he is a big guy, with money. You know the guy—you know who he is."

Really? Who was this guy? Kaarina Pakka finished buttoning her coat. "The father of my son? He is the fashion man, the clothes man...Peter Nygard."

And they were off down the stairs.

+++

In the 1980s, Nygard was a name on the label inside a pair of pants. Rich but not yet notorious. That came later. Peter Nygard created and manufactured at least seven different brands of women's clothes. Never a high-end fashion mogul, he was known as the Polyester King. Over time, Nygard's net worth rose to more than $800 million.

In his heyday, flight attendants would see him show up at the gate minutes before his flight "home" to the Bahamas, telling them to hold the flight. They held the flight. The city of Winnipeg, where his business began in the late 60s, gave him a key to the city, and his photograph at the airport welcomed visitors to Manitoba. He received the Golden Jubilee medal from the Queen, and the little town where, as a boy, he "arrived" in Canada from Finland, named a park after him. Then there was the not-so-public Peter Nygard. Non-payment of child support (he had eight or ten children, accounts vary, by at least eight different women) was nothing compared to what came later. By the end of 2023, Nygard's business had collapsed. He was facing a civil class action in the United States, fifty-seven women and girls accused him of rape and sexual assault. US criminal charges of conspiracy to commit racketeering and transportation of a minor for purpose of prostitution, and sex trafficking by force, fraud, or coercion, had also been laid. In Canada, there were sexual assault and forcible confinement charges pending in Manitoba, Quebec, and Ontario. Nygard had been refused bail, and when he was brought into court from jail, he looked ghoulishly wasted, a shrivelled little man. In December 2023, at the age of eighty-two, Nygard was convicted of four charges of sexual assault in Toronto.

For twenty, thirty years, Peter Nygard had been untouchable. Plenty of women will say that everyone "knew" about Peter Nygard, but no one—except Kaarina Pakka—spoke out or challenged him. Women were either intimidated, shamed, or legally gagged by what were known as non-disclosure agreements (NDAs).

NDAs came out of California's Silicon Valley in the 1980s as a way to protect trade secrets, a tool of business. Over time, non-disclosure agreements became the invasive species of contract law, ubiquitous in dispute settlements, in consumer contracts, in burgeoning "relationships" with the rich and sometimes famous. The trade-offs were straightforward. In return for an increased severance package, don't talk about the business. In exchange for a reduced fare on the cruise, don't tell the other passengers how much you paid. Quick, sign this non-disclosure agreement before we go on our first date.

More insidiously, NDAs expanded to cover what became known as "misconduct claims." Don't talk about what happened in the boss's office when he dropped his pants. Don't talk about the racial slurs, about what happened with the boys on the hockey team. Don't talk and we will protect your privacy and we will pay you to protect ours. *Sign here*. But what was being signed away? A combination of intimidation, manipulation, and non-disclosure agreements kept Peter Nygard's secrets hidden.

+++

The stories about his alleged conduct with the other women served to show [Kaarina Pakka's] courage.... She was fearless.

—Sarah Hampson

Peter Nygard

Kaarina Pakka was, as the headline in a 2006 *Toronto Life* magazine story by Sarah Hampson described her, "The Woman Who Stood Up to Peter Nygard and Won." Pakka was thirty-seven when her son was born. She wanted that baby and fought with Nygard for child support for almost two decades. Realizing that picketing his house wasn't getting her anywhere (Nygard started a libel suit), she thought about the legal bills, swallowed hard, and in 1988, went to court. His sister told Pakka that Nygard had put $200,000 aside to fight her in court. She was not scared off. Along the way, more than one judge referred to Nygard's "abusive" litigation tactics. Pakka had to prove paternity, and Nygard launched a constitutional challenge to paternity testing. He dragged things out interminably.

The last time Nygard and Pakka were in court in 2002, Nygard asked the judge not to reveal his identity. Ontario Superior Court Judge Frances Kiteley was having none of it. "Whether the payer is wealthy...or the payer is of lesser means, the rules with respect to openness ought to be the same," she said and granted a temporary support order of more than $15,000 a month—the largest child support award ever made. The case came back to court to determine who would pay the very large legal bills. This time it was Madame Justice Ruth Mesbur on the bench. She said, "Mr. Nygard fought everything, every step of the way. The proceedings were difficult because he made them so." She ordered Nygard to pay Pakka's legal bill of more than a million dollars. Pakka had beaten him at his own game. "Everyone was rooting for her," said one of the other mothers.

When Sarah Hampson wrote about Kaarina Pakka's legal battles for child support, she knew there was more to the story, more going on with Peter Nygard. Seventeen years after her 2006 *Toronto Life* article, she posted on Instagram: "Everything about that story stank, the stories about how he acted in his office, and his relationship with women...the disturbing stuff about sexual assault—and there was a lot—it was all bits and pieces. People were scared."

Stories of harassment connected to Nygard—the parts of Hampson's story that "stank" and that she couldn't get at—had been circulating for the preceding decade. In 1996, journalist Jan Wong, back in Canada after six years as the *Globe and Mail*'s China correspondent, was looking for a new beat when her editor suggested a lunch-with-celebrities series, with edge. Wong came at everything "with edge"—that, to her, was journalism. Peter Nygard was intended to be her first "lunch guest." Wong was in Winnipeg promoting her recent book on China when she was quietly told that three Nygard employees had gone to the Manitoba Human Rights Commission the previous year alleging "sexual discrimination"—harassment in the workplace.

Canadian law around workplace sexual discrimination had begun to be defined, coincidentally, in Manitoba, in the early 80s as Nygard was building his commercial empire. Two young women, Dianna Janzen and Tracy Govereau, who had been waitresses at Pharos Restaurant in Winnipeg, went to the Manitoba Human

Rights Commission independently of each other. "Tommy the cook," Janzen testified, would regularly touch her breasts, her crotch, her buttocks. When she complained, the restaurant manager said, "You need a fuck anyways." Govereau's complaint was much the same. The Manitoba Human Rights Commission found that this was harassment, and harassment in the workplace constituted discrimination on the basis of sex. "Agreed," said the Court of Queen's Bench when the restaurant appealed. "Disagreed," said the Manitoba Court of Appeal. Mr. Justice Huband of the appeal court said he was "Amazed to think that sexual harassment has been equated with discrimination on the basis of sex." Mr. Justice Twaddle added, "It is nonsense that harassment is discrimination." What really raises eyebrows today is that the Manitoba Court of Appeal held that "no one had to provide a workplace free of harassment." In 1989, the Supreme Court of Canada turned the judgement of the Manitoba Court of Appeal on its head and ruled that workplace sexual harassment was

Jan Wong

discrimination. Somehow, Nygard, busy building his empire, would seem not to have heard that message.

In 1996, Wong and David Roberts from the *Globe*'s Winnipeg bureau found out that the Nygard employees had complained to the Manitoba Human Rights Commission, saying that Nygard made constant sexual comments and "touched their bodies inappropriately." Wong, preparing for her "Lunch with Peter Nygard," also got to know Kaarina Pakka, who handed over some of her legal files. Putting the two cases together, Wong felt she had enough to confront Nygard. She invited him to lunch. To be accurate, he invited her to his office for sandwiches. He showed her his aquarium. She asked him about his perfect, whiter-than-white teeth ("they're bonded," he said), and she walked behind him up the stairs carefully checking if, as was rumoured, he wore lifts in his shoes. (He was five-foot eight.) She concluded that he did. It was when Wong asked him about his meagre, or nonexistent, child support payments—not only for his son by Pakka but also for others of his children—and broached the subject of sexual harassment, that he showed her the door. She wrote,

> As I fetch my coat, I ask about some sexual harassment complaints filed last spring with the Manitoba Human Rights Commission. Nygard, who says his company paid the three complainants to avoid further legal expenses, denied any wrongdoing. His company paid the women about $18,000 in damages and lost wages and agreed to establish a sexual harassment policy. The commission did not proceed with the case.

Nygard "calls the complaints 'blackmail' for bigger severance payments," Wong wrote. The women were paid and they withdrew their complaints. Hush money, some called it. The legal term was non-disclosure agreement.

+++

All kinds of things today are being hidden in non-disclosure agreements.... They're just bad things that one of those two parties doesn't want the public to know about.

—Julie Macfarlane

The dam broke in 2017. On October 5, the *New York Times* published its first Harvey Weinstein story. Eighty women came forward with allegations of sexual harassment, rape, and assault against movie producer Weinstein. There had been a sea change.

Women all over the world were spilling secrets that they had kept to themselves for years about millions of men. The #MeToo movement had taken flight. The hashtag had been created in 2006 by American activist Tarana Burke, and revived in 2017 when actress Alyssa Milano tweeted, "If you've been sexually harassed or assaulted write 'me too' as a reply to this tweet." The hashtag was retweeted nearly a million times in forty-eight hours. On Facebook, 4.7 million users created more than 12 million MeToo posts and comments. It was a giant support group. An international social media movement born in the United States inevitably had repercussions in the law.

As allegations against high-profile public figures—politicians, media personalities, sports leaders—multiplied, there was a growing recognition that these NDAs had effectively kept women quiet, covered up "misconduct," in some cases, possible criminal behaviour. The #MeToo posts on social media told of everything from a slap on the butt from a sporty boss, to the project supervisor who snuck a peek and then jumped women in the washroom, to a judge who had a habit of pinning young women lawyers against a bookcase in the reference library, to childhood sex abuse. Some women had laughed it off, whatever "it" was; others had kept silent and buried the hurt. Some complaints were valid, others weren't. But it became clear that many women and some men had come forward, settled their grievances in private, and signed non-disclosure agreements. The grievances covered not only sexual misconduct but all manner of discrimination. Those agreements traded payment for silence, undertakings that the complainant would not talk to *anyone* about what had happened and that often extended to family, doctors, therapists, and priests.

The broad use of non-disclosure agreements had also been encouraged by a shift in the legal system. Gradually, the eat-'em-for-breakfast, winner-take-all, adversarial justice system had shifted to a system where negotiation, spurred by a drastic need to streamline an overloaded, underfunded justice system, was paramount. Criminal cases are plea bargained; child custody cases (or "decision-making responsibility cases," as they are now called) are talked through and solutions agreed upon. Courts look very sternly at both sides of a civil dispute (where one person sues another) if they aren't able to come to an agreement. By the end of the twentieth century, more than 95% of cases never saw the inside of a courtroom. They were negotiated, settled between the parties.

The consensus is that settling a dispute is a good thing; it is faster than a trial and leaves everyone further ahead financially and emotionally. The complainant (under an "agreement," it is never admitted that a complainant is a "victim")—moves on with some money in their pocket and the other side, everyone hopes, has admitted nothing but learned a lesson. If things work well, there is contrition and forgiveness. But, despite safeguards and ethical considerations, mediation and settlement are not without its detractors. Settlement has been seen as the "privatization" of the justice system. Transparency disappears, case law and precedent shrink. Ultimately, what really got people, and women in particular, up in arms was that NDAs meant the powerful could and did get away with wrongdoing. NDAs were being misused. British writer Catharine MacMillan wrote that #MeToo kick-started inquiries into the use of non-disclosure agreements. She argued that the negative implications of NDAs go beyond the individual: "When a powerful individual silences their weaker victim with a non-disclosure agreement, they begin to change the way in which law is applied to citizens. A private contract between two individuals has worked to create a situation where one is now above the law."

Inevitably, a move to limit NDAs began to develop.

+++

Harvey Weinstein

If you end up signing an NDA…you haven't really achieved anything. The person who will have done the misdeeds is free to continue.

—Julie Macfarlane

Julie Macfarlane, a professor for forty years in the law faculty at the University of Windsor is not against settling disputes or using non-disclosure agreements in the right circumstances. She has written textbooks about "alternative dispute resolution," as it is known, and she has been lauded by the International Academy of Mediators. What Macfarlane objects to is the misuse of NDAs and it's misuse if the agreement hides bad deeds, misconduct. Forty years after the fact, Macfarlane sued the Anglican Church for sexual assault by a minister in England where she grew up and she refused to sign an NDA. The Church accepted her decision. Years later, when she was teaching

Julie Macfarlane

law at Windsor, students came to her with stories about a predatory faculty member. She took the complaints up to the president, the university investigated, and the law professor's employment was terminated. Then, Macfarlane said, "The penny dropped that having done the right thing, my university had done the wrong thing in giving him a non-disclosure agreement." He left the university with a letter of recommendation—the speculation is, it was in return for a reduction of severance pay and/or to avoid putting complainants through a public inquiry. None of this was ever discussed outside the room where the deal was negotiated. The law professor simply went away. Later, Macfarlane got a phone call from another university in another country asking why this professor would have left a good job in Canada. She told them what she had been told by her students only to be hit by a defamation lawsuit. She, as a university employee, was covered by the terms of the university's non-disclosure agreement with the professor. The High Court of Trinidad and Tobago awarded Emir Crowne $100,000 in damages against Macfarlane. NDAs can weave a very tangled web.

Macfarlane was not merely disillusioned but angry with the way NDAs were being used.

> All of the stepping forward, all of the disclosure that the #MeToo movement encouraged, that Black Lives Matter encouraged, where people have been told that you should stand up, you should report this kind of wrongdoing is now being concealed again by use of NDAs.

Julie Macfarlane, together with Harvey Weinstein's British assistant, Zelda Perkins—the first woman to break a non-disclosure agreement with Weinstein—established "Can't Buy My Silence," a group that lobbies to limit the use of NDAs. In 2022, the US passed federal legislation banning NDAs to silence sexual harassment and assault allegations, and so have a growing number of American states. In Canada, 94% of the delegates to the 2023 annual general meeting of the Canadian Bar Association approved a resolution to "discourage [NDA]...use to silence victims and whistleblowers who report experiences of abuse, discrimination, and harassment in Canada." But to date, only Prince Edward Island, the tiniest jurisdiction in the country, has passed broad-based anti-NDA legislation.

Federally, things came to a head when court documents revealed that Hockey Canada had used public money to settle a $3.5 million lawsuit brought by a young woman alleging sexual assault by members of Canada's 2018 World Junior hockey team. Senator Marilou McPhedran seized that opportunity. McPhedran, a fiercely determined woman of many causes, had chaired multiple inquiries into sexual abuse of patients by health professionals before she

Marilou McPhedran, Senator.

became a Senator. She says that she "saw the use of NDAs as a way to allow members of regulated health professions to stay in practice." There were too many locked-away secrets for her liking. McPhedran wanted a bill that, like the PEI legislation, would ban NDAs when they concealed sexual misconduct. Her "Can't Buy Silence Act" would make it impossible to use federal monies by way of pay-off in non-disclosure agreements. It was introduced into the Senate in 2021 but has not become law.

+++

It was the beginning of November 2022, and in Toronto, Jan Wong was wearing a red sweater jacket that matched her big, red-framed glasses. The camera, angled up, showed her at her most authoritative and confident. Wong was on a Zoom call to Manitoba's Standing Committee on Legislative Affairs as it considered a private member's bill to restrict non-disclosure agreements. Julie Macfarlane had Zoomed in earlier in the evening.

Wong was there to talk first and foremost about NDAs and Peter Nygard, but she was painfully and personally familiar with their use. More than ten years earlier, Wong had been diagnosed with clinical depression, taken time off work, and ultimately been dismissed by the *Globe and Mail*. There were months of negotiations, a settlement was reached, and a non-disclosure agreement signed. Wong subsequently wrote in general terms about that settlement and was ordered by the courts to pay the money back. She had violated the NDA. Ironically, because Wong paid the money back, she can now disclose that the *Globe* paid her $210,000 to go away and keep quiet. But Wong's non-disclosure agreement with the *Globe* did not concern or conceal acts of misconduct.

Then there was the Peter Nygard story. In Winnipeg, the legislative committee and the few other people in the committee room watched as Wong, in her Toronto house, smiled, looked down at her notes, and began: "NDAs affect public discourse, freedom of the press and freedom of information, in short they affect the health of democracy," she said. Then she talked about Peter Nygard and those three women, Nygard employees, who had complained to the Manitoba Human Rights Commission all those years ago, and whose complaints were suddenly withdrawn when a non-disclosure agreement got in the way. When she wrote her "Lunch with Peter Nygard" article, she told the committee, "I could only report on Nygard's version of events.... Imagine a quarter-century ago if those three brave women who went to the Manitoba Human Rights Commission could have spoken freely to me. The problem was that no one could get past the NDA." And, she went on, "This is the damage of NDAs. It gives free rein to predators. It creates more victims and more ruined lives."

If those complaints had been heard, Peter Nygard might have been charged, he might have been censured twenty-five years ago. Perhaps other women would not have been assaulted. There might not be pending criminal charges in Canada or a class action lawsuit in the US. There were a great many "ifs," "perhapses," and "mights" in that argument. But her point was well taken.

Eight months later, the Manitoba Law Reform Commission recommended against restricting non-disclosure agreements. NDAs, it said, give "complainants" privacy, enhance their bargaining power, protect them against the trauma of reliving what had happened. Without NDAs, hearings would take forever and there was a strong possibility there would be no money at the end of it for the complainant.

Sure, said a group of lawyers in their submission, bad things happen in Manitoba and there are the high-profile serial sexual offenders like Weinstein, Jeffrey Epstein, and Nygard, and instances like the Hockey Canada scandal, but "such examples are thankfully extreme outliers and represent a tiny percentage of the cases." That submission went on to say, "Our sense is that well intentioned outrage over these high profile events is driving [the proposed legislation]." Should there not be outrage?

The Commission in its final report quoted from a clear, painful, and sad letter sent by a childhood abuse survivor:

> Silence is being traded for money. It's awful, it's disgusting. But it's the reality. And, it's an undeniable fact

> that without an NDA and the corresponding secrecy parties would have less incentive to enter into agreements with victims.
>
> And they are reprehensible. But just because they are reprehensible doesn't mean that the alternative wouldn't be worse.

It was a lesser of two evils argument. The Manitoba Law Reform Commission reported that it searched in vain for any case where the courts had judged the legality of a non-disclosure agreement. So far, it reported, courts have not said a word.

\+\+\+

When Judge Kiteley heard Kaarina Pakka's action against Peter Nygard for child support, she said with the wisdom of experience, "it is probable that the war will continue to be waged at great cost to both parties." Financial and emotional cost. Kaarina Pakka testified that when their son was three, Nygard told her that "If I continued with the litigation, he would have nothing to do with [his son] and only think of him as an expensive fuck." She was in her mid-fifties when her child support battle with Peter Nygard finally ended.

There was plenty of muttering publicly and privately that Pakka was only it for the money. "I don't see myself as a gold-digger." Pakka faced the criticism head-on. "If you are going to have children, then you have to take responsibility." When a settlement was finally reached, she was, not surprisingly, asked to sign a confidentiality agreement that forbade her from talking about the case. "I fought hard not to sign it," she told Sarah Hampson, but she did. She paused and added, "I have a right to my own story and my own life."

Kaarina Pakka—the woman who stood up to Peter Nygard—raised her son and never disclosed the terms of her settlement. Peter Nygard celebrated his eighty-third birthday in jail in the summer of 2024. A few weeks later, he was sentenced for his convictions in Ontario. He will be in prison until he is 90, and there are more charges pending. As far as anyone knows, the three women who complained to the Manitoba Human Rights Commission nearly thirty years ago never broke free of their non-disclosure agreements. Non-disclosure agreements are for life.

EPILOGUE

On a crisp fall day in 2023, a woman leads twenty or so graveyard explorers, mainly women, on a tour of Mount Pleasant Cemetery in Toronto. There were the predictable stories of the rich and famous buried in their marble vaults, and some new stories. In recent years, the very modest grave marker of long-suffering Eliza "I did not commit adultery" Campbell has become a must-see.

Eleanora Tudor-Hart's grandaughter-by-marriage, Edith Suschitzky Tudor-Hart, the Soviet spy, has also gained recognition. Her great-nephew published her biography in 2015, the year after her MI5 files were released, and Kim Philby's granddaughter—Philby was the British intelligence officer whom Edith Suschitzky recruited to spy for the Soviets—has written a novel, *Edith and Kim* about the pair of them. Charlotte Philby pointed out that even in the world of espionage, women got short shrift. The Soviets did not pay Edith Suschitzky a penny. Her photographs of working people have become collectors' items.

Slowly, these women who were connected with the court battles that, one way or another, shaped the lot of women in Canada, have attracted more attention. It hasn't all been positive.

In 2021, someone dumped a can of red paint over the statue of Emily Murphy that stands in the park named for her in Edmonton. To make the message clear, the word "racist" was painted on the base. The statue of the Famous Five on Parliament Hill—Murphy standing beside her chair with Henrietta Edwards, Louise McKinney, Nellie McClung, and Irene Parlby—remains undisturbed.

The docudrama series *L'affaire Chantale Daigle* made it to Apple TV in 2023 and into the awareness of a whole new crop of young Quebecoise. A bursary was established in the name of Jane Hurshman at Mount Saint Vincent University in Nova Scotia, songs have been written about her, and domestic abuse education projects created. Jeannette Corbiere Lavell has been recognized with honorary degrees and awards and today lives quietly in eastern Ontario.

It is easy to label many of these women tragic heroines, women destroyed by their own actions. Jane Hurshman, Stella Bliss, and Racheal Baylis died young, and Florence Murdoch and Chantale Daigle both hid themselves away from the world after their court cases ended. Legal battles can be brutal. In 1980, a woman named Rosa Becker won her claim for half the beekeeping business she and her partner Lothar Pettkus had built, but she, like Racheal Baylis, never saw a cent. Lothar Pettkus was all too adept at avoiding payment. Rosa Becker shot and killed herself and blamed the legal system in her suicide note. The law is far from perfect.

There are less dramatic stories that have pushed women's rights. Ontario midwives weren't recognized as professionals until 1994. Even after this recognition, they continued to be paid substantially less than doctors who did similar work. The Association of Ontario Midwives filed a gender discrimination complaint, and in 2022, the Ontario Court of Appeal said "Yes, you're right." This is systemic discrimination. The Ontario government was ordered to end the gender wage gap.

Then too are rights-of-women questions that were beyond the contemplation of the legal system not so long ago. N.R. was a young, veiled Muslim woman whose relatives, she alleged, sexually assaulted her as a child. She wanted to wear her niqab, a garment that covers all but her eyes, when she testified against them. The accused argued that there is a "deeply rooted presumption" that seeing a witness' face is important to assessing their honesty and asked the court to order her to take off her niqab. When the case got to the Supreme Court in 2012, Madame Justice Rosalie Abella said:

> To those affected, this is like hanging a sign over the courtroom door saying "Religious minorities not

> welcome...." The harmful effects of requiring a witness to remove her niqab, with the result that she will likely not testify, or bring charges in the first place...is a significantly more harmful consequence than the accused not being able to see a witness's whole face.

Judge Abella was on her own in that opinion, however. Two judges said N.R. should never be allowed to wear her niqab while testifying. Chief Justice Beverley McLachlin and the majority of the court carved a middle path and said that, in some circumstances, a woman would be allowed to wear a niqab while testifying, but, "Where the liberty of the accused is at stake, [and] the witness's evidence central," she must remove her niqab.

It could be another story of veils and religious symbols that prompts a legal reckoning of the unfulfilled promise of Section 28 of the Charter of Rights and Freedoms, the section legal feminists of the last century were so proud of: "Notwithstanding anything in this Charter, the rights and freedoms referred to in it are guaranteed equally to male and female persons."

In 2019, Quebec passed legislation that said no public servant is allowed to wear any religious symbol, seen or unseen. No kachera, the white underwear required of Sikhs; no wigs or head coverings for Orthodox Jewish women; no crucifix hidden under a sweater; and definitely no veils—hijabs, niqabs, or burkas. The stated objective was the "laicity," secularization, of the province. Quebec, foreseeing a human rights challenge, invoked a province's right to create law that violates Charter rights, the more familiar notwithstanding clause. A young Muslim woman named Ichrak Nourel Hak, together with the Canadian Civil Liberties Association, launched a judicial challenge, saying this is "a horrendous law that violates human rights and harms people who are already marginalized." A young teacher, Messaouda Dridj, said, "My hijab is me. If I take it off I am no longer me." If the case makes it to the Supreme Court, and as of this writing, the court has not granted Leave to Appeal, there will be push for the court to finally decide what Section 28, the gender equality notwithstanding clause, means.

Canada has always had to balance more than one legal system—common law in English-speaking Canada, civil in Quebec. Now different Indigenous laws are being recognized, taught, and incorporated into the Canadian judicial system. How will that affect women?

And who will be considered "man" or "woman?" What is gender identity? LEAF, the organization that, for years, worked for the equality of women under the law, has expanded its mandate to include "trans and non-binary people." It took decades before there was human rights law in Canada, and years more before discrimination on the grounds of "sex" was prohibited. Gender identity and expression were added comparatively quickly, yet neither are (or can they be?) defined in human rights legislation.

Complicated questions might well be in the offing.

Thankfully, there is an ever-present crop of women, often young and frustrated because the law *can* be an ass, who are prepared to put themselves and their stories forward. It is the stories, the "this-is-how-it-started" stories, the tenacity and credibility of the women and men telling those stories, that will lead to new legal thinking, and to change.

Seldom is there a happily-ever-after for the person who cuts the path through the forest. It's those who come next who benefit.

ACKNOWLEDGEMENTS

I did my first degree in law more than forty years ago. The dean of the law school was a man who, I now realize, was only in his mid-forties, yet he seemed to believe that the world should, or, more to the point, could never change. It was as though he got out of bed in the wrong century. We were a class of sixty-five, including nine women, and one Black and one Chinese man. The dean was perpetually surprised and a little confused, it seemed, to find women (or either of those men of colour) in his class, never quite getting our names right. None of us thought anything of it at the time. After all, there had been even fewer of us oddities the year before. "Later, it became so obvious," to quote Lynn Smith.

We were taught the law as it was, not how to make change. Change in the law, inventiveness among its practitioners is always exceptional. The determination, pig-headedness—call it what you will—of the women at the centre of the cases in this book who pushed themselves and their lawyers forward was nothing short of remarkable. These women were elusive. There were scraps of information in their obituaries and in media stories and I am indebted to families and journalists and to judges who chose to write legal decisions that told something of their stories.

Legal reports of the important cases are all available online. There is a mass of academic material to back them up. (There is a full bibliography of my sources online at secondstorypress.ca/pages/footnotes.) I am no legal analyst—perversely, Supreme Court decisions became my recreational reading for this book—so I am very grateful for the work of Constance Backhouse and other feminist legal scholars. They laid the groundwork. My deepest thanks to Beth Atcheson, my legal sounding board and confidence booster from beginning to end of this project. It was Beth whom I called when things didn't make sense, who gave me contacts, suggestions, and hours of her time.

Lynn Smith, Raj Dhir, and Jeannette Corbiere all dredged their memories for details of events that took place decades ago. Janet Crosby, mother of Racheal Baylis, graciously answered my cold call and shared her memories of her daughter. Both Jan Wong and Senator Marilou McPhedran recounted their very different efforts to establish new legislation limiting non-disclosure agreements. And the network of left-wing women from the West Coast proved their worth once again in referring me from one friend to another until eventually, I found Pat Barter in Powell River. A particular thanks to Ulryke Weissgerber, who was able to prompt Jean Rands's memories of Stella Bliss. I am also grateful to David Mossop of the Vancouver Community Legal Assistance Society for his reflections on that period.

Along the way, I discovered that a growing number of professional organizations and unions have come to value and build a substantial library of oral histories. Brenda McCafferty at the Legal Archives Society of Alberta went above and beyond the call of duty, and Paul Leatherdale at the Law Society of Ontario Archives and the BC Labour Oral History Project were of great help. My gratitude as well to Sarah Ferencz, archivist of the Whitby Public Library, and to the town of Whitby for creating and maintaining a fully digitized record of the *Whitby Chronicle*.

It's often the little things that make all the difference. Lois Cromarty of the Help and Legal Centre of Northumberland passed on material about early legal aid clinics in Ontario; in Nova Scotia, Rose O'Brien hosted me and put countless calls in to friends on my behalf; Kelly Ann Hamshaw of Harbour House in Bridgewater searched through forty-year-old files; and Deborah Jones, Cynthia Wine, Wendy Annand, and the late Dianne Crowell shared their recollections of Jane Hurshman. My old classmate Justice Richard

Mosley gave me a detailed description of the robes worn by Federal Court judges, and Ron Doering and Bernard LaPrade shared memories of cases they had been part of. Dodi Weppler in England, whom I came to know through a previous book, helped track down the story of Edith Suschitzky Tudor-Hart, and my neighbour, Dr. Neil MacDonald, stopped to chat in the parking lot one day and provided a vivid description of the Verdun Protestant Hospital for the Insane and tertiary syphilis patients.

Thanks to the professional generosity of Angela Cameron for sharing her interview with Irene Florence Murdoch's lawyer, Ernest Shymka. There was added value in not only reading the transcript but also hearing his voice. And to Dawn Lavell-Harvard for the discussion of the early days of the First Nations women's movement. My appreciation to my friend, former flight attendant, and Cotswolds walking partner Malise Albrecht. And a special thanks to my daughter, Jennifer, who tolerated my laptop at the end of her dining room table for days on end, and to my friends for putting up with my irritability when things wouldn't go right.

I would also like to express my appreciation and gratitude to the Ontario Arts Council and Access Copyright Foundation (Marian Hebb Research Grant) for their assistance.

Once again, there would be no book were it not for the support and professional acumen of my editor Gillian Rodgerson, and the team at Second Story Press, led by the indomitable Margie Wolfe.

My thanks to all, and where there are mistakes, for mistakes there will always be, they are mine alone.

PHOTO CREDITS

All photos not listed below are public domain.

Page 8 - Photo taken by author

Page 10 - Whitby Public Library

Page 16 - McCord Museum

Pages 31, 40, and 143 - Library and Archives Canada

Page 37 - © Estate of W. Suschitzky, courtesy of Fotohof

Pages 43, 46, and 52 - City of Edmonton Archives

Pages 48 and 132 - University of Calgary Archives

Pages 49 and 156 - Courtesy of the Archives of the Law Society of Ontario

Page 60 - Provided by Parks Canada. All efforts have been made to find the copyright holder without success.

Page 62 - Glenbow Archives

Pages 66, 82, 91, and 94 - Courtesy of The Legal Archives Society of Alberta

Page 80 - Ottawa Jewish Archives. I0209. Rt. Hon. Bora Laskin fonds (OJA 1-588-05).

Page 84 - Courtesy of the United Farmers Historical Society

Page 97 - © Supreme Court of Canada. Photographer: Larry Munn

Page 99 - Courtesy of the Regina Police Services

Page 106 - Provided by the City of Vancouver Archives. All efforts have been made to find the copyright holder without success.

Page 111 - "Sorwuc. Local 7," Fonds Sorwuc, uOttawa Library's Archives and Special Collections, 10-062-S2-F7.

Page 113 - Simon Fraser University Archives

Page 118 - Courtesy of Lynn Smith

Pages 126 and 190 - © Supreme Court of Canada. Photographer: Michel Bedford

Page 130 - Courtesy of Calgary Police Interpretive Centre and Archives

Page 141 - Courtesy of Indspire

Page 149 - Supplied by the Office of Senator McPhedran

Page 159 - © Canadian Press

Page 162 - Courtesy of The Legal Archives Society of Alberta. Photographer: Jean-Marc Carisse

Pages 169 and 193 - Courtesy of the late Dianne Crowell

Page 201 - Photographer unknown, provided by Harrow Early Immigrant Research Society

Page 204 - Provided by the family of Racheal Baylis-Flannery

Page 208 - Courtesy of Raj Dhir

Page 214 - Courtesy of Elizabeth Atcheson. Photographer: Christina Gapic

Pages 222 and 228 - Shutterstock

Page 224 - Courtesy of Jan Wong, Jenna Muirhead Photography

Page 229 - Courtesy of Julie Macfarlane

Page 230 - © Senate of Canada

SELECTED BIBLIOGRAPHY

BOOKS

Backhouse, Constance, *Two Firsts: Bertha Wilson and Claire L'Heureux-Dubé at the Supreme Court of Canada* (Toronto: Second Story Press, 2019).

Gray, Charlotte, *Nellie McClung*, Extraordinary Canadians (Toronto: Penguin Canada, 2008).

Gruben, Vanessa, Angela Cameron & Angela Chaisson, "'The courts have turned women into slaves for men of this world'; Irene Murdoch's Quest for Justice," Tucker, Eric, James Muir & Bruce Ziff eds., *Property on Trial* (Toronto: Irwin Law, 2012).

Macfarlane, Julie, *The New Lawyer: How Settlement is Transforming the Practice of Law* (Vancouver: UBC Press, 2008).

MacGregor, Alasdair Alpin, *Percyval Tudor-Hart, 1873–1954: Portrait of an Artist* (London: P.R. Macmillan, 1961).

Mander, Christine, *Emily Murphy, Rebel: First Female Magistrate in the British Empire* (Toronto: Simon & Pierre, 1985).

McLachlin, Beverley, *Truth be Told: My Journey Through Life and Law* (Toronto: Simon and Shuster, 2019).

Sheehy, Elizabeth A., *Defending Battered Women on Trial: Lessons from the Transcripts* (Vancouver: UBC Press, 2014).

Strauch, Timothy Edgar, "Walking for God and Raising Hell; The Jubilee Riots, The Orange Order and The Preservation of Protestantism in Toronto, 1875," Thesis (Kingston: Queen's University, 1999).

Vallée, Brian, *Life with Billy* (Toronto: Key Porter Books, 2008).

ACADEMIC PAPERS

Cavanaugh, Catherine A., "'No Place for a Woman': Engendering Western Canadian Settlement," (1997) 28:4 Western Historical Quarterly, online: https://doi.org/10.2307/969883

Crenshaw, Kimberlé W., "Demarginalizing the Intersection of Race and Sex: A Black Feminist Critique of Antidiscrimination Doctrine, Feminist Theory and Antiracist Politics," (1989) University of Chicago Forum.

Kootnekoff, Susan, "When the Legal System Fails," (11 December 2020). Inspire Law, online: https://inspirelaw.ca/when-the-legal-system-fails/

Lessard, Hester, "Farce or Tragedy?: Judicial Backlash and Justice McClung," (1999) 10:3 *Constitutional Forum* 65, 1999 CanLIIDocs 270, online: https://canlii.ca/t/t2hg

Pal, Leslie A. & F. L. Morton, "*Bliss v. Attorney General of Canada*: From Legal Defeat to Political Victory," (1986) 24:1 Osgoode Hall Law Journal, online: https://doi.org/10.60082/2817-5069.1881

Smith, Julia, "An 'Entirely Different' Kind of Union: The Service, Office, and Retail Workers' Union of Canada (SORWUC) 1972–1986," (2014) 73 Labour/Le Travail, online: http://www.jstor.org/stable/24244245

Wilson, Bertha, "Will Women Judges Really Make a Difference?" (1990) 28:3 Osgoode Hall Law Journal, online: https://doi.org/10.60082/2817-5069.1764

NEWSPAPER AND MAGAZINE ARTICLES

"Abortion rights: significant moments in Canadian history," *CBC News* (13 January 2009), online: https://www.cbc.ca/news/canada/abortion-rights-significant-moments-in-canadian-history-1.787212

"Balcony Rapist's Jane Doe refuses to be victimized," *CTV News* (23 February 2007), online: https://toronto.ctvnews.ca/balcony-rapist-s-jane-doe-refuses-to-be-victimized-1.230673

DiManno, Rosie, "Will predator's reign come to an end?" *Toronto Star* (23 September 2008), online: https://www.thestar.com/news/will-predators-reign-come-to-an-end/article_e819433d-038e-58ce-8f2b-f4110fbf868e.html

Gunter, Lorne, "Courtship in monosyllables: Poor manners distract us from the high court's sophistry," *The National Post* (1 March 1999).

"Now and Then – Dr. Jeannette Corbiere Lavell," *The Manitoulin Expositor* (2 March 2022), online: https://www.manitoulin.com/now-and-then-18/

Tison, Marie, "L'affaire Chantale Daigle: Coupe de tonnerre à la Cour suprême," *La Presse* (5 March 2023), online: https://www.lapresse.ca/societe/2023-03-05/l-affaire-chantale-daigle/coup-de-tonnerre-a-la-cour-supreme.php

ONLINE

Philby, Charlotte, "Edith Tudor-Hart: The 'grandmother' of the Cambridge Spies," online: https://charlottephilby.com/features/edith-tudor-hart-the-grandmother-of-the-cambridge-spies/

Steigerwald, Stephanie, "The Use of Non-Disclosure Agreements in the Settlement of Misconduct Claims," Manitoba Law Reform Commission (June 2023).

The Joint Federal / Provincial Commission, vol. 3: Violence, "Turning the Tide Together: Final Report of the Mass Casualty Commission," (2020) Nova Scotia Mass Casualty.

ABOUT THE AUTHOR

KARIN WELLS grew up in BC and now lives in eastern Ontario. She is best known as a CBC radio documentary maker and is a three-time recipient of the Canadian Association of Journalists documentary award. Her work has been heard on radio networks around the world and has been recognized by the United Nations. Wells worked—briefly—as a line worker in a pea factory, a school teacher, and an actor. She is also a lawyer, and in 2011, was inducted into the University of Ottawa's Common Law Honour Society.

Wells has documented the lives of influential (but often overlooked) Canadian women in her books: *The Abortion Caravan: When Women Shut Down Government in the Battle for the Right to Choose* (finalist for the Shaughnessy Cohen Prize for Political Writing and winner of the Ontario Historical Society's Alison Prentice Award) and *More Than a Footnote: Canadian Women You Should Know*. *Women Who Woke up the Law: Inside the Cases That Changed Women's Rights in Canada* is her third book.